MAY 1 '92

D0605632

39092 00714793 9

PLANETREE GG 106 C 1991

DATE DUE

JUN 29 1992	NOV 03 '94	
OCT 9 1992	SEP 26 95	
OCT 24 1992	AUG 08 '96	
FEB 12 '93	APR 29 1997	
MAR 03 '93	NOV 17 1997	
JAN 03 '94	ILL CAMP	
FEB 10 '94	sent 12/2/97	
	JAN 24 1998	
MAR 23 '94	FEB 09 1998	
APR 08 '94	JUL 08 1998	
JUL 15 '94	JUL 28 1999	
AUG 23 '94	JUL 27 2001	

GAYLORD   No. 2333   PRINTED IN U.S.A.

Withdrawn.

PARK COUNTY LIBRARY
1057 SHERIDAN AVE.
CODY, WY 82414

Kid Fitness

BANTAM BOOKS
BY KENNETH H. COOPER, M.D., M.P.H.

AEROBICS

THE AEROBICS WAY

THE NEW AEROBICS

THE AEROBICS PROGRAM FOR TOTAL WELL-BEING

THE NEW AEROBICS FOR WOMEN
(with Mildred Cooper)

KID FITNESS

Dr. Kenneth H. Cooper's Preventive Medicine Program
CONTROLLING CHOLESTEROL

PREVENTING OSTEOPOROSIS

OVERCOMING HYPERTENSION

Kid Fitness

A COMPLETE SHAPE-UP PROGRAM
FROM BIRTH THROUGH HIGH SCHOOL

Kenneth H. Cooper, M.D., M.P.H.

Bantam Books

New York   Toronto   London   Sydney   Auckland

PARK COUNTY LIBRARY, CODY, WYOMING

Fitness, diet, and health are matters which necessarily vary from child to child. Your pediatrician or family physician will be the one to make the final determination on the state of your child's health and fitness, but the information in this book is designed to make parents more knowledgeable about danger signs to watch for and, especially, about ways in which they can help to ensure that they are raising children who are both healthy and fit.

KID FITNESS
A Bantam Book / September 1991

Grateful acknowledgment is made for permission to reprint the following:

Growth charts reprinted with permission of Ross Laboratories, Columbus, OH 43216, from *NCHS Growth Charts,* © 1982 Ross Laboratories.

The drawings on pages 130 and 131 were adapted from *Children Moving,* second edition, by George Graham, Shirley Holt/Hale and Melissa Parker by permission of Mayfield Publishing Company. Copyright © 1987, 1980 by Mayfield Publishing Company.

All rights reserved.
Copyright © 1991 by Kenneth H. Cooper.
Book design by Beth Tondreau Design
Illustrations of Tanner stages by Enid V. Hatton.
No part of this book may be reproduced or transmitted
in any form or by any means, electronic or mechanical,
including photocopying, recording, or by any information
storage and retrieval system, without permission in
writing from the publisher.
For information address: Bantam Books.

LIBRARY OF CONGRESS CATALOGING-IN-PUBLICATION DATA
Cooper, Kenneth H.
Kid fitness: a complete shape-up program from birth through high
school / Kenneth H. Cooper.
p.   cm.
Includes bibliographical references (p.) and indexes.
ISBN 0-553-07332-X
1. Physical fitness for children.   2. Exercise for children.
3. Children—Nutrition.   I. Title.
RJ133.C66   1991
613.7′042—dc20   91-9024
                                                   CIP

Published simultaneously in the United States and Canada

Bantam Books are published by Bantam Books, a division of Bantam Doubleday Dell Publishing Group, Inc. Its trademark, consisting of the words "Bantam Books" and the portrayal of a rooster, is Registered in U.S. Patent and Trademark Office and in other countries. Marca Registrada. Bantam Books, 666 Fifth Avenue, New York, New York 10103.

PRINTED IN THE UNITED STATES OF AMERICA

RRH   0 9 8 7 6 5 4 3 2 1

DEDICATION

This book is dedicated to those parents, teachers, and children who are concerned about the fitness and health of our youth.

It's my hope that the information and recommendations in these pages will provide much-needed practical guidelines to help these adults establish exercise, nutrition, and basic health programs for their children.

Acknowledgments

As a specialist in preventive medicine, I often encounter situations that require the advice and counsel of other professionals. In this particular book, I've been fortunate to have the assistance of those who are experts in the health and fitness of children. Dr. Marion Graham, a highly qualified pediatrician, brought his expert knowledge of pediatrics into these pages. Dr. Charles Sterling and Dr. Marilu Meredith, both specialists in exercise programs for children, not only contributed the Fitnessgram materials, but also helped develop the age-group exercise programs.

In the highly controversial field of childhood nutrition, I sought the recommendations of two very well qualified experts: Donna Israel, Ph.D., R.D., and Robyn Wimberly, R.D., L.D. Their contributions were organized and shaped under the skillful hand of Georgia Kostas, M.P.H., R.D., L.D., who is director of nutrition for the Cooper Clinic. Georgia has been an adviser for the nutrition sections of all my books in the preventive medicine series. I am deeply indebted to her and the other members of her staff, including Brenda Reeves and Veronica Coronado, as well as Cindy Savage of the transcription department.

My agent and personal friend for more than 25 years, Herb Katz, provided unlimited direction, support, and editorial review of this book, as he has for all 10 of my previous books.

My editor at Bantam Books, Coleen O'Shea, did a super job, even though she had to stop long enough to have a baby! Congratulations, Coleen, to you and Timothy.

My executive assistant, Harriet Guthrie, again showed expertise in being the "world's greatest organizer" as she kept my travels, lectures, patient care, research, and book-writing activities from developing into one enormous headache. Thanks, Harriet, for another job well done.

The one who deserves the greatest accolades in the preparation of this book is my friend, adviser, and writing consultant, William Proctor. Bill has worked with me for almost 10 years, and his dedication to a project, unrelenting research, tireless working habits, and ability to handle stress-producing deadlines continue to amaze me. Without Bill, this book would never have been published.

Mr. Jay Colt Weesner, staff artist for the Institute for Aerobics Research, was responsible for many of the illustrations in this book.

There are many others who deserve credit and to whom I would like to express my appreciation. Even though they are too numerous to name, their contributions were essential to the development and completion of this project. Heading the list of that group, I would like to name three: my wonderful wife, Millie; my lovely daughter, Berkley; and my talented son, Tyler. Their patience and understanding of the time demands of twenty-five years of book writing exceed even my expectations. Thanks, family. You are the greatest!

Contents

Foreword

One of my recent films, *Kindergarten Cop,* introduced me in vivid terms to the excitement *and* joy that exercise can provide for even the youngest children.

The movie was about a policeman who had to go undercover as a kindergarten teacher. In one of the scenes, the children in the movie do some exercises—and they really got into the program! The more activity we requested, the more fun they had as they yelled, ran, jumped, and, in general, enjoyed themselves. As a result, we actually added more exercise sequences than we had originally planned.

This experience impressed me in several ways. First, it's clear that most children are *naturally* drawn to vigorous physical activity. Also, the more exercise children do, the more they *want* to do. In other words, if given the opportunity and guidance, they easily acquire the exercise habit.

Physical fitness experts such as Dr. Kenneth H. Cooper, author of this book, *Kid Fitness*, emphasize that habits and lessons learned early are more likely to stay with us throughout life. The main idea is to help children get started on a fitness program and then to support them as they find the particular activities or sports that seem most interesting.

As the chairman of the President's Council on Physical Fitness and Sports, I believe that one of the major goals of any sound physical fitness program should be to benefit as many children as possible. The best approach will focus on promoting challenging but achievable levels of health and well-being for the nonathlete as well as for the child who will go on to play competitive sports. Again, I support one of Dr. Cooper's key themes in these pages, that kid fitness must be available for every child at every developmental level.

In this vein, it bothers me that there is only one state, Illinois, that requires daily physical education for all youngsters, from kindergarten through grade 12. When I was growing up in Austria, everyone who went to school had to do one hour a day of exercise. Also, we had sports programs three times a week for those who wanted to engage in athletic competition. I long for the day when this approach to fitness will be commonplace in the United States. To make this vision of kid fitness a reality, several prerequisites are necessary:

• *All* of us should learn to distinguish between sports programs and physical education programs. As Dr. Cooper says, achieving good health and reaching a high level of conditioning for sports are not the same thing. So we must be sure to devote as much thought, energy, and money to promoting basic fitness as we do to athletic prowess.

• Our school systems and community programs must expand and improve their fitness efforts with an eye toward drawing in all children, not just the elite few. We need to focus on improving the average youngster, not just on helping the one who can lift 500 pounds, or run 100 meters in 9.9 seconds, or play varsity basketball.

• Parents must make fitness a family affair. How can Mom and Dad help? They can participate in exercise activities with their children. They can turn off the TV and encourage all family members to get out into the yard or on the street for a brisk walk. I'm especially gratified that Dr. Cooper has included several sections on how parents can participate with their children and motivate them to exercise.

We have a saying at the President's Council on Physical Fitness and Sports: "It's just as important to grow up fit as it is to grow up smart." That's the basic principle for transforming the health and well-being of our children. All that remains is for parents, teachers, coaches, and children to commit themselves to a workable program that prescribes sound exercises, good nutrition, and other fitness guidelines that can make the principle a reality.

In this invaluable book, Dr. Kenneth H. Cooper gives us the prescription for reversing the health crisis now facing American youth.

—Arnold Schwarzenegger
chairman, President's Council on Physical Fitness and Sports

Introduction

"We'll look back and see heart disease as unique to the twentieth century," predicts Dr. Edward Schneider, a gerontologist at the University of California.

That prediction of the future has significant basis in present fact. Since 1968, the death rate from coronary heart disease has fallen 48 percent, and the American life expectancy has risen 5 years, to almost age 75.

And there are indications that these trends may continue: "If a federal program to lower cholesterol takes off, we could have another dramatic fall in coronary death rates in the next 15 years," according to Dr. William Castelli, director of the famous Framingham Heart Study.

If we are to reach such goals, we must continue to whittle away at the coronary heart disease risk factors that caused the danger in the first place. The most important ones include cigarette smoking, high blood pressure, high cholesterol, unmanaged stress, and inactivity.

Put this another way: it's estimated that nearly two-thirds of the reduction in deaths from coronary heart disease during the last 20 years are the result of lifestyle changes, *not* modern medical technology. Clearly, our emphasis should be focused on lifestyle in the twenty-first century.

In a book for children, why is it necessary to talk about coronary risk factors? Heart disease is characterized by years and years of incubation and by seconds in a terminal event, such as a heart attack. This disease doesn't just happen. It takes more than 20 years to develop.

In fact, it's common to see signs of heart disease and atherosclerosis (hardening of the arteries) in children. Yet these deadly developments often go undetected because the heart is "masterful in disguising its problems" and early atherosclerosis can develop without symptoms for many years.

If the twenty-first century is to be free of cardiovascular threats, we must concentrate on the health of our children *now*! Unfortunately, the enthusiasm of many adults for wellness and lifestyle changes has not carried over to their children. Kids are heavier and less fit aerobically now than 15 years ago.

The reasons for this decline? There are many. Often, children no longer take physical education in all 12 years of their schooling. They drive or are driven to school, rather than getting there by foot or by bike. Far too many hours are spent watching television or being mesmerized by video games. Due to the prevalence of fast foods, the diets of our children are much higher in fat and cholesterol than they were in the past.

Unless we concentrate on these excesses and deficiencies in the lifestyles of our children, there is no way that we can expect to see further improvement in the health and longevity of our people. Our children, as well as our adults, must get fit, keep fit, and join the ongoing fitness and wellness movement. If they do, we can expect to see even *greater* progress during the next century.

This book is not a textbook dealing with all of the medical aspects of youth. Rather, it's been designed to concentrate mainly in two areas: exercise and nutrition. If the parents and children—from preschoolers to teenagers—can follow the guidelines suggested in these pages, then many of the health problems of our youth will never materialize. Instead, we'll learn to control serious youth health problems and, in many cases, cause them to disappear. Lifestyle changes include getting back to the basics, and I believe exercise and nutrition are the basic building blocks for any fitness or wellness program.

I trust that the information in this book will inspire parents, care givers, and children to get excited about building strong and healthy young bodies. As adults who care about children, we should remember that if we "train up a child in the way he should go, when he is old, he will not depart from it" (Prov. 22:6). In the final analysis, that's what *Kid Fitness* is all about.

—Kenneth H. Cooper, M.D.

CHAPTER ONE

A Generation of Unfit Children

Millions of our children—the majority of them in middle- and upper-middle-class homes—face the prospect of serious diseases and shortened life spans because of sedentary living and poor nutrition. And the situation appears to be worsening.

The main reasons for this pressing health crisis? First of all, our society is beset by chaotic and conflicting notions about child health, with no strong public voice advocating a consistent and sound kid fitness strategy. Second, the pervasive confusion and lack of information has wreaked havoc on parental understanding and motivation. The end result has been a chronic failure of adults to provide sound guidance to their children.

The implications of these developments are staggering. At least 30 to 35 percent of school-age children are at risk for heart or circulatory disease and for premature death as adults, according to research being conducted by our Institute for Aerobics Research in Dallas. Other studies support and extend our findings:

• One-third of all youths, ages 10 to 18, don't engage in sufficient physical activity to give them any aerobic or endurance benefit, reports the 1987 National Children and Youth Fitness Study.

This situation is nothing short of tragic in light of a recent, widely publicized study conducted by the Institute for Aerobics Research. This longitudinal study of men and women unequivocally established that there is an independent relationship between low fitness and a higher risk of death (see the *Journal of the American Medical Association,* vol. 262, November 1989, pp. 2395–2401).

• Today's children, beginning as young as age 6, weigh more and have considerably more body fat than did children 20 years earlier.

For example, a 1987 study of 22,000 children conducted by the Harvard School of Public Health found that since the 1960s, obesity has increased by 54 percent among children aged 6 to 11, and by 39 percent among children in the 12 to 17 year age range. Obesity was defined as the child's being 20 percent above the ideal weight for his age, sex, and height.

• According to the National Children and Youth Fitness Study, the health and fitness of young people is "significantly associated with certain physical activity behaviors of the children and their parents."

Yet that same study reported that fewer than 30 percent of mothers and fathers of first- through fourth-grade children participate in moderate to vigorous exercise three days a week—the basic requirement for health benefits. More alarming, about 50 percent of the parents interviewed said they *never* engaged in vigorous exercise!

• Children with average athletic abilities increasingly begin to drop out of organized sports and games beginning at about age 9. A major cause: they perceive that they can't keep up with their more physically skilled and gifted peers. By age 13, most boys, and an even greater majority of girls, are no longer participating in organized athletics or any type of regular physical activity.

Yet this movement toward inactivity is so unnecessary! Various studies show that many of these early dropouts are simply late bloomers. If parents and other adult authorities will just continue to work on fitness and athletic skills with these kids, most will eventually catch up with their peers in physical and cognitive development.

• Only 32 percent of children aged 6 to 17 meet minimum standards for cardiovascular fitness, flexibility, and abdominal and upper-body strength: that was the conclusion of a 1989 national study of 12,000 youths sponsored by the Amateur Athletic Union and the Chrysler Corporation. These findings represent a steep decline from 1981, when 43 percent of the children were in acceptable shape.
• A shocking 40 percent of children ages 5 to 8 have at least one heart

disease risk factor, according to the President's Council on Physical Fitness. The factors identified included physical inactivity, obesity, elevated cholesterol, and high blood pressure.

• Only the state of Illinois requires that all students, kindergartners through high-school seniors, attend physical education classes daily, reports the American Alliance for Health, Physical Education, Recreation and Dance.

These trends all point toward one inescapable and disturbing conclusion: our children are currently on a fast track to becoming unhealthy adults. It is evident that parents must bear the brunt of the responsibility to correct this situation.

The local, state, and federal governments won't do much unless we prod them. But even if public agencies *do* respond with more constructive programs, it will still be up to you and me, the individual father and mother, to take the initiative in the home and exert firm guidance in developing viable strategies that will improve the fitness of our children.

I've occasionally heard parents say, "My son isn't athletic" or "My daughter refuses to do anything to increase her physical activity." But I don't buy these excuses. The children *will* respond positively *if* we, as parents, formulate interesting fitness programs and make an effort to motivate our children to follow them.

CHILDREN *WANT* TO BE FIT

Our children *by nature* gravitate toward healthy activities and habits. At the most fundamental levels, they genuinely *want* to have strong and sound bodies and minds. Yet in many cases the forces of unwise nutrition, sedentary living, and lack of knowledge among parents have contrived to deprive children of the very benefits they desire so deeply.

The contrast between what many children will *naturally* do if left to their own devices in constructive surroundings, and what they *actually* do in their homes, schools, and recreational settings can be startling. Most specialists in child behavior will tell you that children are born with a love for physical activity. Left alone, they'll usually keep playing or moving at rates far beyond the capacity of most adults—as the parents of any 5 year old can tell you!

But most kids are offered TV and video games as prime leisure activities or after-school options, rather than exercise or sports. The average 2 to 5 year old watches more than 22 hours of television per week, and the typical 6 to 11 year old takes in nearly 20 hours weekly. Furthermore, all kids need vigorous exercise, consisting of at least three 30-minute workouts each week, such as steady running, cycling, or other activity that promotes endurance. But only two-thirds of our children participate at that level.

The same paradox prevails with food. With minimal adult guidance, young children seem to head naturally for nutritious and appropriate food and drink to satisfy their hunger and thirst. Yet studies in the food industry have shown that children account for more than one-fourth of the market for salty snacks, processed meats, and other easy-to-prepare fatty foods. Also, kids eat more than one-third of all frozen novelties, fruit drinks, and pre-sweetened cereals. Ironically, a Gallup poll has revealed that half of children from ages 12 to 17 tried to avoid high-cholesterol foods—but they didn't know which items were good and which were bad!

It's no wonder that 11 million children from ages 6 to 17 are considered obese. Excess weight would seem inevitable from their lack of knowledge about fitness, their minimal exercise, and their high-fat, sugary diets.

Why is it that most children, when given a chance, are ready to do the healthy thing—and yet so many now suffer from chronic fatigue, little energy, and unfit bodies, and face the prospect as young adults of coronary artery disease and other ills? For one thing, sedentary living and bad eating habits have to be *learned*. Either by following bad role models or pursuing the same unwise activities over and over, kids get used to an unhealthy lifestyle. Also, when children head for the sofa in front of the TV or for the fast-food lines, they're taking the easy way out. They are simply giving in to readily available temptations.

So the goal of parents should first be to create an environment that is conducive to optimum health. Then mom and dad must encourage children to take a hand in designing their own appropriate exercise and fitness programs.

WHY PARENTS ARE SO IMPORTANT IN KID FITNESS

As the parent of an athletic college-age son and daughter, I've been exposed firsthand to the joys and pitfalls of introducing children to sound nutrition and exercise programs. As a doctor, I, and my staff, have worked with countless parents and children in developing individual kid fitness programs. Among other things, several members of our staff at the Institute for Aerobics Research have spent years studying and developing fitness testing and exercise programs for children of all ages, from preschoolers to teenagers. One of our evaluation systems, the Fitnessgram, has been used by thousands of youngsters in many school systems around the country.

I speak with some authority when I say that parents are *essential* players in any successful conditioning scenario.

Just how important parents can be comes across rather clearly in the contrasting experiences of the following boy and girl.

The Boy—and Parents—Who Gave Up.* A well-known celebrity sent her son, Josh, to our clinic in Dallas for an evaluation, and we soon concluded that the boy was in extremely poor shape. At the age of 13, Josh was 40 pounds overweight, with about 45 percent of his total body weight consisting of fat. By the standards we use to measure fitness of children, his body fat should have been no higher than 20 percent, and preferably lower. Also, Josh's cholesterol levels were too high—195 milligrams per deciliter (mg/dl) when the count should have been less than 170.

Overall, Josh reported that he had relatively little energy. He tired easily after moderate physical activity and was often too exhausted to do his homework at night.

"I'd like to play sports, maybe football or wrestling," he said, "but I never have been able to keep up with the other guys during a workout."

Our experts opened the conversation by stressing the improved health and other benefits that a kid fitness program would produce. "You're really going to feel and look great!" they said.

At first, the boy seemed like a promising candidate for a fitness program that could have revolutionized his life. He knew he was in bad shape, he wasn't satisfied with himself, and he said he wanted to improve.

But when we got into the details of the strategy that would be required to get him into condition, a subtle interaction began to occur between the boy and his parents. It all began when a member of my staff began emphasizing some of the hard realities: it was going to take at least two to four weeks for Josh to begin to see real progress in losing weight and improving his endurance capacity. He was in such poor shape that we couldn't expect the almost immediate, positive response usually experienced by the average child.

In addition, we explained that Josh's eating habits—including his devotion to fatty, high-calorie fast foods—would have to change. In particular, he'd have to cut back on those sugary desserts and greasy French fries!

I felt we had presented these exercise and dietary challenges in exciting, upbeat terms, highlighting the conditioning benefits that would soon be

---

*I've changed the names and identifying details of the parents and children I write about in order to protect their privacy, but the people and their experiences are real.

his. But throughout the latter part of the presentation Josh's parents were rolling their eyes and sending out negative signals. Almost anyone observing this scene would quickly have noticed that Josh picked up on his parents' skepticism. He had been alert and interested at the beginning of the discussion. But before long, taking a cue from mom and dad, he settled into a "show-me" mode that said, "Okay, I'm listening but you have to sell me on this deal!"

"Boy, this is going to be tough!" his father said at one point. "You think you can do this, Josh, with that sweet tooth of yours?"

Needless to say, his parents' reaction caused Josh to reconsider the whole fitness proposal. He started focusing on what he had to *lose,* rather than on what he had to *gain.* As a result, he was already complaining and offering excuses as he walked out of the door with his parents.

The family said they would think it over, but the outcome had already been determined. The program seemed too unpleasant and too much work to Josh. His parents, for their part, didn't want to deal with the hassles they saw on the horizon—even though they had played a key role in laying the groundwork for these future problems. Unfortunately, both the boy and his parents gave up on the program before they even got started.

The Girl—and Parents—Who Prevailed. In contrast to Josh, 8-year-old Leslie and her parents approached her shape-up with a completely different attitude.

Leslie's problem wasn't being overweight: her percentage of body fat was about 25 percent, or what we consider to be only on the borderline of normal for a girl her age. She had little endurance; she quickly became tired when she was required to run or play vigorously. As a youth soccer team member, she frequently had to be taken out of games and replaced by a substitute because she couldn't keep up with the other children.

Consequently, Leslie had begun to expect less of herself, and she displayed a decided lack of self-confidence on the playing field. She had already mentioned several times to her parents that she thought she wanted to quit soccer, and her mother and father now viewed the prospect of her dropping out as inevitable.

Of equal concern to her parents was the fact that Leslie seemed unusually susceptible to colds, ear infections, and other childhood illnesses. Typically, she would have to visit the doctor six or seven times a year for treatment, and she often missed school because of these health problems.

Then Leslie's parents learned some interesting facts from a woman, who had a son a couple of years older than Leslie. This boy had suffered from almost exactly the same problems that Leslie was facing: a lack of endurance, a low self-image, and an unusually high incidence of minor illnesses. His mother, however, had not been willing to settle for such a situation. With the help of a professional, she had designed a conditioning program for the boy.

Following the advice they received from this boy's mother, Leslie's parents presented a similar program to their young daughter. Their attitude was that this would be an exciting adventure in which the whole family would participate.

Her mother said that she and Leslie would attend gymnastics classes for kids during the week. The parents also instituted a simple calisthenics routine at home, with special rewards when Leslie performed her assigned exercises with some regularity. In addition, the father spent a few minutes several evenings a week working on the girl's soccer skills.

This program produced near-miraculous changes in Leslie's fitness, overall health, and sports performance. Within only about a month, she was able to perform at much higher endurance levels. Now, she no longer had to rely on substitutes in her soccer games, and she could keep up with any child on the playground.

Her attitude toward exercise and athletics changed dramatically. She constantly chattered about her soccer team's standing in the league and made it clear that she wanted to continue playing the following year.

Perhaps most important in the parents' view, Leslie's improved fitness apparently bolstered her overall health. In addition to increased levels of energy, her susceptibility to illnesses virtually disappeared. She went for an entire year without even suffering from a cold!

What lessons can the experiences of these two children teach us? First of all, *both* the parent *and* the child must somehow get involved if the kid fitness program is to succeed. Young children are unlikely to embark on a long-term, comprehensive conditioning program without the backing and guidance of a supportive mother or father.

Josh is a prime example. His parents were unenthusiastic about his conditioning program; so predictably, the boy began to complain and resist as well. Yet with a little work by parent and child, major improvements in fitness and self-image would definitely have been possible.

Leslie, in contrast, got involved in a life-changing fitness regimen *primarily* because her parents were committed themselves. They recognized that their daughter needed to get into better shape and improve her athletic skills, and they were willing to spend the time necessary to help her achieve these goals.

As a result, this mother and father helped their daughter make it safely through an age when many young girls drop out of sports and become completely sedentary.

This is not to say that a parent must participate in every fitness activity or accompany a child on every athletic endeavor. Certainly, my wife, Millie, and I haven't been present every time our daughter, Berkley, or son, Tyler, have run in a race or played soccer or basketball. But successful kid fitness *does* depend on the parents' enthusiastic involvement and example. For this reason, I've always done everything I could to arrange my schedule and business trips to allow me to attend track meets or other events that were particularly important to our kids. Whenever possible Millie and I have planned family fitness runs, walks, hikes, and other outings.

Kid fitness must be fun. Leslie and her parents enjoyed engaging in more intense physical activity—and their program paid off. As for Josh and his parents, they decided at the outset that they weren't going to enjoy themselves. They looked on fitness as hard work and deprivation. As a result, their program never got off the ground.

After hearing the stories of Josh and Leslie, and after considering some of the facts that show many of our kids are woefully out of shape, you may find yourself pondering a very basic question: "How exactly can the experts tell whether or not a child is fit?" Or to put this in more personal terms, "What tests or standards should I use to evaluate the health and fitness of my child?"

HOW CAN YOU TELL IF YOUR CHILD IS FIT?

"Fitness without exercise" is a concept gaining popularity in this country, as was the quip "Be lazy and be fit" a few years ago. Such statements, which often become book titles, are valid only if you limit the definition of fitness so that it means only the absence of disease.

To me, fitness has always meant more than that. When I classify a child or an adult as being fit, I'm referring not only to the absence of certain symptoms, but also to the quantity and, even more important, the *quality* of life.

It's possible, as I'll demonstrate later, that even minimal activity, or simply avoiding inactivity, is capable of reducing the risks of mortality and increasing longevity. Yet this approach doesn't produce the quality of life so commonly seen in people who have achieved a high level of endurance or aerobic fitness.

Because I'm such a strong advocate of aerobic fitness—and all the benefits that go with it—all of the programs in this book have been designed to produce a high level of endurance, strength, and flexibility. The only requirement is that the child—and that includes those from the preschool to teenage years—follow them faithfully. If he does, he'll become fit in the most comprehensive sense of the word.

But the pressing question remains: "How can I *tell* if my child is really fit? How do I evaluate her or him?" The best way is to use a variety of established tests and measurements, a number of which you'll find in later chapters of this book. These tests—which can be used to check the fitness of children from the preschool to teenage years—will help you identify a number of important points, including your child's particular level of physical and cognitive development or maturity—factors that decisively influence athletic performance and the design of an effective kid fitness program:

- Aerobic or endurance capacity
- Muscle strength and stamina
- Body fat percentage
- Flexibility
- The degree of nutritional balance

You'll learn how to interpret in lay terms the various procedures that a physician usually performs during his regular checkup. These include cholesterol and other blood measurements, a blood pressure evaluation, and the additional components of a child's complete medical examination.

As I mentioned at the beginning of this chapter, we have concluded at the Institute for Aerobics Research that because of poor fitness, *at least* 30 to 35 percent of the school-age population are at risk for early heart or circulatory disease and premature death as adults. These are frightening numbers. These percentages translate into millions upon millions of out-of-shape children, undoubtedly including many you know personally. Yet those 30 to 35 percent at risk can reduce or eliminate that risk by becoming and staying active.

How about the fitness of your own child? Is there any cause for concern about the health of your son or daughter, now or in the future?

Beginning in chapter 7, you'll learn how to evaluate a child's basic physical condition and you may find that some adjustments are required in eating, exercise, or general health habits. But first, you must settle on your ultimate goal in formulating a kid fitness program. In addition, you need to know what physical performance you can and should expect from your child, given his current level of development.

WHAT'S YOUR FITNESS TARGET?

Every kid fitness program, *without exception,* should encourage health habits that will last a lifetime. This must always be your main goal, even if you're now mostly interested in enhancing your child's athletic performance or accomplishing some other short-term purpose.

To put this another way, I want your kids to build early habits that will *carry over* to adulthood—and lead to the fitness that produces a better quality of life and even greater longevity. There's a growing consensus among medical experts that children who develop sound, positive exercise habits will be more likely to continue them as adults. In particular, those who *enjoy* their physical activities as children—as opposed to those who are forced against their will to "be healthy"—can be expected to try to re-create those enjoyable times as adults.

If your child does develop fitness habits that carry over to adulthood, you'll be giving him one of the most valuable gifts possible—a longer and healthier life. That's precisely what we found in our study as reported in the November 1989 issue of the *Journal of the American Medical Association.* One of our conclusions is particularly encouraging for those who consider themselves active but not athletic. If you simply *avoid inactivity or a sedentary lifestyle* you can expect to see a reduction in all causes of mortality. Specifically, the least-fit people in the bottom 20th percentile (as determined by their measured level of fitness, according to age- and sex-adjusted standards) were more than twice as likely to die of all causes as those in the next 20th percentile!

Also, we found that the more fit a person is, the more protection from fatalities he or she enjoys. The least fit, in the bottom 20th percentile, were more than three times as likely to die as those in the top 40th percentile.

Finally, the higher levels of fitness offered the participants protection not just from heart attacks and strokes, but also from deaths involving all health causes, including cancer.

What does it take to avoid the inactivity that can lead to an increased likelihood of death? Not much. The equivalent of taking a brisk walk 30 to 45 minutes three to five times a week enables a person to move up from the bottom 20 percent to at least the next 20 percent!

There's an important lesson here for parents: If you want to provide your children with the gift of a longer, more productive life, you must help them *now* to become accustomed to activity rather than inactivity. At the earliest age possible, they must learn attitudes, physical skills, and sports that will be with them in later life.

THE RULE OF RHYTHM

To get your child started on an appropriate kid fitness program, it's necessary to understand what I call the "Rule of Rhythm." The rule may be stated in simple terms like this:

> *Every child has a personal, inner principle of pace that drives his or her physical and cognitive development and that must serve as the foundation for any effective conditioning program.*

An important corollary to the Rule of Rhythm: Kid fitness is for *all* children—nonathletes and athletes, girls and boys, "normal" kids and those who have limiting disabilities. But even though any child can and should become fit at any age, fitness won't necessarily translate into athletic achievement. A highly fit child with poor motor skills will probably never experience a high level of athletic achievement.

Let's put this another way. Your child's ability to play competitive sports well or otherwise engage successfully in physical activity is determined more by his *developmental age* than by his chronological age. In this regard, experts have long acknowledged that different children reach their full physical potential at different times. That's the scientific basis for saying some are "early bloomers," and others are "late bloomers."

The Rule of Rhythm has a direct bearing on the parent's expectations for the child, as well as on the child's self-image and self-confidence. For example, if a child is slow to develop athletic skills or seems to lag behind his peers on the playing field, a mother or father may conclude, "Well, he's just not a physical person. He's not an athlete." Needless to say, it doesn't take the child long to begin to believe the same message: "Well, I'm just not a physical person. I'm not an athlete."

A number of parents I know have gone one step further. They've decided that because their children lack certain athletic skills at a certain age, there's no point in encouraging them to engage in any form of vigorous exercise. Hence, the genesis for the next generation of couch potatoes!

Yet as you'll see in the following chapter, such unscientific, wrongheaded conclusions can rob a child of the joy and high energy that fitness can provide—not to mention the eventual opportunity to excel in some form of athletics.

Various studies have confirmed what many coaches and parents have known all along: some children are simply slower than others to develop basic physical skills like catching or hitting balls or executing movements that require agility. In a few instances, the boys and girls who learn these skills earlier, say at ages 4 to 5, may have a natural ability that others lack. In many cases, though, certain children merely grow and develop faster than the rest, or their parents do more to train them at a young age. The others can still catch up—*if* they are just given a chance!

Tragically, this message hasn't been communicated to many parents, or to some coaches and physical education instructors. There is increasing evidence that a significant number of students, beginning in about the third grade, start withdrawing from physical activities that lead to fitness. The tendency to give up on exercise reaches a crescendo in early adolescence, as the majority of students fail to develop good conditioning habits that carry over to adulthood.

In addition to physical development, there is also a *cognitive* factor that influences how well a child can perform in sports and games. Some children can concentrate and focus on tactics and athletic skills at a relatively young age, ranging from about 7 to 9. Many more don't develop this capacity until they are at least 10 to 11, or older.

The Kid Fitness Shape-Up Program takes the Rule of Rhythm into account in our exercise and nutrition plans by utilizing what might be called the "catch-up effect." First of all, I recognize that certain children take longer than others to develop their physical abilities. Second, I encourage a commitment to patience on the part of the parents. They must be willing to hang in there with the child, by providing consistently good nutrition and vigorous exercise opportunities until his physical or mental growth catches up with that of the other children his age.

PARENTS MUST PREPARE FOR THE ADOLESCENT SLUMP

Another expression of the Rule of Rhythm involves what I call in chapter 3 the Adolescent Slump—or a tendency for the fitness of many children to go downhill after about age 11 or 12. Also, the slump is often characterized by a fitness decline in girls that may begin even earlier and may plummet at an even greater overall rate than that for boys.

The Disturbing Outlook for Teenage Girls. Young girls often enjoy a fairly strong start with fitness, but then they fade fast as adolescence approaches. Our studies at the Institute for Aerobics Research show that at age 7, 86 percent of girls can pass a basic 1-mile run test and 57 percent can pass an upper-body strength test. But by age 15, girls' fitness levels decline precipitously: only 49 percent can pass the 1-mile run requirement and a dismal 27 percent pass the upper-body strength test.

And Boys Are Not Much Better. Seven-year-old boys begin below girls on the mile endurance test and slightly ahead on the upper-body strength test. Then their fitness drops gradually over the years, although at a slower rate than that of the girls. Specifically, 76 percent of the 7-year-old boys passed the 1-mile run test, while 60 percent passed the upper-body strength requirement. At age 15, a less-impressive 62 percent met minimum standards for the 1-mile run, and 50 percent passed the upper-body strength test.

It is obvious that we face a major problem with both boys *and* girls when they move into adolescence—but what can we do about it? In more personal terms, what can *you,* the concerned parent, do to enhance the physical condition of your child, now and in adulthood?

THE ANSWER FOR CONCERNED PARENTS: THE KID FITNESS SHAPE-UP PROGRAM

First of all, parents must move to head off the high drop-out rate from organized sports and other fitness activities beginning at about ages 9 to 10 and culminating with the onset of adolescence. Various studies have identified several reasons many kids give up:

- Constant failure in competition
- Mismatching children at different developmental stages in team sports
- Too much organization and practice drilling, and too little time for fun (see Rainer Martens, 1980)
- Emotional stress from placing excessive performance demands on children
- Negative feedback from coaches and parents
- Not getting to play in sports events

Here's a case in point. In a study exploring the motivation to participate in recreational sports, 314 boys, 6 to 10 years of age, rated these items the highest: (1) "learn to do my best," (2) "learn and improve skills," (3) "have a coach to look up to," and (4) "get stronger and healthier." Surprisingly, "win games" and "become popular" were rated least important (see H. Patrick Stern, M.D., et al., February 1990). These and related factors will be featured in chapters 4, 5, and 6 as part of our exploration of effective strategies for parental involvement in kid fitness and child motivation.

In the second place, parents of an adolescent girl must become more sensitive to her special problems. Dr. Bruce Watkins, professor of sports management at the University of Michigan, reported in a 1989 study in *Child Development* that girls 11 to 13 leave fitness activities in part because they resist being in competition with boys. Watkins has also identified a tendency in girls to rate themselves lower in athletics than their natural abilities would warrant.

Using the fully tested approaches developed by our Institute for Aerobics Research, I've provided in chapter 8 a comprehensive set of exercises for different ages and developmental levels. These include progressive play sessions for younger children and a variety of aerobic activities for older children, such as walking, running, jogging, cycling, and swimming. Also, there is a graduated program of strength and flexibility exercises, featuring activities like gymnastics and child-oriented variations on the traditional sit-ups, stretching routines, and modified pull-ups.

I've developed a point system that enables boys and girls to monitor their own progress—an especially important habit for later self-monitoring in adult fitness efforts. To stimulate interest, the points the children earn can be awarded in the form of stickers, stars, inexpensive toys, increases in a weekly allowance, or special ribbons or patches. The overall objective is to develop from a young age aerobic capacity, strength, and flexibility—but without boring or overloading children, or endangering the growth process.

I've included plenty of special topics on exercise, such as:

• How to deal with differences between boys and girls in fitness activities and sports competition
• Recommended ages and techniques for special strength training, including the use of weights
• Safe distances for runs for children of different ages—and suggested precautions to protect against heat problems and muscular and skeletal injuries
• How to tell whether your child is ready for a relatively disciplined exercise regimen, or whether you should stick to a more informal program
• A comprehensive plan for the elite child athlete—and guidelines for parents of these physically gifted children

My overall goal has been to help you, both parents and young people, to become self-starters in formulating and applying an individualized kid fitness program. Kid fitness should always begin with a powerful parental presence. But then the child must be empowered to take control of his own fitness program.

To lay the groundwork for effective parental guidance, you'll need to "depressurize" the atmosphere in your home and open the door to more relaxed, intimate interactions. So in chapter 14 I've described:

- Ways to establish a low-stress lifestyle in your home
- Guidelines to identify and evaluate the most serious stress events in your child's life, including divorce, entering a new school, and failing to gain the approval of peers

A cornerstone of any complete child conditioning program must be a sound eating plan. To this end, chapters 9 and 10 include:

- A program to make smart eating second nature for the fast-food generation
- Strategies to control the consumption of fast foods and junk foods, such as a "semimonthly splurge" (e.g., letting the child have a serving of a less-nutritious food about once every two weeks, or in some cases, once a week)
- Preparation instructions for health-promoting "kid recipes"
- Programs to combat obesity and eating disorders
- Guidelines to deal with the question of cholesterol management and low-fat diets for children

Finally, in chapters 7, 8, 11, 12, and 13 I'll provide you with basic fitness and medical standards and information:

- A comprehensive compilation of charts and tests on children's health and fitness
- An action plan to help parents influence school systems and politicians in strengthening good public nutrition and exercise programs
- A checklist for a comprehensive physical examination
- Immunization schedules for children at every age level

Although this information represents the latest scientific thinking in the field, my primary concern has been not the experts, but rather, *you,* the parent or care giver. I want you to have at your fingertips the essential facts and practical guidelines that you need to encourage your child's natural inclination to be healthy and fit.

Our joint goal should be to instill in that boy or girl the enthusiasm and vision that must accompany any successful kid fitness program. But before you can act effectively, you need to know approximately where your child stands right now, in the broad sweep of physical and emotional development. In short, you need to understand how the Rule of Rhythm applies to your own youngster's growth cycle.

CHAPTER TWO

The Development Factor in Kid Fitness

For a kid fitness program to work, parents must begin with an understanding of their child's level of physical and emotional development—a concept that is quite different from chronological age.

Different children reach developmental plateaus at different ages. That's why age, while important, isn't by any means the only determining factor in the pace of growth.

So the parent must become aware of the peculiar *rhythm* of growth, as a particular boy or girl moves from one physical and emotional stage to the next. Every human being develops according to a highly individualized time clock, a biological schedule that helps determine readiness for various fitness activities and sports, as well as the ability to participate in planning and executing a fitness program.

This Rule of Rhythm—which I introduced in the previous chapter—is the fundamental principle on which any exercise, nutrition, or athletic plan for a child must be based. But so many parents, coaches, and even physicians fail to recognize that each child has his own appropriate time and pace for certain fitness activities and programs. Here are some cases in point:

• At age 8, Jay was small for his size and lacked many ball-handling skills that were required to do well on a Little League baseball team. Yet his parents, who were big baseball fans, pushed him to participate in a league that included 8 to 10 year olds.

During the season, Jay never got a hit—or even swung at the ball, he missed numerous easy fly balls and grounders, and he became the target of catcalls from opposing players: "Easy out! Easy out!"

As a result, Jay dropped out of baseball for good after the season ended. He also lost confidence in his ability to play other sports and avoided all vigorous exercise that would have improved his physical fitness.

• Twelve-year-old Amy had done fairly well as a soccer player in a youth league, and she frequently won races sponsored by organizations that ran family fun runs and peewee olympics. But she had just experienced menarche (first menstruation), was becoming more interested in boys, and was finding it difficult to maintain her interest in athletic competition.

As a result, she dropped out of her athletic activities as a seventh grader and failed to replace them with another fitness program. Soon her aerobic capacity and muscular strength declined, and she put on 10 pounds of unwanted fat.

• Tim, who was big and muscular for a 10-year-old, displayed advanced skills as a tennis player, and he won practically every tournament that he entered in the 10-and-under classification. But his parents resisted putting him in tournaments for older players, even though he wanted to, because they worried that they might be "pushing him too much."

The result: by the time he was 12, Tim had lost interest in tennis and was focusing on other sports that gave him more opportunities for personal control and offered more challenge.

• An 11-year-old female gymnast, Becky, complained to her physician about a 3-month-old pain in her left wrist. The doctor found that the grip she was using on the parallel bars had caused her to fracture her wrist in the epiphysis, or growth plate. This was a potentially serious injury that could interfere with her bone growth. Apparently, the break had occurred as a result of constant stress during her long 3- to 4-hour daily workouts.

The doctor's prescription: Becky had to quit gymnastics entirely for 6 months and allow the injury to heal. Fortunately, at the end of that period the fracture was repaired and the bone began to grow normally again.

• About 10 years ago, a 6-year-old boy entered a marathon and managed to complete 15 miles. At this point he collapsed from exhaustion and severe dehydration.

Fortunately, after several days' hospitalization the symptoms associated with heat exhaustion and dehydration passed, and the boy's health returned to normal. But as far as we've been able to tell, he never ran a race again.

• At about 95 pounds 9-year-old Art was very heavy for his age. But much of that weight was fat. Because of his size, his parents encouraged him to go out for a local kids' football team, even though he feared he wasn't skilled or fit enough to meet the requirements.

As it turned out, the first practice demonstrated that Art was right and his parents were wrong. Although he was certainly heavy enough to play on the line, he wasn't sufficiently strong or fast to keep up with the other boys. In one particularly violent play, he sprained his ankle and was pronounced by his doctor to be out for the season. This unpleasant experience confirmed Art's belief that there was no point in him trying exercise or sports.

In each of these cases, the children failed to participate in sports compatible with their *developmental* age, even though the activities may have been appropriate for others of their *chronological* age. Consequently, they became discouraged, bored, or injured. Yet such results are entirely unnecessary *if* parents can begin to understand the development factor in their child's fitness.

THE TRANSFORMATION OF THREE FAMILIES

Many times, parents botch kid fitness efforts because they don't realize how important it is to know the child's developmental stage. Lives can be changed for the better when parents are better informed as can be seen rather clearly in the experiences of the following three families.

Like Father, Like Son? In the Johnson family, the tall, thin father regarded himself as "unathletic" and took the same view of his son, who was built much like dad.

"It's in the genes," the father sighed. "I was always a lousy athlete, always the last picked when they were choosing sides for a game in school. And my son's exactly the same. It's history repeating itself."

That was an unfortunate attitude especially because the son was only 9 years old when the father made those comments! It's true that the boy was tall for his age and gawky and had considerable trouble handling balls or controlling his body on the playing field. But this parent was on the verge of making a major mistake: he was assuming that his son could never measure up to his peers physically, simply because he lacked certain athletic skills at this particular point in time.

The Catch-Up Effect. Among other things, he was ignoring what I sometimes refer to as the "catch-up effect" in child fitness and athletic development. The catch-up effect may be summarized this way: *many* young children are less competent in sports than others in their age group, at about age 8, 9, or 10. But by the time they turn 12, 13, or 14—or in some cases, 16 or 17—they not only catch up but they are sometimes in a position to surpass the same classmates who seemed hopelessly far ahead of them years before.

But note: I say they're "in a position to catch up" because in many cases, they *don't* catch up. There is a simple reason. Parents, coaches, or other care givers fail to encourage them to keep fit and work on their physical skills.

To be sure, slower children, or late bloomers, often function for a time on the playing fields at levels well below others in their age group. But if they work to achieve a high level of strength and aerobic conditioning and continue to hone their athletic skills, they'll build a physical platform that will allow them to take off when the rhythm of their development intensifies later in adolescence. Also, getting into good fitness habits and acquiring sports skills during youth will help these late bloomers experience a carry-over effect of physical fitness to adulthood.

Professor Vern Seefeldt, director of the Youth Sports Institute at Michigan State University, places special emphasis on the development of athletic skills as a means to enhance fitness for children, including those late bloomers. He says: "If we concentrated at an earlier age on developing fundamental motor skills, which are the ABC's to movement, then children are likely to become more involved in the games, dances, and sports of their society and to maintain fitness in that way. . . . Fitness is really a foreign concept to children. We must persuade them to move, and movement generally has to be fun or children won't do it" (Kathryn Simmons Raithel, October 1988).

Raising the Johnsons' Spirits for Sports. Now let's return to the problem in the Johnson family. As in many other homes, a below-average sports performance by the son discouraged the father. So dad decided to ignore the development of the boy's athletic motor skills and physical fitness entirely. Instead, he urged the boy to concentrate *exclusively* on academic and musical skills.

Now, I'm all in favor of promoting academic and musical excellence, but *not* at the expense of creating an unbalanced and less-than-healthy youngster. If this boy has the potential to be a fine scholar or violinist, then certainly, he should consider devoting most of his time and energy to these disciplines.

But the child will ultimately be adversely affected if he completely neglects minimum exercise and good nutrition.

Here are some further arguments that convinced the Johnsons to stick with sports: French and Canadian studies have shown that children who are physically fit tend to perform better in their academic work. In France, children with 8 hours of physical education (PE) per week did better in the classroom and also demonstrated more maturity and independence than a control group of students with only 40 minutes of PE per week.

In Canada, children with 5 hours of vigorous activity each week were tested against a group who worked out only 2 hours per week. Here are the results: the more active children showed more progress in cardiorespiratory fitness (endurance), strength, *and* academic performance in French, math, natural sciences, and English (William B. Strong and Jack H. Wilmore, April 1988).

Remember our recent findings at the Institute for Aerobics Research. Those adults who spend only enough time and effort to be placed in a moderately active category of fitness live significantly longer and are healthier than those who are completely sedentary. It's certainly preferable to be a long-lived, energetic musician than one who dies or loses his health at an early age!

The Johnsons Become Believers. We're still working with the Johnson family, and I'm optimistic because the father has begun to take a broader look at his son's overall development. The boy, who is now 11 years old, is still doing extremely well with his school grades and his music, and I expect he will become quite accomplished on more than one instrument. At the same time, however, he is spending time in less-competitive sports programs, such as a gymnastics class for children who aren't planning on participating in meets, and also a B-level basketball league.

The father, with his son's help, is also designing a family fitness program. Mr. Johnson has become quite enthusiastic that his son is much more physically fit than in the past, is acquiring a valuable fitness habit, and is also slowly developing sports skills. As he says, "Who knows, with his height, he may even become a good basketball player someday!" This possibility is not at all far-fetched, as the next two illustrations of the Rule of Rhythm show.

From String Bean to Superstar. Julie was only of average height, and she was extremely thin until about age 13. Then she shot up to a height of nearly 6 feet, though she remained a "bag of bones," as she disparagingly described herself. She had been only an average athlete on the community teams she had joined over the years.

Fortunately, though, Julie continued a sound nutrition program and a calisthenics regimen that her parents had established for her when she was about 10. In the early years of this home program, the parents had to encourage her and schedule her time so that she ate regularly and exercised properly. During the time she followed this plan, Julie continued to add very little body mass or fat. But the exercises kept her aerobically fit and relatively strong and agile for someone so tall and thin.

Her height and conditioning finally caught the eye of both the girls' basketball and volleyball coaches during tryouts for her junior high school. Before long, Julie was playing on both teams, although she finally elected to specialize in volleyball.

With the onset of menarche at age 14, her body filled out. Now, far from being a string bean, or bag of bones, she turned into a tall, fit, and attractive young woman. By the time she reached high school, Julie had become a certified star at her chosen sport. Furthermore, she was a recognized leader in her school, with a satisfying social life. When the time for college applications arrived, she even became a candidate for a variety of athletic scholarships.

What's the secret to Julie's success? I have to give most of the credit to her parents. They encouraged their daughter to continue with sound nutrition, a thorough fitness program, and athletic skill development even though for years there was no dramatic payoff. Many mothers and fathers would have lost interest when they saw their child's muscles fail to fill out immediately. But Julie's parents had the long-term view of kid fitness and a surprisingly incisive understanding of the rhythm of child development. Most important, their daughter is now reaping significant benefits from their insights and commitment.

How Fat Freddy Became Fred the Flash. Another less-dramatic, but still highly encouraging, story involved a boy named Freddy, who at age 10 was grossly overweight. His body composition measurements revealed a 40 percent body fat level—far above the minimum 20 percent we recognize as healthy for boys his age.

Fred's personal history showed that he possessed certain natural athletic abilities, although they weren't necessarily exceptional enough to make him a contender for a varsity team. In particular, he had always had a good sense of balance. Among other things, he had been one of the first children in his neighborhood to learn to ride a bicycle, ice-skate, and roller-skate.

Fred's problem was that with his excess weight, he had become the butt of school and neighborhood jokes. Every time he put on a T-shirt or donned a bathing suit, he elicited some comment about "Fat Freddy," or "Mr. Roly-Poly." When he tried to play sports with other children, he was always one of the slowest runners and had little endurance.

Finally, Fred told his parents he wanted to quit a couple of the teams he played on, including a junior hockey league team. His excuse: "It's not as much fun for me as it used to be." Translation: "The other kids are teasing me more than ever, and I tire so easily that the games seem to be more work than play."

His parents, rather than give in to Fred's assessment, put him on a weight-reduction program that involved both better nutrition *and* systematic fitness training. The exercises involved the lowest level of aerobic conditioning, beginning with vigorous 30-minute walks three times a week. Also, they started him on a graduated calisthenics program, which included sit-ups, stretching exercises, modified pull-ups, and modified push-ups.

To motivate the boy, they established a system of rewards, such as inexpensive toys and tickets to attend special sports events when he did a minimum number of workouts or moved up to a new fitness achievement level. Perhaps the most powerful motivation tool of all, though, was the parents' attention as they supervised his exercises, and their approval and praise when he finished each session.

Within one month, Fred had lost about 5 pounds, his muscle strength had improved somewhat, and his endurance had increased significantly. The most important motivator of all, however, was Fred's *belief* that he was improving physically. This growing confidence enhanced his performance on his sports teams and in playground activities.

It's been four years since Fred began this program, and now, at age 14, he's a completely changed boy. During the intervening years, he grew several inches. This growth spurt, as often happens with adolescent boys, combined with his exercises to hasten the loss of "baby fat" that had accumulated around his midsection.

What's Fred's current fitness level? His body fat is now less than 20 percent, he can run a mile in under 8 minutes, and his capacity for doing sit-ups and other exercises is well above average.

He has elected not to go out for his interscholastic school sports teams, but he does participate regularly in less-competitive community hockey and basketball leagues. In those, he is always a competent player and sometimes a star—or "Fred the Flash," as some of his friends now call him.

One thing I especially appreciate about Fred's story is that he hasn't become an outstanding athlete and probably never will. But he is in the process of establishing some solid fitness and nutritional habits that are likely to carry over to his later life.

The main secret to his transformation was his parents' commitment to a program designed to change him over a period of years, as he moved from one developmental stage to the next. When they began, Fred was lagging well behind his peers in athletic performance and confidence. By launching a kid fitness program at an early age, however, the parents succeeded in improving his physical condition immediately. Most significant, they prepared him for better physical performance in later years, when he had moved through the important adolescent growth phase.

Each of these three families illustrates an essential overriding principle: because children develop at different rates, parents must be perceptive, patient, and systematic in designing a kid fitness program that matches the individual maturity level of a child.

In many instances, mothers and fathers have to be prepared to work over a period of years on basic fitness and physical skills development if they hope to maximize their child's health and athletic potential. But ultimately, persistence will pay off—I can guarantee it!

How can you become more perceptive, patient, and systematic in dealing with your child? The first step is to learn where he or she now stands in the broad spectrum of physical and cognitive development.

HOW TO IDENTIFY YOUR CHILD'S DEVELOPMENT PHASE

Child development is an extremely complex subject—one which pediatric and sports medicine experts continue to research and argue about. But two points are certain:

• Different children develop emotionally and physically at different rates— or at different "rhythms."
• To be generally effective for most children, fitness programs must first take into account the particular child's current level of development.

But how can parents, coaches, and others concerned about kid fitness determine a given child's developmental standing? To help you answer this question about your own child, I've identified six major phases of child development, as they relate to kid fitness. These categories will assist you in performing what pediatric experts often call a "maturity assessment" of your child.

As you read about each of these stages, however, I don't want you to approach them as you would a textbook. Instead, imagine that you can actually *see* your boy or girl at each of these stages. Picture him as an infant, then in the First Skills Phase, then in the Basic Fitness Phase, and so on.

Obviously, because your child is currently in a particular development phase, you can't retrace the steps you've already taken with him. But try to remember him or her at those past levels and phases of development, and then project his probable development a few years into the future. That way, you'll understand better the significance of where you've been, where you are now, and where you may be going.

An important fringe benefit of this exercise is that you'll begin to think of your child's fitness as part of a *long process,* rather than a point-in-time issue. By understanding the broad sweep of a child's physical and mental changes, a parent is more likely to become perceptive, patient, and systematic in guiding that child toward better health and fitness.

Within each of the six development phases, I've included three sections. *The Body* section includes changes and developments you can expect in your child's physique. *The Mind* section focuses on transformations that take place in his mental processes and emotions. *The Fitness Considerations* part contains suggestions and tips to keep in mind as you oversee your child's personal fitness program. Specific fitness programs for each developmental level can be found later in this book, in chapters 8, 15, and 16.

An understanding of *all* these factors—body, mind, and fitness considerations—will be decisive in helping you design the best kid fitness program for your child.

NOTE: I've included some general references to typical age ranges, which often apply to children at each of these developmental levels. But these age indications should *only* be taken as broad indicators, *not* as precise predictors about where your child should be at a given time in his life.

In other words, many children between ages 5 and 8 may fit into the developmental descriptions I've used for the Basic Fitness Phase. Then, at age 8, they move beyond them. But if your child *still* has some of the Basic Fitness Phase characteristics at ages 9 or 10, there is nothing to worry about. He may just be a little slower than his peers at this point. There's every likelihood that if you work with him on his fitness and athletic skills, and help him maintain good nutrition, he'll eventually catch up.

Finally, as you read through the descriptions of the six developmental phases, you may find it helpful to make a note of those characteristics that describe your child. This exercise will make analysis easier when you later attempt to classify and evaluate your child's state of development.

#1. The Postbirth Phase During this first phase of development, which roughly ranges from birth to age 2 for most children, major changes are occurring in your child's body and mind.

The Body. Most children reach half of their adult height by 22 to 24 months. In fact, many pediatricians suggest that parents multiply their child's height at 23 months of age by two to get a general idea of how tall the youngster will eventually become.

The child's organs are also growing at a rapid rate. The brain, for example, nearly triples in size between birth and 1 year and reaches about 80 percent of its adult size by age 3. The heart nearly doubles in size by the first birthday, the lungs more than double, and the stomach nearly triples. These major changes in the child mean that his potential to develop strength, endurance, and physical skill increases at an exponential rate during the first 2 years of life. Such possibilities present a major challenge to parents, who are trying to monitor and channel their child's explosive growth.

The American Academy of Pediatrics and other sources suggest the following milestones for physical development at different ages in the Postbirth Phase. If your child is a little ahead or behind the indicated age level don't worry. But if the physical milestone fails to occur more than a couple of months past the suggested age, you should notify your pediatrician.

Age 3 Months:
• While lying on his back, your child moves each of his arms and legs equally well.
• The child's hands are often open.
• When you hold your child in a standing position, she can support her head more than a moment.

Age 6 Months:
• The child can roll over at least twice, from the stomach to the back or the back to the stomach.
• The baby responds to sounds.
• The baby can see, pick up, or otherwise respond to small objects, like dust, insects, or crumbs.

Age 9 Months:
- Your child responds to quiet sounds or whispers (e.g., by turning his head toward you as you creep up quietly behind him).
- The baby attempts to stand and support some of his own weight when you hold him under his arms, with his feet on the floor or your lap.
- While on his stomach, your child can support his weight on his outstretched hands.
- Your youngster holds her bottle unassisted.

Age 12 Months:
- Your child can crawl on her hands and knees.
- He can pull up to a standing position.
- She can walk while holding on to some solid object, like furniture.
- He can identify sounds by turning his head in the direction from which they come.

Age 18 Months:
- Your child can hold an adult cup or glass without help and drink from it without spilling the contents.
- He can walk without support or help all the way across a large room without falling or wobbling from side to side.
- She can take off her shoes.
- He can feed himself with a spoon.

Age 2 Years:
- Your child can take off his clothes, such as pajamas or pants, by himself.
- She can run without falling.

The Mind. Mental development is also moving along swiftly in the Post-birth Phase. Here are some typical signals you should watch for. Again, the indicated ages are just general guidelines; you shouldn't worry if your child is a few months late or early in manifesting these signs.

Age 3 Months:
- Your child makes sounds other than crying, such as cooing, gurgling, or babbling.
- He follows moving objects, such as toys or hands, with his eyes.

Age 6 Months:
- Your child plays with her hands by touching them together.

Age 9 Months:
  • Your child is interested in children's picture books, at least for a few minutes at a time, when you point out the images to him.

Age 12 Months:
  • When you hide behind something, such as a corner, and then you reappear, your baby looks eagerly for you to show yourself.
  • Your child repeats identifiable sounds, such as *mama*, or *dada*.
  • She can say at least one real word.

Age 18 Months:
  • Your child can say two words other than *dada* or *mama*.

Age 2 Years:
  • Your child can say at least three words, other than *dada* or *mama*.
  • She can occupy herself for several minutes looking at pictures in a picture book.
  • He is able to tell you in words or sounds what he wants.
  • Your child often repeats words spoken by other people.
  • He can point to at least one named body part.

Fitness Considerations. Contrary to what you might think, there's a lot you can do for your child's physical fitness during the first two years of life. At this age, it all begins with good nutrition, a topic that we'll cover in detail in chapter 9. Among other things, I advocate that children drink whole milk, breast milk, or formulas with no restrictions on fat content, a position that conforms to the views of most pediatric nutrition experts.

In addition, it's important for you to encourage your child to be active, but the emphasis should be on play and fun and not on a systematic fitness regimen. Still, the more you encourage your child to be physically active during this period, the stronger and more energetic you can expect him to become, and the more quickly he'll develop skills in using his muscles. I don't recommend that you rely on excessively organized "superbaby" exercise programs or "baby swimming" classes. But you might try such activities as these:

  • Playfully and gently help your infant to roll over, if she can't do this already. The more you show her how to perform new movements, the faster she'll learn.
  • When your baby passes the 4- to 6-month mark, allow him to push as hard as he likes against you or the floor with his legs. Encourage him to hold

on to your fingers and pull up toward you, from a reclining position. Help him to sit up by himself.

• Get her to play games, such as picking up objects with both hands.

• As he moves into the last half of his first year, begin to hold him in a standing position and walk him around. But only continue this exercise as long as it's fun for the child!

• Put some enticing item, such as a colorful ball, just out of reach so that your child will begin to crawl toward it. Then, when he reaches it, knock it a little farther away so that he keeps moving. You'll be able to tell if this activity is fun if your child laughs or shows an inclination to chase the object.

• The development of fine muscle movements becomes important in the last half of the first year. So you should encourage activities such as allowing your child to begin to feed himself (as messy as that can be at first!), using crayons, and playing with toys that have moving parts.

• As your child approaches her first year of life, you'll be able to roll balls toward her and teach her to roll them back.

• As he gains some facility in walking by himself, show him how to walk backward, walk up steps, and stand on his toes.

• As he approaches age 2, work on throwing and catching large balls. Then, when he gains some expertise with the large object, move to one that's a little smaller.

• Continue to work on fine motor skills, such as stacking toys or blocks and retrieving objects in cartons or other containers.

• At this age, many children also become interested in "helping" with housework. Encourage this inclination, even though the youngster may require the adult to slow down the pace of cleaning.

• At age 2, enjoyable fitness activities include "dancing" to music in imitation of adults, learning to jump, and becoming more adept at balancing, such as by standing on one foot.

• Fine motor skills can be fine-tuned as the child plays with malleable claylike substances, puzzles, and other small items. (CAUTION: Be sure the objects she plays with aren't small enough to be swallowed!)

Of course, there's no way to predict precisely what your child's interest in athletics will be at such a young age. But still, if you learn at this stage to observe your child closely, you'll begin to see certain strengths and tendencies that may become the foundation for a later fitness program.

For example, if your child walks early, that may be an indication he has good balance—an aptitude that could enhance certain fitness activities like cycling or skating. I can recall several cases where a child began to walk at 9 or 10 months, learned to ride a bicycle by age 4, and started ice- and roller-skating shortly afterward. These youngsters were able to derive considerable fun *and* aerobic benefit from more rigorous skating and cycling as early as age 6 or 7.

#2. The First Skills Phase For many children, this period of life encompasses the preschool period, from ages 2 to 5. Others may begin to show signs of this First Skills Phase even *before* age 2, however. Still others may be 6 or 7 or even older before they move completely out of this second phase.

The Body. Children in the First Skills Phase are beginning to develop basic motor skills, including those large-muscle and small-muscle physical abilities that can be used later in general fitness activities and sports.

Many experts regard this First Skills Phase as critical for the full success of the child's later fitness efforts. The reason? The skills he learns now provide the groundwork for later, more complex abilities that are essential to the enjoyment and the efficient performance of exercise.

As Professor Vern Seefeldt of Michigan State University says, we should teach all the basic motor skills—such as catching, kicking, throwing, and running—as early as possible so that children will have a physical-skill base for successful athletic performance later in their lives.

To put this another way, it's no fun to play catch if you don't know how to catch or throw! Likewise, if you can't kick a ball reasonably well, soccer and kickball can quickly become boring or frustrating. Even a relatively simple activity like running may require some practice before the faster style of movement becomes efficient.

So beginning at least by this second phase of development, parents should introduce their children to the basic motor skills for athletic performance. As a handy checklist for parents of First Skills Phase children, here are 21 such key skills identified by Professor Seefeldt and others.

N O T E : Most children can make a good beginning with *all* these skills before age 5 or 6. But in the majority of cases, it's necessary for the parent or another concerned adult to take the initiative and help the child with those movements that seem particularly difficult.

OBJECT CONTROL SKILLS: (1) kicking, (2) throwing overhand, (3) throwing underhand, (4) catching, (5) punting, (6) dribbling (or bouncing a ball several times in succession), (7) striking a ball with a bat or racket, (8) trapping with the feet (stopping a ball with a foot as it rolls toward you, as in soccer or speedball).

LOCOMOTOR SKILLS: (9) running, (10) jumping over an obstacle, (11) hopping, (12) skipping, (13) balancing (as on one foot, on a narrow surface, or on a two-wheel bike), (14) galloping, (15) leaping forward (which involves executing a running jump off one foot and then landing on the opposite foot), (16) rolling forward (somersaults), (17) rolling backward (backward somersaults), (18) sliding while in a standing position, as on an icy or slick surface.

NONLOCOMOTOR SKILLS: (19) pushing, (20) pulling, (21) lifting.

Obviously, these are very basic physical skills, but each provides a foundation for later, more complex movements that are required for many sports. If your child can learn each of these movements at an early age, he'll also be more likely to build on them at an early age. This means that he'll become more adept at playground activities, at pick-up games during recess and physical education class, and later, at team sports.

In addition to these sports-related skills, there are also some common physical benchmarks that pediatricians often look for at different age levels (*Your Child's Growth: Developmental Milestones,* American Academy of Pediatrics, 1987). Their purpose is to ascertain whether a child's development is in the general range of "normal."

But remember, the listing of an age is only a general guideline. Your child may be perfectly healthy and normal, yet still be a little late or early with any of these abilities. In any event, here are some of those common changes you can expect in your child's body and physical abilities during this First Skills Phase:

Age 3 Years:
• Your child can throw a ball overhand (as opposed to sidearm or underhand) toward your stomach or chest for a distance of about 5 feet.
• She can help put her toys and other belongings in their proper place.

Age 4 Years:
• Your child can pedal a tricycle at least 10 feet forward.

Age 5 Years:
• She can button some of her clothes or her doll's clothes (snaps don't count).
• He can lace his shoes.
• She can walk down stairs alternating feet on each stair step.
• He can execute a broad jump—a leap forward, either from a standing position or while on the run.
• He can point as he counts at least three different objects.

The Mind. During the First Skills Phase, the brain and nervous system continue to develop dramatically. They increasingly provide the cognitive foundation that's necessary to use physical skills effectively.

PARK COUNTY LIBRARY, CODY, WYOMING

For example, the child's interest in new activities and new skills, and his capacity to be motivated to participate in these activities, begin to emerge clearly in this phase. Also, the ability to understand and follow rules is an essential ingredient of successful play on the playground or athletic field.

Here are a few of the mental and behavioral guidelines that pediatricians look for at different ages during the First Skills Phase. These points are necessarily general because of natural variations in children at these age levels.

Age 3 Years:
- Your child can name at least one object or animal when you look at common picture books together.
- He can answer simple questions you ask him.
- She can begin to relate simple stories about herself.
- He can ask simple questions.
- He can understand and indicate simple opposites, such as up and down.
- She knows her gender.
- He can name and identify at least one color.

Age 4 Years:
- He is able to play games where he is required to take turns and follow rules, for example, hide-and-seek, cops-and-robbers.
- He can name many pictures in books or magazines.
- She can describe the action that's taking place in a given picture.
- She uses numerous action words—i.e., verbs.
- He plays with an imaginary companion.
- He can begin to understand the alphabet.

Age 5 Years:
- He interacts well with baby-sitters—although he may still complain or cry initially when you leave home.
- He can memorize songs and rhymes.
- She can name at least three colors.
- He can name at least one coin correctly.
- He can identify simple numbers, such as dots on dice.

Fitness Considerations. Once again, good nutrition is a primary consideration during this phase of development and it will continue to occupy a key role as the child gets older. Unlike the normal adult, the child should continue to eat more meats, dairy products, and other foods relatively high in fat. Growing muscles, bones, brain, and nervous tissue have special needs for the nutrients in these foods. For this reason—as I'll explain further in chapter 10—children up to age 5 should *not* be vegetarians. After age 2, however, they *may* reduce the fat content in their diets by using only milk products containing 2 percent milk fat.

As far as exercise is concerned, the child in this phase of development should continue to be highly active and should be given plenty of opportunities for running about and exercising growing muscles. It's also important for parents to become more aware of the importance of limiting television time.

To stimulate the child's interest in physical activity, it's essential for the parent to make a systematic effort to teach important physical and athletic skills. Look back at the list of 21 motor skills mentioned earlier in this section. Your goal should be to help your child get a good start on *each* of those skills during this First Skills Phase. My program for fitness and for skills development during the preschool period is covered in some detail in chapter 8.

If your child can show significant progress with all these skills by age 4 or 5, you may have an outstanding future athlete on your hands! In any event, your youngster will be in a good position to enjoy almost any physical activity during childhood.

On the other hand, you shouldn't worry if your child is a little slow developing certain of these skills. Some late bloomers become the most avid and committed fitness buffs in later life. The main idea at this early age is just to *get your child started*—and to develop a fitness routine that can ensure good physical habits for the remainder of his life.

#3. The Basic Fitness Phase At this transitional time of life, which roughly runs from about age 5 to 8, children become more interested in organized group play and team sports, like community leagues for soccer and T-ball. Their physical and cognitive skills and development haven't quite prepared them for serious competition. But in many neighborhoods, these youth teams provide a major vehicle for becoming physically fit and skilled at various sports. Just as important, being in shape often helps efforts at socializing and builds self-esteem.

WARNING: This third phase may be *absolutely pivotal* for the future fitness and athletic endeavors of many children. Most dropouts from fitness programs and sports seem to occur later, from about age 8 through the early adolescent years. But much of the groundwork for dropping out or losing interest is laid during this earlier Basic Fitness Phase.

The Body: Boys and girls remain on a relatively even level during this period of their lives. As a result, they can play together satisfactorily or compete against each other successfully.

Boys, for instance, range from a median height of a little over 42 inches at age 5 to slightly over 51 inches at age 8. Girls' median heights are comparable: nearly 43 inches at 5 years, to about 50.5 inches at age 8. It's a similar situation with weight. Boys range from a median of 40.5 pounds at 5 to a little more than 60 pounds at 8; girls are 40.5 pounds at age 5 and slightly above 58 pounds at 8.

Like the height and weight measurements, however, the various organs of the body still have a long way to go before they reach adult size. The heart is only about 30 percent of adult size and the resting heart rate of the 6 year old is still quite high—95 beats per minute on average, as compared with about 72 beats in adulthood. The lungs are about 20 percent developed, and the stomach is less than 40 percent of the adult size.

The 6-year-old child's skeleton is also far from mature. *No* child has all his carpal bones in the wrist. The growth plates—the sensitive sites known as epiphyses, where bone growth occurs throughout the body—are just beginning to unite in a very few areas. These locations include a part of the hipbone and the pubis bone, just in front of the pelvis. In many other parts of the body, however, the growth plates continue to be highly active *and* vulnerable to injury.

Bones in children during this phase also tend to be smaller and more fragile than those in the adult. On average, for example, the chest circumference at 6 years is only 22.5 inches, in contrast to the adult male average of 34.5 inches.

Overall, then, children at this stage of life are physically *very* immature. They typically do quite well when they play with and compete against those at a similar stage of development. But they are quite susceptible to injury when they are pitted against children who are more mature, even when those children are at the same chronological age.

What can you expect of a child physically at this phase of development? According to the American Pediatric Association, by age 6 the average child can dress himself completely. Also using only his hands, he can catch a small ball such as a tennis ball on the bounce. In addition he can skip with both feet and can copy a circle on a piece of paper.

As your child moves through this Basic Fitness Phase, his physical and athletic skills should continue to develop and improve. For example, by age 6, parents should introduce their youngster to riding a bicycle and using roller and ice skates, if those skills haven't already been learned.

Also, the 21 basic skills that he should already have developed can now serve as the foundation for more complex movements and abilities. For example, many children at this age have learned to wield a plastic bat or stick and strike stationary objects on the ground. So now is the time to begin to roll the object toward the child and encourage him to hit it on the move with his bat.

In addition, if he joins a T-ball league, he'll learn to hit a ball with a heavier baseball bat off a stationary position from a waist-high tee. Finally, parents should give the child increasing practice in hitting balls on the fly with a bat or racket. The same sort of approach should be taken with all the other motor skills.

The ultimate goal with these exercises, by the way, is *not* to turn every child into a superathlete. Rather, the more reasonable and modest objectives for most parents should be threefold:

• To provide your child with plenty of opportunities for enjoyable and vigorous exercise with those at his developmental and maturity level

• To help her develop the motor skills that will enable her to reach her full physical and athletic potential

• To provide your child with basic skills and habits that will make it more likely that fitness and sports activities will be more enjoyable and compelling during adulthood

If you achieve these three goals, your child's body will be well on the road to becoming strong and aerobically fit. Furthermore, he will possess motor skills that should help him to perform much better in the playground and on the athletic field. As an important by-product, his improved athletic performance will almost certainly help him feel better about himself.

The Mind. The child's mental processes move along rapidly during the Basic Skills Phase, and in some ways cognitive development is even more important at this point than physical progress.

What exactly is happening inside your child? At age 6, the brain weighs nearly 90 percent of what it will eventually weigh in adulthood. Also, the central nervous system, although largely in place, is still maturing and "making connections" with muscles and other parts of the body.

The degree of maturity of the nervous system and the thinking processes has a direct bearing on how well a given child can perform in a fitness activity or sport. Younger children, for instance, are not usually as capable as older kids and adults of activating the various muscles in the body. As a result, according to research by Dr. Cameron J. R. Blimkie of McMaster University in Ontario, Canada, they can't generate the muscle force that you might expect from their weight and height. In part, this is because different children reach different plateaus of neurological development at different chronological ages.

The implications of these findings are profound. A child whose nerve development is delayed may be the same age, size, and weight as many of his peers. But he may be unable to get off to a quick start on the playing field, shift directions easily, or kick or hit a ball with much force. In a few years, however, this situation may change dramatically. After his neurological development "catches up," he may be able to perform as well as or better than his peers.

A Year-By-Year Scenario. Now, let me illustrate these mental and neurological events in more detail by providing you with a year-by-year view of the average child's physical and cognitive development from age 5 to 8. But remember, these references to chronological age are merely *general* indications of what most children are doing or thinking during a particular year of life. If your child is a little behind or a little ahead, that doesn't mean anything is seriously wrong. Rather, his developmental age right now is just a little different from that of his peers—a fact that's important to keep in mind as you design a kid fitness program.

In other words, your child may be 5 years old, but her cognitive development may be at the 6- or 7-year level in many ways. If that's the case, you may want to enter her in an athletic program that caters to older children.

Or your son may be 8, but right now, he's operating at a 7-year level. In this situation, parents should lower their expectations for his performance for the time being and be patient until he catches up with his peers.

Here, then, are some thoughts about characteristics of the average child in each year of the Basic Skills Phase:*

AGE 5: Although the typical 5-year-old has developed many physical and sports skills—such as running, throwing, and jumping—he's often slow in executing various movements, at least by the standards of older children or adults. Also, children at this age are easily distracted and may seem to forget instructions, even seconds after they're issued. This can be a frustrating phenomenon for coaches who are trying to get children this age to work together as a team!

The youngster may be able to eat with regular table utensils, but it takes

---

*The following descriptions are based on my own research and observations, on insights provided by experts at the Institute for Aerobics Research, and also on points made by the American Pediatric Association and by Dr. George H. Lowrey in *Growth and Development of Children,* eighth edition, 1986.

a little while for food to get to the mouth efficiently. Or he may be told to throw a ball in a certain direction, but the movement doesn't come automatically. Despite repeated coaching, he must stop, think, and then execute the movement.

Another 5-year-old may be able to hit the ball, but then he stands and watches it rather than immediately running toward first base. Still another may be directed to play defense in soccer by kicking the ball away from her own goal and toward the sidelines when it comes to her. But then, in a real game situation, she may fail to kick it at all, or even kick it toward her own goal.

The 5-year-old's interests are more in fun and play than in competition or winning. He mainly focuses on his relationship with his parents. He wants very much to please them, whether at home or on the playing field. Playing at home, though, is often more interesting for the 5-year-old than playing on an organized team. Also, there's enough routine and rule following for this child at school. Fitness activities will be compelling and interesting *only* if they are enjoyable and stress free, and if they offer plenty of opportunities to unwind.

Finally, never forget that the child at this level is still gaining basic intellectual skills—a fact that parents and coaches should keep in mind when trying to communicate game rules and strategies. The typical 5-year-old can usually name at least four colors; draw a rough, but recognizable, figure of a human being; and identify pennies, nickels, and dimes. But he *can't* figure out complicated athletic strategies or coaching instructions!

One soccer coach told a group of 5-, 6-, and 7-year-olds, "You've got to be more aggressive when you're in a defensive posture!" They just looked at him blankly and continued to play the same way they had been playing. Even if they had understood his vocabulary—and they didn't—most lacked the cognitive development to be able to follow his orders.

Overall, 5-year-olds, as well as other children throughout the Basic Skills Phase, are subject to a kind of "Out-to-Lunch" syndrome. Although they are drawn to the social camaraderie and excitement of organized sports, they are easily distracted and periodically lose interest entirely in the game that's going on about them.

I still have a vivid recollection of a 5-year-old on a soccer field who was looking up at the cloud configurations in the sky as a ball was being kicked past him for a goal. Another boy, an 8- or 9-year-old, was playing in the sand in the outfield when a baseball rolled past him for an extra base hit.

To be sure, such antics can be frustrating and even infuriating for parents and coaches. But keep in mind that these children are just that—*children.*

They may seem out to lunch, but that's normal in this stage of development. A few may be relatively focused and competitive at an early age, but these are the exceptions.

It's important for adults to be understanding and patient. Even most of the out-to-lunch types will eventually learn to keep their minds on the business at hand. In the meantime, it's important, quite literally, to let the kids be kids.

Adults can try gently to nudge and guide children into better mental disciplines, and in some cases that may help a little. But pushing for greater skills and playing ability shouldn't get in the way of the main goals at this developmental level: enhancing the child's physical fitness and helping him *gradually* to develop skills he doesn't have.

As far as mental functioning is concerned, most parents and coaches just have to wait it out, until the child moves up to the next developmental plateau.

AGE 6: Children at this level can usually tell their age correctly. They can also repeat at least four numbers in their proper sequence, and may be able to count up to 20 or 30. Obviously, however, most are not ready to figure their batting averages or keep score in tennis!

Physical activity accelerates during this period, and the child may be quite restless and have trouble deciding what to do with his time. Accidents increase, such as spilling food at meals, and outbursts of anger become more frequent. The reason: children are becoming more independent and beginning to exercise their newfound freedom, for better or worse.

Television continues to be a major interest, and the child will probably identify a number of shows that she feels she "just has to watch." Consequently, parents must pay particular attention to supervising television and channeling the child's free time into more productive activities, such as sports and fitness-oriented play.

AGE 7: Those at the 7-year stage are now *mostly* able to dress and undress themselves, although many still need help. The majority can count by twos and fives, can tell time, and are able to tell you the month.

This child, like all others in this Basic Fitness Phase, needs the approval of his peers at school and on the playing field. Most important, he needs the love and support of parents as he develops and improves at his own special pace. Rejection, ridicule, or harsh criticism can discourage the child from wanting to play certain sports or pursue fitness activities at all.

Remember, your main objectives at this stage are to help your youngster increase his level of fitness, reinforce his natural enjoyment of sports, and provide him with further skills to enhance that enjoyment.

At about this point, children also begin to display "spontaneous cuing" according to Dr. Robert Arnot, founder of the Lake Placid Sports Medicine Center and Sportlab. Spontaneous cuing involves the development of the capacity to make complex but instantaneous sports decisions.

For example, increasing numbers of children at the 7-year level are able to hit a ball in a T-ball game and then, without hesitation, run toward first base. Others learn at this age that when they take a shot at a soccer goal, they should immediately follow up on that first attempt in an effort to get a second shot.

This process of integrating physical and cognitive skills becomes increasingly important during later years, when team play becomes more demanding. By the time many children reach the 9- or 10-year level, for instance, they have accumulated sufficient skills and experience to be able to relay a ball from the outfield to home plate, or even execute a fairly efficient double play.

Why are these developments so significant? Improvement at sports—and the fun that accompanies better performance—depends on building steadily on one's current level of skill and understanding. So it's highly significant when your child experiences any breakthrough, such as:

- Following up on a basketball or soccer shot
- Automatically fielding a grounder and throwing it to first base
- Executing a racing turn in the pool

These may seem small physical skill advances to you, but they're giant steps for an elementary-school child. And remember, I'm not mainly interested in encouraging you to turn your child into a top-level athlete. Rather, your main parental objective in this Basic Fitness Phase is to provide your son or daughter with as many physical abilities as possible so that fitness activities become easier and more pleasurable.

If fitness is a chore, or requires the development of skills that the person has never acquired, discouragement and dropping out become more common. But if a child *or* adult knows how to perform certain physical maneuvers and is familiar with the cognitive patterns that accompany them, it's much more likely that his interest will remain high and he'll continue his participation.

AGE 8: The eighth year is a major watershed in the development of most children. But unfortunately, most parents fail to recognize that not every child who is 8 years old chronologically is at the 8-year developmental level. They overlook the fact that some children who celebrate their eighth birthday are at the 6.5- or 7-year developmental level. Other chronological 8-year-olds are ahead of their peers, at the 9- or 10-year developmental level.

Of course, this disparity between developmental and chronological age has been important before age 8. But at this stage it can be *decisive* in shaping the child's attitudes toward fitness and his motivation to pursue vigorous physical activities. The reason? Children at about age 8 become more aware of how they perform in comparison with other children. Also, 8-year-olds are often thrown in with older children on teams and may be subjected to peer criticism in unbearably intense doses: "He can't hit anything!" "She's too small and slow!"

At this age level, peer acceptance and involvement become extremely important, and in the child's view, parents increasingly get in the way. Usually, the 8-year-old will prefer to be away from home and parental authority and in the company of friends. That typically means playing games or sports with peers, either at school, in the playground, in someone's yard, or at an athletic event.

What else is going on in the typical 8-year-old's mind? He is developing significant thinking and intellectual skills, such as the ability to count backward from 20; make proper change for small purchases; and remember dates and times when athletic contests, parties, and other important events are scheduled. His mental powers are becoming more subtle, as he begins to distinguish fictional from factual accounts. As far as sports are concerned, he starts to analyze *why* certain people are able to perform better than others and begins to perceive a connection between athletic ability or fitness and popularity.

Dr. Bruce Watkins, professor of sports management and communication at the University of Michigan, surveyed a group of 8-year-old third graders, in addition to several groups of older children, to determine their beliefs about athletic ability and excellence. The third graders, more than any other age group, believed that the main source of athletic abilities is *effort* or *practice*. They placed relatively little value on innate, natural athletic ability or on the development of mental strengths, like concentration or motivation.

The third graders also indicated they believed there was a relationship between athletic ability and positive interpersonal skills. Watkins notes that sports excellence may be linked to popularity, even at the 8-year age level.

Watkins's findings have important implications for the motivation and emotional well-being of children. Specifically, parents of those at the 8-year age level of cognitive development should recognize that because these children accept the importance of practice, plenty of opportunities for regular physical training should be provided. As parents promote improved athletic performance, they'll most likely see their child begin to enjoy some related benefits, such as greater popularity and social acceptance (more on this in chapters 5 and 6).

Fitness Considerations. As I've already emphasized, all children in this phase can improve their physical skills through regular play and practice and short training sessions with parents and team coaches. As long as the instruction remains relaxed and is punctuated by plenty of vigorous play, the children will be able to perform increasingly difficult and complex maneuvers on the playing field.

All children can improve their aerobic and muscular fitness. Some limited calisthenics may be appropriate, but I don't recommend more sophisticated strength training using weights or other apparatus. Both boys and girls can experience increases in aerobic and muscle power during this phase, but they won't see any real increase in muscle mass. Muscles don't begin to respond significantly to training until about the time of puberty, probably as a result of an increased output of sex hormones (further guidelines can be found in chapter 8).

Children can safely participate in many vigorous sports, with the exception of those such as football or hockey, which involve serious collision between players. The skeletal structure and other organs are too immature in this stage for high-impact sports.

Here is another caveat: children in the Basic Fitness Phase are often expending a great deal of energy, sometimes in hot weather. The danger is that they have less efficient mechanisms than adults to get rid of heat in their body. Research has shown that although they have a larger number of active sweat glands per square inch of body surface than adults, the children's glands put out only about 40 percent as much sweat as those of adults.

Children produce more body heat during a given amount of physical activity than do adults. In addition, the ratio of body mass to total body surface is much lower in 5- to 8-year-olds than in older children or adults— another factor that causes children to heat up very quickly during vigorous sports.

So parents and coaches must *not* withhold water from exercising children, but should encourage them to drink plenty before and during vigorous exercise. As a general rule, children who are racing or running steadily in sports events during hot weather should drink 8 to 12 ounces of water (adjusted to age and body weight) 30 minutes before the start of their activity, and then take in supplemental fluids during the exercise.

■　■　■

The end of this Basic Fitness Phase ushers in a period of high vulnerability when many children begin to drop out of sports and fitness programs. Parental patience and long-term planning are essential to prevent giving up and to minimize discouragement. An understanding of the next three phases of child development will help you meet the most serious challenges to fitness programs that begin at the end of the preteen years and degenerate into what I've called the Adolescent Slump.

CHAPTER THREE

Understanding the Adolescent Slump

T he most serious threat to kid fitness arrives just before the onset of adolescence, when many children are in the 8- to 10-year age range. At this time, a great surge of discouragement and declining interest in sports and fitness grips huge numbers of young people. The walkout continues up into adolescence, and by then the large majority of children have left organized sports and vigorous exercise programs.

What causes the mass exodus and what can you as a parent do to head it off? This question can best be answered by a consideration of the next three stages of child development—the Early Team Phase, the Puberty Phase, and the Final Development Phase.

#4. The Early Team Phase I call this next phase of development the Early Team Phase because children in this category are moving beyond the initial, relaxed exposure to sports into a more competitive, organized team experience. These children are often between the ages of 8 and 10, although some children may be as young as 7 when they enter this phase, and others may be approaching 12 before they move out of it.

For these kids, the team experience usually hasn't yet reached the intensity that will occur when the team's final won-lost standing or a school's athletic reputation assumes overriding importance. But children are now starting to make definite comparisons: "He's the best player on the team." "I hope she shows up because we can't win without her!" "Do we get trophies if we win?"

Furthermore, the sense of being a drag on the team or a poor performer may cause children to become increasingly discouraged at the team athletic experience.

During this period of life, a huge number of children participate in various community, church, and neighborhood athletic and fitness activities. The National Children and Youth Fitness Study (NCYFS) of 1987 revealed that nearly all children—more than 84 percent—participate in physical activity through at least one community organization.

At the same time, there is a dramatic shift toward team sports and competition in school physical education and extracurricular programs for children in grades three to four (or the 8- to 10-year age range). The officials with the NCYFS have said they are alarmed by this trend because with the increased focus on competition, programs that emphasize *non*competitive activities and lifetime fitness habits begin to disappear.

Is the alarm justified? In fact, it is. As the boys and girls in the Early Team Phase confront the challenge of serious team competition, the first big wave of dropouts emerges, usually before age 10. After the exodus starts, various studies show that 80 to 90 percent of all children eventually drop out of organized sports by age 15 or 16.

Unfortunately, very few of the children who leave sports turn to noncompetitive fitness activities as a substitute. Instead, increasing numbers rely on television or other sedentary pursuits to occupy their free time. The growing bodies and minds of these preteens thus miss out on the physical activity they so desperately need in this phase of development.

The Body. The muscle strength of most boys and girls in the Early Team Phase still falls far short of what it will be when they go through their main growth spurt, the "peak height velocity," during puberty. For girls, the average age of the peak height velocity is 11.5 years, and for boys the average age for this big growth spurt is 13.5. This means that most children are well past 10 years of age when they experience the growth spurt that will trigger their main gain of muscle strength.

On the other hand, there are *some* children who experience early strength gains. According to a 1989 report by Dr. Cameron Blimkie in *Youth, Exercise, and Sport,* about 1 percent of boys have a significant increase in muscle power before they reach puberty. More than 10 percent have this strength gain after the onset of puberty, but before their peak increase in height.

In other words, a very small percentage of boys may be only about 10 years old when their muscle power begins to accelerate. This development gives them a significant advantage when they are competing in sports or other fitness activities against those who haven't reached the same maturity level.

Even more girls experience their major strength gain at an early age: more than 15 percent undergo a big muscle power increase before puberty—or as early as 8 or 9 years of age. Another 25 percent, who are in the 10- to 11-year age range, go through the main muscle power burst after the onset of puberty, but before their peak height increase.

There's also another strength factor that may affect children who are playing and competing in sports in the Early Team Phase. Many youngsters in the 8- to 10-year age range have not only failed to go through their major gain of strength, they also lack the nerve connections necessary to *activate* the full force of the muscles that they have.

I've already mentioned this muscle-activation issue in my discussion of the Basic Fitness Phase. But here's some more important information that may relate to your 10-year-old:

Dr. Blimkie reports that on average, 10-year-old boys can activate nearly 90 percent of their elbow flexors, featuring the muscles on the front of the arm, the biceps. On the other hand, some 10-year-olds can only activate 50 percent of their elbow flexor muscles. Obviously, the varying rhythms of development give the first group a major advantage in sports over the second group.

Even more 10-year-old boys are behind older children in the development of their ability to activate the knee extensors—the thighs and other muscles that enable them to straighten out their legs. Dr. Blimkie says that the average boy tested could only activate about 78 percent of these leg muscles and a few were able to activate less than 50 percent of the muscle units.

Such findings have major implications for any kid fitness program for children in the Early Team Phase, which roughly covers ages 8 to 10. For one thing, parents and coaches in charge of these youngsters must expect a wide variation in muscle strength and physical power on any given team. A relatively large child may seem unable to kick or hit a ball as hard as a much smaller youngster. Still another child may be a little slow in starting a race, or may lag in changing direction as she runs for a ball.

In such situations, it's easy to write a late-blooming child off as a poor athlete—but such a conclusion is probably dead wrong! Instead, you may simply be witnessing a developmental delay with the activation of certain leg muscles.

Other key fitness-related physical changes are also occurring in the average 10-year-old boy or girl. The average child's chest circumference has increased to slightly more than 25 inches and there have been significant gains in height and weight.

On the whole, though, at this stage boys and girls still remain about the same physically. The median height for boys now tops 55 inches and the median weight is a shade under 72 pounds. For girls, the median height is about 55.5 inches and the median weight is more than 70 pounds. Overall, these measurements and averages indicate that while growth is progressing during the Early Team Phase, there is still pervasive skeletal immaturity. Furthermore, as Dr. Rainer Martens of the University of Illinois at Urbana-Champaign notes, beginning at about age 10, "the range of individual differences in physical structure . . . is greater than at any other time in the human life span."

To illustrate, he says that boys of the same chronologic age may differ by as much as 60 months in their anatomical or skeletal age. Accordingly, one 10-year-old could have a skeletal age typical of the average boy at age 7.5 and another 10-year-old could have a bone maturity level of the average 12.5 year old. Martens warns that these differences in the physical maturation of children can "present substantial problems in making competition in many sports safe and equitable." I wholeheartedly concur.

What about the sensitive, easy-to-injure growth plates that were present at age 6? They are still open and functioning—and still vulnerable. The remaining bone growth centers, or epiphyses—such as those in the upper arms, wrists, and legs—won't begin to unite until about age 12. Furthermore, the union and hardening (and thus protection) of these plates won't be finished in many children until age 19 or 20.

It's common for active children in the Early Team Phase to complain of lingering aches and pains as a result of blows to the growth plates or overuse of certain skeletal areas during sports. These complaints are usually nothing to worry about, and probably your pediatrician or orthopedist will quite properly just advise resting the part that hurts until healing occurs.

On the other hand, the growth plates *are* vulnerable, and they become even more susceptible to injury as the child gets older. Collision sports like football and hockey may produce serious or even permanent growth plate injuries.

On a more positive note, only about 10 percent of all skeletal trauma in children involves the epiphyses, and few long-lasting effects have been reported. In fact, it's not clear whether intensively trained young athletes are at a greater risk of injury than children who are engaged in free-play activities. Still, your child's training programs involve an increase in intensity and duration, it's wise to use the best protective equipment and take other steps to guard against serious injury.

Some of your child's bones are probably still not even present at this stage of development! In the wrist, for example, the pisiform bone (one of the carpals) is present in only 50 percent of girls at age 9 and in only 6 percent of boys at that age! A few boys still lack as many as four carpals—or half of the eight bones in the wrist—at age 8. The implication for the lack of such bones isn't entirely clear—except that the child will have less skeletal support in these areas and may be more susceptible to injuries.

What about the differences between boys and girls in the Early Team Phase? Although the physical growth of boys and girls is still roughly the same, girls begin to forge ahead at about age 10 in some ways. Their skeletal development is often in advance of boys'. Also, some girls are beginning to enter the initial stages of puberty, with a slight swelling of the breasts and the appearance of pubic hair.

These sexual changes, and the accompanying advances in the girl's skeletal development and overall maturity, mean that girls can often compete *physically* quite well with boys in this phase. I'm reminded of one very tall, heavy, and athletic girl who was one of the most feared forwards and scorers in a soccer league for 10-year-olds. There are also countless serious 9- and 10-year-old female tennis players who can hold their own with the best among their male counterparts.

The Mind. Cognitive functioning, including the capacity to analyze and evaluate one's own performance and that of others, becomes increasingly important in fitness during the Early Team Phase. A major manifestation of this more sophisticated mental operation is the phenomenon of dropping out.

Growing numbers of boys, as well as girls, begin to drop out of fitness activities around the age of 9 or 10 for a number of key reasons.

• Many girls at this stage may drift away from competitive sports, in part because teams are often dominated by boys. These girls may no longer be able to identify with some of their once-favorite sports because the activities don't seem to be "right for a girl."

• Boys or girls may become bored because they are not on the first string and thus find themselves spending too much time on the bench. Studies show that 90 percent of boys who participate in sports would rather play on a losing team than sit on the bench with a winning team!

Something about just *participating* can give anyone, child or adult, a sense of accomplishment, of self-worth and personal success. If you are playing, there's always a chance you'll improve and maybe even win, but there's *no* chance if you aren't playing.

NOTE: A frequent underlying reason for a child's not being able to play is that preference is given to more mature, and thus highly skilled, players. If teams are organized so that children of similar skills and development are matched, many of the problems with being relegated to the bench may be resolved.

• Children quit during the Early Team Phase, as well as later, because they are *told* they are no good. As a result, they may begin to believe that they are not good or even adequate at the sport in question.

In many instances, the source of this problem is coaches or parents who constantly criticize, even when a child is doing reasonably well. This excessive negative feedback can make the child feel that improving or succeeding at the activity is impossible.

• Some children quit because they or their teams frequently fail to win. These kids decide they are no good because they can't beat anyone else.

Parents or other adults may say winning doesn't matter that much. But it's hard for a youngster to become enthusiastic and want to stick with a sport if he rarely or never is victorious.

• Children may drop out beginning in the 9- to 10-year age range because they don't react well to the pressure of competition.

Some children seem to thrive on the demands and stresses of game conditions. They actually perform better when they come up to the plate in the last inning with the bases loaded, two outs, and the outcome of the game hanging on their swing of the bat. Many other children, though, quake in fear at the prospect of such pressure. Their reaction may be so severe, with stomach upsets, rashes, or other physical symptoms, that they simply can't function. If parents and coaches add to these pressures—or at any rate, if they fail to counteract them—stress-sensitive children are likely to follow the swelling wave of departures from youth fitness activities. Probably the best way to combat such pressures is to help the child gain a sense of perspective on each contest, including an understanding that a win or loss isn't all that important.

• Children drop out because they are alienated by heavy training sessions that just *aren't any fun*. Too many practice routines, lectures, or other boring workouts can drive any child from a worthwhile fitness program to another activity.

Now, let's move beyond the drop-out issue and consider a few related emotional and mental factors that distinguish the average child in the 9- to 10-year age range.

Although I may not always agree with the Swiss psychologist Jean Piaget, I think he has a point when he says mental development and emotional development in preadolescent children are quite different from those in adolescents and adults. In particular, children of this age don't employ logical reasoning in evaluating themselves and the world about them. They don't take a certain set of facts and then weave a hypothesis or conclusion from those facts, so as to obtain broader or deeper insights into their day-to-day experience. Instead, from about age 7 to 11, children are locked into *concrete* as opposed to symbolic thinking. They focus mainly on the objective world that they can perceive with their five senses.

To be sure, most children of this age do have a well-developed imagination and active fantasy life. But when it comes to the real world, they are concerned primarily about the facts at hand. They don't speculate or project their conclusions and thoughts much beyond the present. One of the few exceptions is the inclination to look forward to enticing events in the near future, such as their next birthday party, summer camp, or the opening day of baseball season.

So the eyes of the typical 8- to 10-year-old will probably glaze over if you say, "Learning how to play this sport now (or doing such and such a set of exercises now) will help you later when you play in high school."

It may be even more incomprehensible to say to the child, "You have a natural talent in this sport, so why don't you specialize in it, rather than spending so much time on other activities." Likewise, it's fruitless to urge, "I want you to participate in these physical activities because they will make you a healthier and happier adult."

Children in the Early Team Phase just don't care much about the future value of present activity. So trying to appeal to their reasoning ability is a waste of time.

On the other hand, it may very well be possible to get the child to do certain exercises, pursue a certain sport, or otherwise change his behavior *if* the activity can be made compelling on the child's terms. As you'll see in chapter 6, a well–thought-out system of immediate rewards for children can reinforce good fitness behavior, even if efforts to reason with the child fail.

Other general characteristics of children at this stage of development include the following.

- They can accept blame and responsibility for their actions.
- They can complete designated tasks, such as performing to the best of their physical ability in an assigned position on a team.
- They are susceptible to hero worship; are deeply influenced by impressive adults, such as professional athletes, dancers, or others who have mastered physical skills; and can be inspired to pattern their behavior after the example of these heroes. So the more they can be exposed to suitable role models at sports contests or other events and performances, the better.
- They want to please important adults, including parents and coaches—a powerful force in the hands of grown-ups who carefully plan how to use their influence wisely.
- They become increasingly independent and want to spend more time with peers, outside the influence of parents and other adults.
- They deeply desire the approval of their peers, and one way to get it is to perform well in physical contests.
- They become familiar with the demands and needs of teamwork, including helping teammates who may be in a position to score. A sacrifice fly in baseball becomes almost as significant as a base hit, and an assist in soccer rivals the importance of a goal.
- They recognize the importance of following the rules when they play various sports.

Parents who teach their children in detail the rules of various popular games can place a powerful instrument of influence and prestige in the hands of these children. Respect is likely to be accorded the child who knows the details of the infield fly rule in baseball, who can describe the 3–6–3 double play in baseball, or who is able to observe the offside rule in soccer.

Fitness Considerations. Aerobic capacity, which comes through endurance activities like running, cycling, and swimming, is very helpful in the Early Team Phase. As a matter of fact, the National Children and Youth Fitness Study of 1987 revealed that the most popular sports among children in the first through fourth grades were among the most beneficial in developing endurance capacity.

Specifically, both boys and girls said the most frequent sport they engaged in was swimming and the second most frequent was running or racing. The fourth and fifth most popular sports for boys were soccer and bicycling, respectively, and the third most popular for girls was bicycling. With these findings in mind, I've prepared in chapter 8 a number of enjoyable and systematic exercise programs involving swimming, running, bicycling, and other popular endurance activities.

Also, the muscle power of children in the Early Team Phase responds well to strength training, such as the calisthenics plan I recommend in chapter 8. Furthermore, *extremely well supervised* training with weights or other apparatus may be appropriate. As with younger children, you won't see much increase in muscle size or definition in this age range because these children still haven't received the necessary increase in hormones that occurs when they go through puberty. But you *will* usually see significant increases in muscle power and control.

#5. The Puberty Phase Adolescence begins with the onset of puberty—roughly the 10- to 14-year age range when the major sexual and hormonal changes begin to occur in the child.

The Body. This time of life is especially important to understand for those designing a kid fitness program, because puberty triggers various other growth processes, such as major height increases and weight gains. For example, boys who have not entered puberty may find themselves at a severe disadvantage when participating in physical activities with boys who have already started this phase. Among other things, various studies have revealed that boys who are advanced in sexual maturity tend to be stronger and perform better on motor performance tests.

In one unpublished study of Peewee football players, eight of the nine boys rated by their coaches as the best on their teams were midway through the puberty changes. They dominated the key positions of quarterback, fullback, cornerback, and end. The only prepubescent boy in this group was a quarterback who was tall for his age.

Similarly, in a classic study of 112 players in the 1955 Little League World Series, 37.5 percent of the players had entered puberty and 45.5 percent had finished with puberty! As might be expected, the most important positions in the field and batting order were also filled by those who were the most mature sexually.

Another study of 55 participants in the 1957 Little League World Series found that only five of the boys involved had delayed maturity, with delayed "skeletal ages" (i.e., development of bone structure). Another 25 of the boys had maturity levels and skeletal ages in the same range as those of their chronological age. The final 25 boys were *more* mature than their peers, with skeletal ages in advance of the average for those their age.

In analyzing these youthful 1957 baseball players, the researcher W. M. Krogman concluded that "the successful Little League ball player is old for his age, i.e., he is biologically advanced. This boy succeeds, it may be argued, because he is more mature, biologically more stable, and structurally and functionally more advanced" (Robert M. Malina et al., December 1982).

One exception to this advantage arising from maturity is boy hockey players. The majority of 12-year-old boys participating in one international hockey tournament—including tournament all-stars—were of average or slightly delayed maturity status, according to a 1982 report.

Why should boys in prepuberty or early puberty have an advantage in hockey? One possibility is that because they were lighter, they could take advantage of their skating skills more readily than their heavier, more mature counterparts.

On the other hand, the evidence shows that by age 16, all-star hockey players are significantly taller and heavier than boys of a similar chronological age. The reason? Experts speculate that the skill level of the older boys had increased to the point that they are able to make full use of their greater size and strength.

The most advanced fitness programs and leading exercise experts recommend that children—especially boys—be matched in sports according to their degree of sexual maturity. Otherwise, an 11-year-old boy who is developmentally at the 9-year level may be placed in competition with an 11-year-old who is at the 13-year developmental level. Such mismatching can be discouraging and even dangerous for the less-mature child.

NOTE: There are many basketball, baseball, tennis, and other programs that match children according to their skill or developmental levels. Parents with children who are lagging somewhat athletically should seek out these possibilities rather than placing their youngsters on teams that are too demanding for their children's abilities.

For girls, the situation is somewhat different. Delayed sexual maturity may actually work to their advantage in a number of fitness activities and sports.

For example, researchers have found that young female gymnasts and ballet dancers tend to be quite delayed in their skeletal and sexual maturity, including the onset of menarche (menstruation). Female track athletes are also delayed, although less so. Other studies have shown that elite girl athletes involved in ice-skating, tennis, and volleyball move through puberty on about the same schedule as their nonathletic counterparts.

Female swimmers may be the major exception. Some researchers have found that they are slightly ahead of those in their chronological age group in skeletal maturity and the onset of menarche.

What's the reason for the delay in puberty among many female athletes? There are several possibilities:

• Girls who are slow to mature may naturally gravitate toward certain activities like gymnastics and ballet, where it's advantageous to be relatively small and light. Puberty triggers significant health and weight gains, without necessarily bringing on an accompanying ability to control and use the body in these sports.

• Heavy training routines have been known to lower body fat and thus delay the onset of menarche.

• With girls more than boys, the onset of puberty with menarche tends to shut down the growth process. As a result, girls who mature later are more likely to become taller and bigger than those who become sexually mature at an early age. This added period of growth for late maturers can be an advantage during adolescence and adulthood for many sports, including basketball, some track events, and volleyball.

What sort of changes can you expect to occur in your child during the Puberty Phase, and at what age are they likely to happen? First, it's necessary to pinpoint the *sexual* changes that are actually occurring in the child. This isn't such an easy task because with the onset of adolescence, children's need for privacy increases dramatically. Most don't want a nosy parent checking to see what's happening to their bodies!

One possible way to get around this problem is to inform the child about the significance of the Puberty Phase, or perhaps to have him read some of the sections of this book that pertain to him. Then the child can take responsibility for checking himself to ascertain his own developmental status. Another possibility is to have your physician check him during a regular medical exam.

In determining the puberty status of boys and girls, the researcher J. M. Tanner has provided some helpful guidelines by identifying five stages of sexual maturity for both boys and girls (see the accompanying figures that show these stages for both boys and girls).

Tanner's Stage 1 represents the absence of sexual maturity and Stage 5 describes the fully mature boy or girl. Stages 2 through 4 indicate intermediate states of sexual development, which are characteristic of the Puberty Phase. For boys, the stages are based on changes in genital organs and pubic hair; in girls, they are based on genital organs, pubic hair, and breast development.

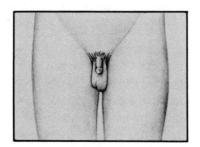

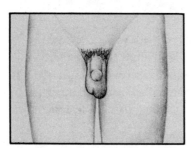

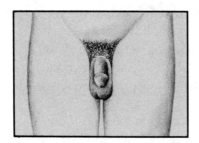

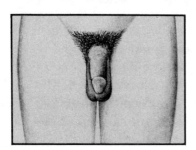

TANNER STAGES 2 THROUGH 5 FOR BOYS: the development of pubic hair and genitalia. Source: Dennis J. Caine and Jan Broekhoff, "Maturity Assessment: A Viable Preventive Measure against Physical and Psychological Insult to the Young Athlete?" *The Physician and Sportsmedicine,* vol. 15, March 1987, p. 69.

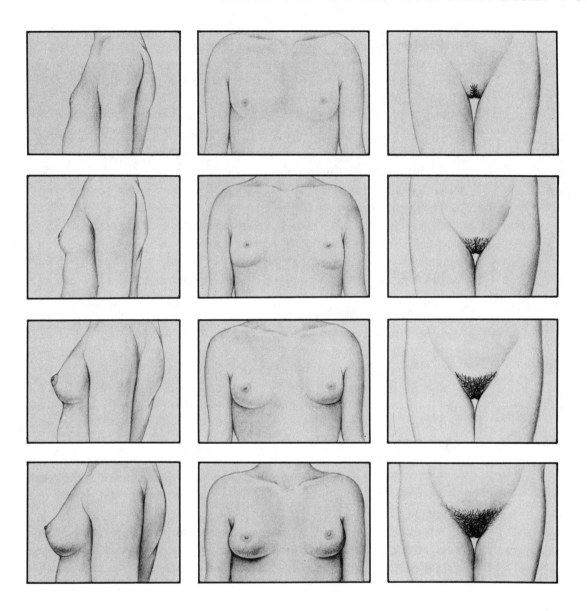

TANNER STAGES 2 THROUGH 5 FOR GIRLS:
the development of pubic hair and breasts. Source: Dennis J. Caine and Jan
Broekhoff, "Maturity Assessment: A Viable Preventive Measure against Physical
and Psychological Insult to the Young Athlete?" *The Physician and Sportsmedicine,* vol. 15, March 1987, p. 70.

REMEMBER: The sexual changes usually signal or trigger other important physical developments, which can be decisive to the success of any kid fitness program or sports effort. Puberty becomes a pivotal development that can turn children either on or off to habits that may make all the difference in their health and conditioning as adults.

Using Tanner's findings and several other sources, I've devised the following composite picture of the sexual and other related physical changes that take place during puberty in boys and girls. If you can monitor where your child now is in this sequence and follow the way she develops, you'll be in a much better position to recommend effective fitness strategies.

The Puberty Picture for Girls.

THE BEGINNING OF BREAST DEVELOPMENT: This change begins between about 10.5 and 11.5 years of age for most girls, although some may be as young as 8 or 9 and others may be older than 12. The characteristics include slight swelling of the breasts and rising and darkening of the nipple.

THE APPEARANCE OF PUBIC HAIR: Pubic hair typically appears on girls beginning between ages 10.5 and 12, with some having this change by age 9 and others after age 12.

THE MIDDLE STAGE OF BREAST DEVELOPMENT AND PUBIC HAIR GROWTH: This stage, which occurs on average between ages 11 and 13.5, involves the continued development of the breasts and nipples, and also a significant increase in the amount of pubic hair—although to a point short of full maturity.

An important event that also occurs during this stage, on average between ages 11.5 and 12, is the major adolescent growth spurt, known as the "peak height velocity." The girl will reach most of her adult height during this height surge.

But there is considerable variation among individual girls. In one Swiss study, for example, the beginning of the growth spurt occurred between ages 6 and 13, and the most intense upward growth occurred between ages 9 and 15.

About a year after the average adolescent girl's major growth spurt, between the ages of 12 and 13, she typically undergoes her greatest gain in weight, because of the increase in sex hormones at this age. Much of this weight is fat, however. As a result, the girl's endurance capacity—the amount of oxygen she can consume per minute during intense exercise at her particular body weight—decreases dramatically.

Also, because much of the weight gain is fat rather than muscle, her strength doesn't usually increase dramatically at this point. In fact, various studies show that girls perform much worse on strength tests, in part because they are held back by extra fatty tissue.

MENARCHE: The arrival of menarche, or the girl's "period," occurs on average between ages 12.5 and 13.5.

As with other aspects of the maturing process, the time when menstruation begins can vary greatly from girl to girl. In one Dutch study, for instance, the most advanced 10 percent of the girls experienced menarche at an average age of 11.7 years. In contrast, a full 50 percent had undergone this change by 13.3, and the most delayed 10 percent still hadn't had their periods by nearly 15 years of age.

The onset of menarche has a direct effect on the girl's growth pattern: increases in height for girls who have had menarche quickly level off, while those with delayed menarche continue to grow taller.

Furthermore, as Dr. Nathan J. Smith, professor of pediatrics and sports medicine at the University of Washington School of Medicine in Seattle, has said, "Elite women athletes in most sports experience menarche later than average. . . . Tallness in women is associated with superior sports performance." He notes one study that showed the height of Olympic medal winners was significantly greater than that of average Western women.

At about the time of menarche, or one to two years after the peak rate of increase in height, the girl begins to show a greater ability to respond to strength training. Muscle development through calisthenics or weight programs, such as those I've included in chapter 8, become quite beneficial at this stage.

FINAL SEXUAL MATURITY: The average girl begins to move out of puberty and toward full sexual maturity between the ages of about 13.5 and 15.5. This stage includes full breast development and pubic hair growth. At this point, the skeletal growth, organ development, and weight increases are almost completed. Consequently, strength and endurance training can have a much greater impact on young women, because the turbulent phase of puberty has passed.

The Puberty Picture for Boys.

THE APPEARANCE OF PUBIC HAIR AND INITIAL ENLARGEMENT OF THE GENITALS: This stage of development typically occurs between ages 11 and 13.5 in our society. The genitals usually increase in size first, and this change is followed by a growth of sparse, long, slightly pigmented pubic hair.

Along with the dramatic changes that begin to take place now in the boy's body, including an increase in height, his flexibility decreases. The youngster's skeleton is still quite immature at this stage, although there is a tremendous variation in body size and strength in boys the same age, depending on the stage of maturity.

Heavy contact and collision sports pose a great threat of injury during puberty. So my advice is for boys at this stage to be extremely cautious participating in wrestling, ice hockey, tackle football, and lacrosse. Also, any strength training with weights should be closely and expertly supervised so as to prevent injury to the immature bones.

The boy's endurance capacity—or cardiorespiratory function—also begins to increase rapidly at about age 13. Investigations have shown that children 10 years old or younger don't react to endurance activities with an increased endurance capacity, as one might expect from teenagers or adults. The trainability of endurance seems to depend on the biological maturity level of growing children. After puberty, however, the effects of endurance training are similar to those reported for adults.

THE GROWTH OF DARKER, COARSER, AND MORE CURLY PUBIC HAIR AND FURTHER GENITAL DEVELOPMENT: On average, boys enter this next stage of puberty between about 12.5 and 14 years. The development is a matter of degree, with further maturity of the genitals and the appearance of relatively coarse, darker, and more abundant pubic hair.

As with the previous stage, the boy should be quite wary of heavy contact sports because of his relative skeletal immaturity. The risk of injury to the growth plates (epiphyses) becomes especially high at this point because growth is accelerating toward the period of peak height velocity. A severe injury to the growth plates in the arms, legs, or elsewhere can actually stunt growth in the affected part of the body.

THE PEAK HEIGHT INCREASE: At ages 13.5 to 15, the boy develops mature pubic hair, but in a more restricted area than is common for adults. Typically around age 14, the boy's so-called peak height velocity begins, as he shoots up at the most rapid growth rate he has experienced since infancy and toddlerhood. As with girls, however, the times at which this big growth increase begins and intensifies can vary greatly among individuals.

In a study of 112 Swiss boys, for instance, the *beginning* of the major growth spurt ranged from just under 8 years of age to 13.5. The *peak* of the spurt occurred as early as 12 and as late as nearly 16.

In a related development, the heart is known to participate in the adolescent growth spurt. A peak increase in the transverse (crosswise) diameter of the heart coincides with peak height velocity during puberty. A personal observation: for more accurate evaluation of the function of the heart, we probably need to develop electrocardiogram tables that take sexual maturity into account.

During this period, boys should continue to be careful about participating in heavy contact sports and other activities that may endanger the growth plates.

THE MUSCLE-AND-WEIGHT STAGE: With the appearance of fully adult pubic hair and genital development, the boy experiences a significant increase in new muscle and body weight. A signal that full sexual development has occurred is the appearance of pubic hair on the inside of the upper thighs. Usually, this stage occurs between about ages 14.5 and 17.5.

The most rapid increase in the boy's endurance capacity occurs at this time, but his muscles at first are still relatively weak and inflexible. Soon, though, the development process will enable him to reach his full muscle power and flexibility.

The Mind. The beginning of puberty also marks the greatest surge of dropouts from fitness programs. As we've seen, this process began in the Early Team Phase, at about ages 9 to 10. But the movement to quit sports teams or otherwise abandon fitness activities now escalates as many children move toward their early teenage years.

Why should this be? What causes boys, and especially girls, to leave fitness programs—and what can be done to keep them in those programs? The answers to these questions begin with the adolescent mind. Boys whose sexual and physical development has been delayed often find they can't compete well with more mature boys. As a result, many just quit sports teams.

Or if they stay on those teams and try to compete, many are *cut* from the teams because they aren't as good as other competitors. In fact, a growing number of experts believe that much of the exodus from sports among 12- to 14-year-old boys is not the result of voluntary dropouts but occurs because the boys have been cut by coaches or are in imminent danger of being cut.

The University of Michigan's Dr. Bruce Watkins raised some interesting questions about adolescent dropouts in his study of children's attitudes toward athletics. He notes that the sixth grade, which typically includes children about 12 years old, is an age of keen social comparison. According to Watkins's findings, these youngsters believe that athletic achievement is rooted mainly in motor skills and "knowing rules." When they compare their current abilities and experience with others—and find themselves falling short—they decide the only logical course is to quit.

But Watkins argues that these children are making their decisions about athletic participation with incomplete data. Older children, for example, rightly emphasize the importance of mental capacities in sports, such as motivation and concentration. But sixth graders apparently don't comprehend the full importance of the cognitive functions.

Also, many 12 year olds are well behind their peers in sexual and physical maturation. If these children—and just as important, their parents—would be patient and give themselves a little time, they might actually develop into competent or even outstanding athletes. Just how parents may play a role in this process is a subject I cover in chapter 4.

My own feeling is that almost *every* normal child, even those who initially may appear uncoordinated or unathletic, can become a competent athlete and develop the skills and fitness needed to enjoy a variety of sports. It's just a matter of believing that they can do it and making a reasonable effort.

So parents and other respected adults must encourage these young people to continue to work on basic fitness and motor skills. Then they must support the children as they *wait* for adequate physical development and maturity to occur. The basic fitness programs I've included in chapter 8 have been designed with these democratic assumptions in mind.

Finally, there are some special gender-related factors that are operating to cause girls to drop out of sports during the Puberty Phase. You'll recall that before puberty begins, boys and girls are essentially equal in their physical development. So most are able to compete on the same teams up to about age 10. After the onset of puberty, however, girls quickly begin to go through the physical changes that increase their body fat and decrease their relative size, endurance, and muscle power in comparison with boys. Continued exercise and attention to diet can limit the impact of these changes, but, of course, the basic transformation that occurs with puberty is inevitable.

When these changes occur, many girls begin to feel inadequate in competition with boys and quit team sports involving both sexes. At the same time, they fail to join girls' teams or pursue other exercise activities, which could enable them to stay fit. As I said in an earlier section, this process begins for many girls at the end of the Early Team Phase—but it definitely picks up momentum as the Puberty Phase unfolds.

Second, many girls, even in our "enlightened" age, are conditioned to feel as they get older that sports are for boys and less-rigorous activities are for girls. In other words, girls may regard fitness activities, and especially competitive sports, as inconsistent with their gender identity.

Fortunately, there is a strong movement away from this way of thinking, but still, many parents tend to deemphasize physical fitness for adolescent girls. To make matters worse, schools and community groups often fail to provide attractive exercise outlets for girls.

Third, there is evidence that girls begin to develop sports skills later than boys and also work less diligently at fine-tuning them. Fourth, girls are more likely than boys to attribute athletic success to social support systems, such as the encouragement of parents, siblings, peers, or coaches, says Dr. Watkins. They tend to underrate the contribution of athletic ability to achievement.

Watkins concludes, "Social support and encouragement are crucial to initially eliciting and subsequently maintaining participation by females."

My conclusion is that parents and coaches must recognize that many girls need great encouragement and positive feedback, apparently even more than boys. Dropping out can be headed off if parents just recognize that their daughters are going through hard times during puberty. At the same time, mom and dad must take steps to provide creative alternatives. Some possibilities are family fitness outings or perhaps the organization of girls' sports teams at their daughters' developmental levels.

Fitness Considerations. The Puberty Phase is the crucial time when the Adolescent Slump emerges in full force. The dropping out of competitive sports and other vigorous activities, which began during the Early Team Phase, now reaches its peak.

Predictably this slump is accompanied by a decided decline in fitness among our adolescents. Our Fitnessgram investigations at the Institute for Aerobics Research shows this deterioration in fitness during the Puberty Phase quite clearly:

• At age 9, 77 percent of boys turned in an acceptable minimum score on a 1-mile run test, but at age 14, only 59 percent could pass the test.

• Girls experienced an even more serious drop on the 1-mile run requirement during the Puberty Phase: at age 9, 72 percent passed, but at age 14, only 49 percent met the minimum standard.

• Both sexes also lost ground on the sit-up test: at age 9, 82 percent of boys and 76 percent of girls passed, but by age 14, 70 percent of the boys and only 53 percent of the girls met the requirement.

The age variations in the upper-body strength tests were predictable, given the changes each sex was undergoing during puberty. Specifically, 57 percent of the 9-year-old boys passed the test, and that increased to 59 percent by age 14—a reflection of the increased muscle development in boys during and following puberty.

As for the girls, 45 percent passed the upper-body strength test at age 9, and that figure declined to only 25 percent at age 14. A systematic kid fitness program could certainly improve the performance of the older girls. But some decline in their upper-body strength has to be expected in view of their accumulation of extra fat and their relatively small increase in muscle strength during early adolescence.

What can parents do to overcome the Adolescent Slump? In a sense, this entire book has been written in response to this question. In particular, we must begin to emphasize fitness for children who aren't interested in highly competitive sports or who have been driven away from athletics for the reasons that have already been discussed. Your children *can* and *should* be taught the basics of sound exercise and good nutrition, regardless of their age, sex, or interest in sports. Most of the following chapters have been devoted to helping you achieve this objective.

#6. The Final Development Phase In general, boys have completed most of their physical development by ages 16 to 17 and at that time are ready to pursue practically any sport, even those involving heavy contact or collision like football and ice hockey. Girls reach their Final Development Phase about one to two years earlier, at ages 14 to 15.

The Body. By age 17, the young person's skeletal maturity is almost complete. Chest circumference has nearly reached adult size, and height and weight are almost at adult levels. The weight and size of various body organs, such as the heart and lungs, are also approaching adult dimensions.

One area that still lags in many children is the closing down and union of certain important growth plates, such as those in the part of the long inner forearm bone closest to the wrist (the distal radius), the section of the long bone of the inner forearm closest to the wrist (distal ulna), and bones in the thigh (femur) and lower leg (tibia and fibula). These growth plates often don't stop functioning until males are between 18 and 20 and females are between 17 and 19.

The Mind. As teenagers move from about ages 15 through 18, a number of important attitudes about fitness may become fixed.

For one thing, those who have been discouraged and dropped out earlier may become more set in their opposition to fitness and sports. Regrettably, they may continue to pursue sedentary practices and develop habits that will be hard to break later as adults.

Also, these young people may adopt resigned, fatalistic attitudes about who can play sports successfully and who can't. Dr. Watkins has found that by the time they reach the senior year in high school (or age 18), only 15 percent of young people believe that a major source of athletic ability is effort, experience, and practice in a sport. As early as age 15, one-third think that sports ability comes mostly from innate natural ability: either you're born with it or you're not.

Such attitudes can work against the participation of many children in fitness activities because they may assume, "I'm just not a natural athlete," or "I'm so bad at sports that I interfere with the other players' fun."

On a happier note, a growing number of high-school seniors—30 percent of those surveyed—believe that sports ability arises from emotional and attitudinal skills, such as determination and setting priorities. Obviously, these cognitive factors *can* be influenced by the young person—a hopeful thought for parents who are trying to convince their teenagers to become more physically active.

Finally, as children grow older, they become more able to analyze their social and physical situation and devise plans to improve themselves. An increased level of physical fitness will lead to greater self-esteem and self-confidence at any age, and older teenagers have the intellectual maturity to understand this fact.

Sometimes, all that's necessary is to point out the link between being in good shape and feeling better about oneself, or being more popular with one's peers. Then the light dawns in the teenager's mind, and she becomes more willing to take independent steps to improve her physical condition. In other cases, of course, such as chronic obesity or eating disorders, more comprehensive measures, such as professional counseling, may be necessary.

Fitness Considerations. In one sense, parents of older teenagers have a difficult task influencing their children to follow wise fitness practices. After all, these young people are more independent than preadolescents. So I recognize that it may be hard to convince a 14-year-old in the middle of his peak height velocity that tackle football may not be the best sport at this time.

To have an impact on your child in these difficult teenage years, it's necessary to embark on a comprehensive parental program, of the type I'll be discussing in the next chapter. Furthermore, it's highly advisable to begin this program *before* the child goes through puberty. That way, it's more likely that good habits will be established, along with a stronger trust relationship between parent and child.

HOW TO APPLY THE CHILD DEVELOPMENT PHASES TO YOUR KID FITNESS PROGRAM

I suspect that you've already been picturing how your child fits into one or more of the above developmental categories. To continue this evaluation in more detail, I suggest that you follow these four steps, which will facilitate your later efforts to formulate an individualized kid fitness program for your child. Remember, to be maximally effective, all exercise efforts, sports programs, and other fitness activities must be keyed to your child's developmental level and rhythm. For most children, the key time to begin this evaluation is in the 5- to 7-year age range.

Step 1. On three separate sheets of paper, jot down these three headings:

- Present Phase of Development for (your child's name)
- Past Phases of Development for (your child's name)
- Preliminary Kid Fitness Strategy

Step 2. Identify where you think your child is *now* in the various developmental phases we've explored. Include as many comments as come to your mind, with notes about your child's evolving physical and cognitive characteristics. Also indicate any delayed or advanced development that you've noticed.

Step 3. Using the description of the different phases, record on the second sheet of paper any milestones you can remember in your child's *past* development. Some sample questions to ask yourself:

- How old was he when he began to walk?
- When did she start riding her bicycle?
- How has he performed on various sports teams?
- What does he like or dislike about fitness activities?
- What motivates him?
- Has she become discouraged or talked of dropping out of sports? If so, describe.
- How involved have you or your spouse been in your child's past fitness activities?

Step 4. On the last sheet of paper—the one labeled Preliminary Kid Fitness Strategy—write down briefly the basic approach you feel your child should take with fitness. Some possible topics:

- Should noncompetitive activities be emphasized?
- Should your child be placed in a developmentally advanced sports group?
- Is he overweight?
- Does she need work on endurance or strength?
- What can you, as a parent, do to help your child?

Obviously, you're just at the beginning of formulating the appropriate Kid Fitness Shape-Up Program for your child. But these thoughts will give you a solid start in ascertaining where your child is developmentally—an understanding that will serve as the foundation for later decisions you'll make about fitness programs, sports participation, and even nutrition.

Also, you're well on your way to resolving the great parental dilemma of what *you* must do to help your child embark on a successful fitness effort.

CHAPTER FOUR

Confronting the Parental Dilemma: A Strategy to Get You and Your Child Started

Parents contemplating a fitness program for their kids usually find themselves on the horns of a dilemma. First of all, mothers and fathers must confront their own lack of motivation and limited time. It's all too easy to give in to the conflicting demands of daily life and make excuses or put off starting a program for a child. Yet all the evidence indicates that most successful programs begin early and proceed with regularity.

Second, parents run into snags with their children, who may resist and argue at every turn about having to exercise more or eat better. Yet nagging and threatening will never produce lifetime health and fitness habits.

However you cut it, then, a successful child fitness effort must begin with the parents. The adults don't have to be in super shape themselves, nor do they even have to supervise all the child's sports outings or conditioning activities. But they *do* have to take an active role in planning a kid fitness program and in motivating their child to follow it.

How does a parent do this without giving up his adult interests—or running himself ragged, trying to keep up with an increasingly active son or daughter? In the next three chapters, I'll describe five fundamental strategies to resolve the parental dilemma in kid fitness:

- Parent-child fitness contracts
- Fitness role modeling
- Parental participation
- The use of qualified surrogates
- Observing the 10 commandments of motivation that can turn a child on

STRATEGY #1. PARENT-CHILD FITNESS CONTRACTS

A great way to get started with a kid fitness program in your home is for you and your child to sit down *today* for a serious talk about the importance of exercise and fitness. This shouldn't be just a general brainstorming session that both of you forget as soon as it's over. Rather, the discussion should lead *immediately* to mutual agreements about fitness goals and a practical action plan. In other words, the time has now arrived to begin to formulate what child psychologists call a "contract" between you and your youngster.

Some parents may object, "Aren't you getting ahead of yourself, Dr. Cooper? Before I can start making formal commitments and plans with my child, I think you need to tell me more about kid fitness. *Neither* of us is involved in systematic exercise or fitness at this point!"

Actually, getting started on a kid fitness program is quite simple and requires relatively little preparation. In fact, to take the next major step in formulating your family's kid fitness program, all you have to do is finish reading this chapter and the two that follow—and then start putting together a preliminary fitness contract with your child!

Granted, establishing a *complete* program will take more time and require ongoing changes, adjustments, and fine-tuning as you acquire more knowledge and as your child moves from one developmental phase to the next. But it's important not to wait to act until you think you've learned all you need to know about kid fitness. If you do that, the chances are you'll never get started. Even the *experts* don't know everything because the field is changing so rapidly!

So the time is fast arriving to begin serious fitness discussions with your child. Before you actually start, however, refer back to the notes you made in the previous chapter about your child's current developmental phase. Also, review your projections about the appropriate kid fitness strategy for someone at his stage of maturity. Then plan how you'll approach your boy or girl about the topic of kid fitness.

Of course, the level at which you conduct such a discussion will depend on your child's age and cognitive development. It's obvious, for example, that the attention span and reasoning ability of the typical 5-year-old will differ dramatically from that of the typical 15-year-old.

On whatever level you operate, however, the style of the discussion should be *negotiation*. The objective of the talk is to reach an agreement under which both you and your child gain something and also, most likely, give up something. The final result will be a *parent-child contract*—an oral or written agreement that says certain acts will be performed in return for specified rewards or consequences.

Unfortunately, most parents have been conditioned to use authoritarianism and threats to get children to change. A common negative alternative to the negotiation-contractual approach to kid fitness might go like this:

> DAD: "Johnny, I want you to go for a jog with me."
> JOHNNY: "No, I don't feel like jogging. I want to play catch."
> DAD: "Jogging is good for you. It's part of your fitness program. So I want you to go with me now and plan to play catch with your friends later."
> JOHNNY: "No! I don't feel like jogging."
> DAD: "You'll go jogging first or you won't play catch!"

Arguments, tears, and probably *no* jogging *or* catch will most likely be the result with this ordering-and-arguing style of directing child behavior. But there's a better way—the contractual approach that emphasizes negotiation and mutual agreement.

There's nothing new about the idea of making contracts with kids. Most people negotiate oral agreements daily with their sons and daughters. For example, here's what a successful interchange between the above father and son might look like:

> DAD: "Let's go for a jog around the block."
> SON: "No, I want to play catch with my new mitt."
> DAD: "Suppose you jog with me around the block, and then I'll play catch with you."
> SON: "Okay."

Here we have a brief oral negotiation and agreement where the father gets what he wants (a jog plus the companionship of his son) and the son gets what he wants (playing catch with dad). But in a sense, each has to perform some service in return for a reward: the father must play catch and the son must join his father on the jog.

As you can see, the underlying fitness benefits in this sort of agreement are enormous. First of all, the contract has resulted in both father and son engaging in a highly rated aerobic activity (jogging). Second, the arrangement has given them an opportunity to work on an important motor skill (catching) that will encourage the boy to participate in sports that will, in turn, further enhance his fitness.

I realize that the word "contract" may conjure up images of impersonal deal making or manipulation. But in parent-child relationships, the contract concept has the opposite effect. The idea is *not* to turn parent-child relationships into a what-can-I-get-out-of-it sort of thing. Rather, the objective is to encourage parent and child to look for ways to reach agreements with one another with a minimum of hassles, arguments, and resistance.

Clearly, the above illustration of an informal oral negotiation and agreement is far superior to the first encounter, which ended in a temporary breakdown in the relationship. That's why I advocate the contract-negotiation approach to establishing a kid fitness program. The parents give a little and change a little, the child gives and changes, and, with both participating, the program succeeds.

Although this simple oral agreement illustrates the way the fundamentals of a parent-child contract work, there's a great deal more to the concept than this. You can often handle isolated, uncomplicated fitness issues by just coming to a quick agreement in a conversation. But your comprehensive kid fitness program—which will serve as the cornerstone for all future fitness efforts—should always be structured as a *written* contract, with sections delineating responsibilities and rewards for both parent and child. That way, there will be no question about what's expected of whom if a question should arise later. Also, you'll have an ongoing record of the performance of specific exercises, goals, and principles you've chosen.

Furthermore, it's best to commit your basic kid fitness program to writing no matter what your child's age. At what age can your child actually begin to *participate* in the negotiation and drafting of such a written contract? Most children must be at least 3 or 4 before they can enter into simple agreements with their parents, and even then, their understanding and involvement will be limited. But even with very young children, the program should still be written down to remind parents of the specifics of the plan and of how the child is progressing.

Although many children can begin to take part in formulating a program as preschoolers, full participation in a written agreement probably won't be possible until they reach school age and gain some facility in reading and writing. But I would urge you to get them involved as early as possible in the discussions and decisions. After all, we're talking about a *kid* fitness program, not a parent fitness program! It *never* works for a parent to try to impose a program on a child, with little regard for the youngster's interests and wishes.

Finally, let me reiterate this point: whatever your child's age, I realize that at this stage in your reading, you don't have sufficient information to draw up a complete agreement. We haven't yet covered many essential topics, such as fitness and skill testing, the specifics of various fitness programs, or the basic guidelines for good youth nutrition. But you and your child can at least get started by putting together a preliminary contract. This exercise will encourage you to think seriously about the kind of program you want. The details can be filled in later, as you finish subsequent chapters of this book.

How to Draft a Parent-Child Fitness Contract Four main steps are required to draft a fitness agreement with your child:

1. You should define your mutual goals.
2. You should each provide two sets of lists—one covering what you expect to do under such a program and the other, what you expect to get out of the program.
3. You must narrow down these lists to a workable written agreement.
4. You should set up a monitoring system to be sure that the terms of the contract are followed by each party (the parent and the child).

Now, here is how these steps can work in formulating a preliminary parent-child fitness contract.

Step 1. Define Your Mutual Goals. In your initial discussion with your child, begin by opening up and giving your son or daughter a close look at what's going on inside you. Discuss how you feel about exercise and good health and what you'd like to see a kid fitness program accomplish. Emphasize that even though the plan is called a "kid" fitness program, *you* plan to participate too! You might mention some of the benefits you expect to enjoy as a parent, such as improved physical conditioning, better eating habits, and a longer life.

Many children are impressed when their parents say something like this: "By letting me join you on this program, you'll help make me a much healthier person!" Even more important, point out the opportunities you and your child will have to spend more time in fun activities together.

Then give your youngster all the time she needs to describe *her* dreams and goals. Maybe she'd like to become a better athlete during recess or gym at her school. At a relatively young age, say 8 or 9, many children can readily understand that they'll feel better about themselves—in adult terms, that their self-esteem and self-confidence will improve—if they become more physically fit.

It may be that your child has a specific objective or need, such as losing weight. Or perhaps she would like to become the best tennis or basketball player in her local community sports program. If so, be sure to list these concerns.

A major objective in this discussion is to let your imaginations run wild as you explore some of the possibilities of greater fitness and better health. To spark your thinking, it may be helpful to show your youngster pictures of well-conditioned athletes from magazines like *Sports Illustrated, Tennis, Runner's World,* or *Sports Illustrated for Kids.*

At the end of this talk with your child, write down on a sheet of paper the goals that you have discussed. Save this paper to use as a guideline when you draft your preliminary parent-child fitness contract later.

An almost certain by-product of this discussion will be increased excitement about the possibilities of a fitness program. And as the excitement escalates, both you and your child will find that your motivation to get started will soar!

Step 2. Parent and Child Should Make Two Lists. The first list will focus on what each person expects to *do* in a kid fitness program—in other words, this will be a statement of your respective responsibilities. The second list will include the rewards or payoffs that parent and child anticipate from the program.

As for the first list, the child may write that he expects to have the following responsibilities:

- Join the family on a regular fitness outing
- Be at a specific place to exercise
- Be ready at a certain time of day for exercise

• Have a set time duration for the exercise
• Provide the parent with the results of the exercise session (e.g., how many exercises were performed, including the number or repetitions and sets)

The parent may list these responsibilities:

• Be available for *every* scheduled family fitness outing
• Remind the child to exercise at a particular time
• Be present to supervise exercises (especially if the child is preadolescent or younger)
• Monitor the results and give the child feedback
• Be an exercise partner
• Provide various rewards for adequate performance

For example, one 11-year-old child wrote, "I will do at least 20 minutes of calisthenics three nights a week, and I won't complain if Mom or Dad reminds me to do them." The parents wrote, "We'll remind Alex to do his exercises, and we'll also schedule at least one physical activity, such as a hike or cycling, every weekend."

The second set of lists centers on what *benefits* each person expects to derive from the program. These items will include some of the main sources of motivation for child and parent. Both should feel free to include any rewards they think they might be entitled to receive as a result of a properly completed weekly fitness program.

NOTE: At first glance, some of the typical benefits listed below may not seem directly connected to a fitness program. But remember, in a contractual agreement, either party can obtain *any* benefit or reward that the other party is willing to provide. So, in return for acceptable fitness performance, a parent may be willing to give a child colored stars, inexpensive plastic toys, a chance to go to a popular movie, or an extra opportunity to use the family car.

The child's list of fitness benefits may look like this:

• Improved athletic ability
• More chances to be around Mom or Dad
• More energy and an increased feeling of well-being
• Toys of various types
• Stickers or stars (for young children)
• The opportunity to take a special course, like guitar or karate
• The chance to stay out later one night
• An increase in allowance

- The right to choose any clothes for school wear
- Permission to wear hair in desired way
- The opportunity to stay overnight at a friend's house
- Driving lessons or permission to apply for a driver's license
- The use of the car on a particular night
- The chance to watch a favorite TV program
- Special foods at mealtime
- Having a friend stay overnight
- The opportunity to play on a particular sports team
- Permission to go to some favorite place or hangout
- A special trip, including family holiday excursions
- A visit out of town to see favorite friends or relatives
- Dinner at a special restaurant
- Permission to go to a popular movie
- A special purchase, such as a piece of athletic equipment or a tape, disk, or recording of a favorite musician
- *Not* having to perform some regular responsibility, such as washing the dishes or the car
- Riding a bicycle or skateboard to a previously restricted location
- Listening to the radio or stereo at a previously restricted time
- Additional use of the phone
- A father-son camping trip
- Accessories for a special hobby
- The right to decorate own room
- Permission to have a party at home

A teenage girl, for instance, said, "Fitness will help me control my weight and look healthier. Also, if I stick to my program, Mom has promised to help me choose and buy a new wardrobe."

What about the parent's list of rewards or payoffs from the contract? Here are a few of the possibilities:

- Better personal health, fitness, and energy as a result of participating in a fitness program with the child
- The satisfaction of seeing a son or daughter improve athletic performance and self-esteem
- Opportunities to spend more time with a child
- A greater sense of family unity, as several or all members of the family participate in the kid fitness program
- The intellectual stimulation of becoming knowledgeable in kid fitness

- The opportunity to become the coach of one of the child's community athletic teams
- The likelihood that the child will be watching less blaring TV and spending less time as a "couch potato"
- A probable decline in the family's health problems and medical expenses

One parent wrote, "I'm going to have more chances to spend fun time with Rod when we're running together and practicing baseball skills. Also, I expect to see his self-confidence grow."

Step 3. Pare These Lists Down to a Workable Written Agreement. Now, it's time to draft your preliminary parent-child fitness contract. First, go over your written statement of goals and your lists of responsibilities and rewards, then check the top four or five items on each list that each of you considers most important. This is the point where the tough negotiating occurs because it will quickly become apparent that not all of the rewards or the responsibilities listed can be included in the final agreement. As a result, some hard choices have to be made.

For example, the child may decide he doesn't want to go along with his parent's entire list of fitness activities, which might include one family weekend cycling trip, one distance swim, three jogs, and a couple of strength-training sessions. The parent, for his part, may think the child's inclusion of a trip to Europe as a reward for fitness compliance is a mite excessive.

The final agreement may be written up in a form that looks something like this:

KID FITNESS CONTRACT

I, (name of child), WILL: _____.

[Include here a brief statement of the goals and fitness activities you've agreed on. At this point, I'd suggest that you stick to some of the family fitness suggestions described in Strategy #3 in the following chapter. A specific conditioning program can be chosen after your child has been tested for fitness and skills in chapter 7 and you've learned more about specific programs in chapter 8.]

I, (name of parent), WILL: _____.

[Include here a brief statement of the activities that you expect to supervise or participate in with your child. Again, at this point I'd suggest that you write down only a family outing of the type we discuss in Strategy #3. The more detailed exercise and nutrition programs can be added later.]

KID'S RESPONSIBILITIES: _____.

[Write down specifically what the child expects to do, the time of the activity, the requirement to show up on time, prohibitions against complaining, etc.]

PARENT'S RESPONSIBILITIES: _____.

[Explain how you'll help plan, supervise, or otherwise engage in the activity.]

KID'S REWARDS: _____.

[List the benefits the child will receive from the activity. If you only list a family outing at this point, the benefits may be simply doing something fun with the whole family. Or maybe you'll tack on something at the end of the outing that is a special treat for the entire family, such as going to a movie together or out to a restaurant.]

PARENT'S REWARDS: _____.

[This can be a brief sentence or two, based on items listed in the parent's written sheet of rewards.]

DATE:_____.

[The day, month, and year when the contract was drafted.]

SIGNED AND AGREED:

_____

(child's signature or mark)

_____

(parent's signature)

NOTE: It's important for the parent *and* the child to sign the contract because signing impresses on both the importance of their agreement. If you've never used the contractual approach with your son or daughter before, you may be surprised at how seriously the child takes it. It really *means* something for him to put his name down on a document! Also, by formalizing the procedure this way, you, the parent, will most likely think twice before you ignore or violate the commitment you've made with your youngster.*

Even more important, by going through the process of negotiating and agreeing to this initial phase of your fitness program, you've both made an important commitment. Your child will sense he's become involved in something serious that won't be neglected or forgotten tomorrow.

As for you, setting up this contract will immediately pull you much more

*For further information on drawing up contracts for kids, see Dr. Bradley Bucher, *Winning Them Over: How to Negotiate Successfully with Your Kids* (New York: Times Books, 1987); *Fitness Contracting Handbook,* Institute for Aerobics Research; A. F. Douds, M. Engelsgjerd, and T. R. Collingwood, "Behavior Contracting with Youthful Offenders and Their Parents," *Child Welfare,* vol. 56, no. 6, June 1977, pp. 409–417.

deeply into your child's fitness efforts. Now, you don't have to worry too much about generating sufficient motivation because this written document, which has taken some time to produce, will probably be enough in itself to keep you moving forward. Furthermore, as you add to the contract from information you learn later in this book, you'll find yourself becoming even more involved and committed.

Step 4. Set Up a Monitoring System. After you draft a preliminary kid fitness contract, only one step remains—making sure the contract works. With a simple preliminary contract, the monitoring should be rather easy. If you only include one or two family fitness outings per week at this point, you just have to be sure that they take place and that everyone is present.

The best way to do this will be to set up a separate monitoring sheet, with scheduled dates of the outings. At the end of each outing, indicate with a check, an "okay," or some other notation that the event did indeed take place. Then, after the date, list the family members who participated, and include comments about the success of the venture and any problems that may have arisen. Here's a sample chart:

MONITORING SHEET

	DATE	TYPE OF OUTING	PARTICIPANTS	COMMENTS
1.				
2.				
3.				
4.				
5.				
6.				
7.				

You can assume that there *will* be problems, by the way! Every written agreement must be adjusted according to the realities of life. You may find, for example, that two scheduled family fitness outings per week are just too much to handle, and so you'll reduce the number to one. Such suggested changes should be noted on your monitoring sheet. But they should be included in the basic contract *only* when all parties, parents and children, have been notified and agree in writing to an amendment.

After all, this contract you've drawn up with your child is serious business! You've agreed to something definite with your son or daughter, and that agreement should be observed until both parties consent to a change.

In every case I know about, it's been possible to work out amendments to these contracts. Children understand as well as adults that sometimes circumstances change and require adjustments to previous understandings.

But suppose you reach an impasse. Suppose, for instance, it's clear that the agreement must be changed because of some fundamental problem, such as the impossibility of compliance by a parent whose work hours have changed. Yet what if the child won't agree to the change? In that case, the original agreement will simply have to be scrapped, and parent and child will have to begin again to draft another contract.

With regular monitoring, you'll find that over time, you can make adjustments and develop a highly effective agreement that becomes part of the basic rules of behavior and activity in the family. Fitness will become something that you do in your household because you've all agreed to the program and have gotten into the habit of following it. Motivation to keep fit will become a built-in feature of your way of life.

CHAPTER FIVE

Rules for Role Models

When drafting a parent-child fitness contract, many parents find themselves under a glaring spotlight that points up their own inadequate physical fitness, eating practices, and health habits. In fact, more than one parent has elected to put off the drafting of a contract until, as one mother put it, "I can get my own act together. Right now, I'm a terrible role model!"

That sort of response is a mistake. None of us is perfect, and if you wait until you get your act together, you'll never enter into a fitness agreement with your child *or* embark on a kid fitness program.

I advise parents not to run in the other direction or hide from a commitment, no matter how tempting the prospect may be. Rather, look on the contract and the fitness program as an opportunity for both you and your child to improve your health and fitness. If you can just make *one* beneficial change this month and another next month, you'll not only be light-years ahead of where you were when you started, you'll also take a giant stride toward resolving your personal parental dilemma with kid fitness. In short, you'll be well on your way to becoming a worthy fitness role model.

STRATEGY #2. BECOME A GREAT ROLE MODEL!

So how can you become a better health and fitness role model for your child, even if you feel you're now hopelessly out of shape?

Being a good role model begins with admitting that in many ways, you fall short of any fitness ideal. Then, after recognizing your shortcomings, look for practical ways to improve, little by little, over the next weeks and months. The parent-child fitness contract is a great vehicle to help parents as well as children improve their health and conditioning.

Suppose you have a problem with eating too many fatty, sweet foods— a weakness that has raised your cholesterol level and increased your percentage of body fat. If you feel you can manage it, you might insert a clause in the contract that binds you to cut down on these harmful foods, just as your teenager may be agreeing to cut back on fast-food meals. The same approach may be used with smoking or any other practice that you feel not only harms your health but also is a bad example for your child.

Above all, don't be discouraged or give up if you fall short in your efforts to improve your health. You can *expect* to violate your commitments in the contract, just as you can expect your child to miss exercise sessions or eat the wrong things. These failures will be noted during the monitoring phase, but they are *not* cause for terminating the contract or making you feel as though you're a bad person.

The important thing is to set your goals and responsibilities, try your best to live up to them, and monitor your failures as well as your successes. When you fall short, pick yourself up and try again! Your child will be more impressed and encouraged by your ongoing effort and commitment in the face of failure than if you could somehow present him with a perfect record of success.

What are some of the specific characteristics a parent should strive toward in becoming a better fitness role model for his child? Here is a checklist of some important qualities and practices that I've gleaned from the medical and scientific literature. You'll probably find you need to work on several of these, but don't despair if you can't immediately correct all of your bad habits! As I've said, becoming a good role model for your child is a process that takes time, often years, and will never be entirely completed.

- Parents should be involved in their OWN regular exercise program.

Various research has established that the actual involvement of parents in sports activities seems to be decisive in the sports involvement of their children. Specifically, parents who engaged in an exercise program and had a positive attitude toward fitness motivated their adolescent children to want to engage in vigorous exercise (see *Research Quarterly for Exercise and Sport,* vol. 58, no. 4, 1987, p. 323).

This may seem a simple and obvious point, but it's startling how many parents *aren't* involved in their own program. The National Children and Youth Fitness Study of 1987 reported these facts:

1. Only 28.6 percent of mothers of children in grades one through four exercise moderately to vigorously three or more times a week, the minimum required for optimal physical fitness.

2. Less than 30 percent of fathers of these children participate in moderate to vigorous physical activity three or more times a week.

3. Even more shocking, more than 42 percent of the mothers and 48 percent of the fathers don't participate at all in moderate to vigorous physical activity!

The main adults to whom children look for their values, habits, and lifestyles are their parents. Even when teenagers go through a period of rebellion or the drive to separate from mom and dad and assert their independence, they still often retain many of the characteristics and values of their parents. How often I've heard adults in their thirties and forties say, "Even though I thought I was rejecting my parents when I left home, I find now that I become more like them every year!"

So the place to begin with fitness role modeling is your own exercise program. If you talk a good health line *and* practice what you preach, that will be one of the most powerful influences you can exert on your child.

• Teach your child the physical skills you know—and try to develop additional skills you can pass on to him.

Remember the point made by Professor Vern Seefeldt, director of the Youth Sports Institute at Michigan State University: if parents concentrate on the early development of basic motor skills, like catching, batting, and kicking, "then children are likely to become more involved in the games, dances, and sports of their society and to maintain fitness in that way" (see Kathryn S. Raithel, October 1988).

Parents—even those who never regarded themselves as particularly good athletes—can be a rich source of guidance, information, and training for a child's fitness program. Practically any parent is better than his 5-year-old child at catching, throwing, and kicking, and when a child sees this superior parental skill exercised, that will give him a model to emulate and a goal to shoot for.

Furthermore, even if they can't execute certain movements themselves, mothers and fathers are in a better position than their children to understand the mechanics, strategies, and rules of exercise and sports. It's the same with nutrition: parents have a broader educational background and life experience, which give them an advantage in investigating and using principles of good eating.

All that's required is to do a little homework, such as learning some of the facts I've included in this book, and you'll become an instant expert to your child. Show your child that you "know your stuff" about fitness and health and are trying your best to improve—*that* will make an indelible impression.

- Emphasize fun and fitness, not winning and hard work.

An increasing number of experts are recognizing that making physical activity fun is an absolutely necessary component to kid fitness. Take the 1987 report of a group of researchers from the University of Texas published in the *Research Quarterly for Exercise and Sport* (vol. 58, no. 4, p. 301). They concluded that "activities must be highly enjoyable, thereby fostering positive attitudes toward physical activity that may carry over into adulthood."

The best image for the parent to project is that exercise, good nutrition, and the other components of a healthy life are enjoyable and interesting—*not* that they are difficult or laborious. If your child's main impression of you at exercise is that you're huffing and puffing and groaning about stiff muscles, you can bet she won't want to get involved. On the other hand, the child will be more likely to be drawn into the activity by the mom or dad who bursts through the door after a workout and says, "That felt great! I'm ready for the day!"

Of course, even if you *say* you had a wonderful time running 3 miles at the crack of dawn, that won't automatically convince your child to get involved. Increasing anyone's fitness and aerobic capacity so that he can run for 2 or 3 miles without feeling discomfort *does* take some training and work. Any child will immediately recognize the negative part of the experience during his initial outing as he jogs his first few hundred yards.

So in addition to just telling the child that exercise is great, you'll probably have to include a "sweetener" or two to get him started and keep him going. Rewards of the type I've mentioned in the discussion of parent-child fitness contracts are one possibility. We'll go into this concept in more detail in chapter 6, which includes the 10 commandments for turning a child on.

- Limit FAMILY television time.

A great deal has been said about placing restrictions on the *child's* television viewing. Yet the *Nielsen Report* says that the average *household* with a TV spends more than 7 hours in front of the set every day! How can *parents* who are constantly in front of the set expect their boy or girl to be reasonable and moderate in the use of TV?

As we know, the TV problem with our kids is approaching the critical level. The National Children and Youth Fitness Study of 1987 concluded that the "amount of time a child spends in watching television seems to be related to how active the child is." The less television a child watches, the higher the level of activity. Furthermore, increased television viewing has been associated with increased obesity in children. A 1985 study, for instance, found that each hour of television viewing by adolescents was associated with a 2 percent increase in the number of obese teenagers.

In any event, it behooves the concerned parent to examine first his own television habits and then to map out a television policy for the *entire* family, not just for the child.

- Eliminate smoking from the home.

There are several problems with parents who smoke. In the first place, the link between smoking and heart disease, cancer, and many other serious medical conditions is well known and not necessary to document in detail here. Suffice it to say that the parent who smokes may not even be around to enjoy the final results of the kid fitness program he helps to create!

Second, smoking around kids sets a bad example. If mom or dad do it, their child is more likely to assume that the practice is acceptable.

Third, increasing numbers of studies show that passive or side-stream smoke can have a devastating effect on nonsmoking members of the household. For example, passive smoking has been associated with an increased prevalence and severity of asthma in children. Also, smoking by the mother has been linked to fetal and infant deaths. It's been estimated that if all pregnant women stopped smoking, the number of these deaths would be reduced by about 10 percent.

- Limit your use of fast foods.

Every second, an estimated 200 people in the United States order at least one hamburger, and on a typical day nearly 46 million Americans are served in fast-food restaurants. Perhaps your family has been among these numbers at one time or another—I know mine has!

We'll explore the nutritional problems with the fast-food industry in more depth in chapter 9, which deals with good nutrition for kids. For now, I'll just summarize my basic recommendations. Limit your family's use of fast-food restaurants to *no more* than once a week, and preferably only twice a month. That way, you and your child will have the benefit of an occasional "binge," but the effect on your blood cholesterol and bodily functions will be minimal.

■   ■   ■

There's much more that could be said about being a good role model for your child, but the above points are enough to get you started. In fact, any parent who can abide by these modeling principles most of the time will be far along the road to setting a good example of fitness and sound health.

On the other hand, if you keep lapsing back into bad habits on one or more of the items in this checklist, don't give up! As I've already said, it takes most people years to make major changes in their lifestyles. All you need to communicate to your child is that you have a set of fitness standards, and you're trying your best to maintain them. He'll respect you for that. He'll also look up to you as you pursue the next parental strategy for meeting the challenge of kid fitness—being more of a *participant* in your child's program.

STRATEGY #3. GET INVOLVED!

Parental participation may be the prime prerequisite for a successful kid fitness program. In fact, a 1986 report in *The Physician and Sportsmedicine* concluded that parental support was the "major factor that influenced the child's interest in participation" in two child fitness studies.

One of the best ways to get involved is to launch a *family* fitness program. Your presence, interest, and support will greatly reinforce the commitment of your child. Also, once you get started, you'll find that both parent and child will make the transition rather easily to a more complex and comprehensive regimen.

N O T E : To institute a relatively *complete* family fitness plan, it will be necessary to include the fitness and skill testing procedures described in chapter 7. Also, you'll eventually want to include a specific exercise program and nutritional commitments, as outlined in chapters 8 and 9. But I'll encourage you to begin with a simpler approach when you finish this chapter and then to plug in additional components and details later.

Here are the guidelines I'd suggest to help you get started with your family fitness plan:

1. Call the family together for a discussion.
2. Explain that you want to start doing some enjoyable, vigorous activities together but that everyone—parents and children—must agree before you make a commitment. Tell them that for future reference

you'll record the final commitment on a sheet of paper, as described in chapter 4, on parent-child contracts.

3. Ask for suggestions about possible family activities that will involve moderate to vigorous exercise. As the ideas occur, write them down. Let your imagination soar. If someone wants to climb mountains or go on long canoe trips, include those fantasies. The chances are, one or more of these top 12 favorite sports activities will be suggested:

Jogging, running, or walking
Swimming
Bicycling
Bowling*
Tennis
Table tennis*
Roller-skating
Basketball
Ice-skating
Waterskiing
Golf*

*The items *without* stars are better fitness choices. Those that have been starred are good, but they are primarily recreational. That is, they provide little or no aerobic benefit—although they may be a means to unify the family in a nonsedentary, enjoyable activity.

4. Select an activity. In making this decision, you should ask the entire family these questions, as well as any others that you feel are relevant to choosing an activity:

• Which activities will give us the most fitness benefits?

It's best to choose an activity that provides as much fitness improvement as possible, such as those *not* starred in the above list of 12. If you do pick bowling, table tennis, or golf, try to pair it with a sport that's more aerobic or endurance oriented in nature.

• Do we all have enough time for the activity?

If an activity will take all day Saturday, but dad or mom has to work many half-days on Saturdays, the time factor will effectively eliminate one parent. Also, you'll have to decide whether you want to participate once or twice a week, or more often. My suggestion is to move ahead slowly. Select an activity that you can complete during one weekend morning or afternoon.

- How much money can we spend?

Some families plunge into a fitness program without counting the cost. Then much of their momentum is lost when they have to pull back after finding the activity they've chosen is going to be too expensive. So estimate the cost, and eliminate those activities you find you can't afford.

- Can we all get there conveniently?

Again, it may be a great idea to go for long hikes or canoe trips in the backwoods. But even if you have the time, do you have adequate transportation to carry the family *and* the equipment?

After holding your family meeting and answering these questions, write down your choice on your parent-child fitness contract. Include the various rewards and responsibilities connected with the activity. For example, Who organizes or carries the necessary equipment? Who makes and carries the lunch? Where do we meet and at what time? What are the rules about complaining and whining? Is there a "sweetener" linked to the activity, such as a movie or eating out after we've finished?

5. Get started! Remember, once you've gotten into the habit of partici-pating in a limited, relaxed fashion in a family fitness activity, you'll find it's much easier to move into more disciplined, vigorous exer-cises.

STRATEGY #4. SELECT A SUPER SUBSTITUTE

No one parent can do it all for a child. Consequently, when there are two parents in a family, it is important for both to get involved in kid fitness.

Of course, even two-parent families often face such heavy work loads and other responsibilities that it becomes impossible for either mom or dad to devote adequate time to implementing the child's fitness program. The pres-sure increases with single-parent families, when the one care giver, who is the mother 90 percent of the time, finds she simply can't do everything for her child.

Whatever your situation, there's absolutely no reason to feel guilty if you find you have to enlist a friend, grandparent, or sitter to take your child to an athletic event or engage in a workout. The important thing is that you participate when you can and that your child be given the opportunity to get into shape—and to enjoy himself while he goes about it.

In one family I know, the working mother loved baseball, hated soccer, and was lukewarm on basketball, but her 11-year-old son was keen on all three. To compound the problem, mom was divorced and had limited time to take the boy to his activities or play with him when his peers weren't available. In this situation, the mother had three options:

- She could neglect her work and try to be a "perfect" parent by giving her full personal attention to all three sports.
- She could require her boy to choose only one of the activities.
- She could enlist the aid of a surrogate, such as a sitter, relative, or other friend to take her place when she couldn't make it to an event.

This mother chose the last option because she was fortunate enough to know a high-school boy who lived in the neighborhood and was looking for extra spending money. She hired this youth to take her boy to his soccer and basketball practices and games, and she even arranged for them to play and work out together on other weekdays. As a result of this setup, her son actually got more attention in his fitness activities and developed more quickly than if his mother had tried to operate alone.

A few caveats and guidelines are in order with this surrogate issue, however:

- The parent should have a serious talk with the surrogate about the goals and requirements of the fitness plan. For example, if the surrogate doesn't like the fitness activities that the child likes, another person should be chosen.
- Punctuality is essential, especially if the child is committed to playing on teams with scheduled starting times for games.
- The surrogate should be provided with *specific* written instructions and schedules. For example, "Johnny must be on the field to warm up for his soccer game by no later than nine thirty A.M. Saturday. The kickoff is precisely at ten A.M." "Susan needs to work on her hitting and catching. Spend 15 minutes practicing hitting and 15 minutes practicing catching. Then take as much time as you like practicing something else or playing a game."
- Unless you know the surrogate well, references should be required and checked.
- Monitor the surrogate's performance. You should periodically ask your

child's opinion about how things are going with the surrogate, including the existence of any problems or complaints. If your child is dissatisfied, you should switch sooner than later. Otherwise, your youngster will sour on fitness as well as on the care giver.

I'm reminded of one 8-year-old boy who liked his baby-sitter during the evening hours because she was interested in playing games around the house with him. But this same sitter *hated* sports. When she was given a daytime assignment that involved vigorous physical activity, she would arrange things so that she and the boy did more sitting in the shade than running around. When the parents found out, they were wise to seek out the services of a more energetic sitter for daytime play.

• Don't allow the availability of a surrogate to keep you from participating with your child when you are able. The surrogate, by definition, is only a substitute, not the actual parent. There are usually limits on how far he can go in providing parentlike guidance and emotional support.

These four strategies for resolving your parental dilemmas with kid fitness have focused on what it takes to get *you,* the concerned mother or father, effectively involved. You've learned how to draft a parent-child fitness contract, and you've considered the rules for becoming a participating role model in your child's program. Now, let's turn our attention more directly on the child as we explore a strategy to "turn on" that son or daughter to kid fitness.

CHAPTER SIX

The 10 Commandments for Turning a Child On

An envelope that was placed on my desk contained letters from Heather and Amy, two fourth-grade classmates from North Carolina. In response to their questions about a project on the benefits of exercise for a school science fair, their teacher, one of my former patients, had directed them to one of my books on aerobic exercise.

One of the first things that caught my eye was a fragment of free-form verse under Heather's byline:

> Running is free, so like the wind.
> When the sun comes up and dawns on the mountains,
> You better get up and run before your dreams beat you!

Now, I'm the first to admit that my books are intended for the person who is *serious* about some aspect of his health, whether it's controlling cholesterol, preventing osteoporosis, or designing a personal fitness program. Casual readers usually look elsewhere. But these two 10-year-olds were sufficiently motivated to pick up one of these books, read it, and begin applying it in their lives!

Listen to what else Heather had to say:

> Dear Dr. Cooper,
> Hello! My name is Heather. I am ten years old. I'm in fourth grade. At my school we had a science fair. My friend, Amy, also did the same project . . . on running. Our teacher, Miss Kempfer, said she had gone to you for her health. So we took your advice. . . . I agree with you on running. Everyone should. We found out we needed a longer period of

time for the project. We only had a week. I love to run, and I hope I will always be able to.

> Love,
> Heather

Her classmate Amy became equally involved in the project. She wrote:

> We ran for a week, and our health did change, even in a week. . . . What would you recommend for good health for children my age? Well, I got to go.
> Your friend,
> Amy

These messages still move and amaze me, as do the poems, essays, and photos that accompanied them. Too often, we adults assume that elementary school students are too young to understand how a fitness program can change their lives. Yet the testimonies of such children suggest that some exciting things can happen in the presence of:

- A respected adult role model—in this instance, a teacher
- The yearning of children of *every* age to do what's right for their health
- The capacity of improved fitness to catch on and take on a life of its own, even with someone very young

I've summarized these and other principles for motivating children in the following final strategy for resolving your parental concerns about a kid fitness program. (The first four strategies have been described in the previous two chapters.)

These 10 commandments for turning a child on aren't by any means exhaustive; as you're reading through the points, you'll probably think of several others I haven't mentioned that would apply to your child. My main purpose here has simply been to provide a number of solid suggestions that many child development experts, pediatricians, parents, and surrogates have found to be effective motivational tools.

STRATEGY #5. THE 10 COMMANDMENTS FOR TURNING A CHILD ON

First Commandment: Use a Token Economy System The term *token economy* refers to the use of rewards to encourage a child to perform a task or learn some new skill. A reward is the "token" that is used to generate give-and-take in the family "economy," or the execution of tasks and responsibilities by parents and children.

The reward might be as simple and nonmaterial as a kiss or a pat on the head, or it might involve some item or service that costs money, such as a toy, a movie, or an increase in allowance. In every case, however, the token should be positive.

In other words, a threat of punishment to force the performance of certain fitness responsibilities won't produce desirable long-term results. But the use of *positive* rewards to reinforce good behavior—such as those listed in chapter 4 under the discussion of parent-child contracts—is an established way to encourage productive performance and development.

Here's the way the token economy concept worked in one family: The parents decided to try the approach with their oldest child, a 6-year-old boy named Donny, who seemed to be lagging behind some of his peers in physical and athletic development. Donny's father first focused on short jogs with his son over a course of about a mile to a mile and a half. But he quickly found that Donny wasn't at all inspired when dad just said, "Let's go for a run." Instead, the father found he really got the boy's attention when he suggested, "Let's go for a *toy* run."

What was this father talking about? He had decided to hide small plastic soldiers and other inexpensive toys at regular intervals on the route he and his son took through the neighborhood. When they reached the site of one of the hiding places, the boy, following hints from Dad, would discover one of the prizes and would be off and running toward the next location.

To vary the program as Donny got older, the father got into the habit of writing "secret messages" to the son and stashing them with the toys. These messages directed the boy to do a certain number of push-ups or sit-ups before jogging to the next spot. In effect, what we have here is a kind of parcourse, which combines aerobics and strength training.

A common question that is asked about this token economy approach is Does the child still want to exercise when you take away the reward? The answer is yes and no. In the case of Donny, it was yes, he did continue to exercise when he no longer cared that much about toys. But no, he didn't do it without any reward at all. In fact, we *all* need rewards to continue exercise.

For adults, the reward may be a greater feeling of well-being, greater self-confidence, a more attractive physique, or the prospect of longer life. For Donny, the most compelling rewards as he grew older were his improved athletic performance and the increased sense of self-esteem he enjoyed as one of the fittest members of his class. In other words, a kind of "substitution effect" occurred. The principles behind the token economy system continued intact; it's just that the specific nature of the rewards and positive reinforcement changed.

Some parents have found that their presence and participation in fitness activities is enough of a reward to keep their child going. Others have instituted a formal point/purchase system, which is a classic tool of behavioral psychology. A point system, by the way, like any other agreement between parent and child, would be included in the fitness contract.

Although a comprehensive point system for a kid fitness program is described in more detail in chapter 8, here's how a relatively simple point method might work. Suppose the young person accumulates points for regular fitness efforts. Then he is entitled to "buy" certain privileges, such as attendance at a special movie or a professional sports event. For example, suppose that your kid fitness program, among other things, calls for your child to do some simple calisthenics at least three times a week. Specifically, he is supposed to do five things—push-ups, sit-ups, chin-ups, and two stretching exercises. Under your agreement with him, doing the required number of repetitions on each exercise earns him one point, or a total of five points for each session during which he completes the entire program.

You and he have agreed that when he earns 30 points—or the equivalent of six complete exercise sessions—he will be entitled at your expense to take a friend to a movie. Or he can apply his points to buy other rewards or privileges.

The transactions under such a point system can become quite complex, but a number of parents have found that having a formal arrangement like this removes much of the hassle and argument from fitness programs. Instead of arguing or threatening when the child resists doing exercises on a certain night, the parent can just say, "Okay, you let me know when you want to earn some more points so you can get that new baseball glove." Such a reminder is usually enough to get a positive response.

Second Commandment: Use Video Aids—But Don't Be Used by Them We've gone into some detail about the drawbacks of television, but there are also some positive possibilities with the video screen. Because most children are drawn naturally to the tube, parents should look for ways to use it to promote the kid fitness program. Here are a few thoughts and suggestions:

Check Sports Programming for Family Viewing. Sometimes, the networks or cable channels that specialize in sports will offer exciting, instructive programming that will reinforce what you're trying to teach. Parents who make the best use of these opportunities will sit with the child and interject comments on the performance or behavior of the athletes. Some typical comments:

- "Did you see the way he faked to the left and then drove to the right toward the basket?"
- "She's in better shape than anyone else on the court—that's one reason that she's a champion."
- "The key to that goal was the pass the left wing made to the center forward."
- "He always loses concentration when he starts arguing with the umpire."

Parents often tell me that their children want to go out and play the same sport they've been watching on television. I know of one girl who started playing tennis regularly after having been inspired by a performance of Steffi Graf at Wimbledon. In another family, a young boy launched an enthusiastic intramural basketball career after regular viewing of pro games. Take advantage of this stimulus!

Find Some Inspiring Sports Movies or Other Tapes You Can Show on Your Videocassette Recorder. One 7-year-old boy began a two-year "career" of watching on his VCR *Chariots of Fire,* the dramatization of the 1924 Olympics. He viewed this video 30 or 40 times during this period and became much more enthusiastic about jogging and sprinting in his spare time. His father even noticed that he had begun to mimic the running style of the great Scottish sprinter Eric Liddell!

Another boy viewed the basketball movie *Hoosiers,* about how a small-town in Indiana wins the state championship in the 1950s. He insisted that he wanted it for his birthday, and his parents enthusiastically went even further. They bought it *before* his birthday, showed it at the party, and then arranged for the boy and his friends to go out and play a real basketball game at a local park. This event led to other neighborhood games and, eventually, involvement in a team that played in one of the community leagues.

Such experiences show that television can, indeed, be a positive force if parents are just careful and creative about how they use it. You can expect your younger children to latch onto a favorite video and watch it over and over, and I see nothing wrong with that *if* the messages being conveyed are positive and constructive. In fact, when the values in the films are sound and the story is inspiring, videos can become an extremely useful adjunct to any fitness program.

Third Commandment: Put Your Child in Charge Your child must be an active participant at the very beginning of any kid fitness program and should gradually become more and more independent in pursuing it. The parent-child contract, and the negotiations leading up to it, are designed to get your youngster involved in initial decision making. Then his participation will increase during the self-evaluation process that we'll be discussing in chapter 7, on fitness testing, and chapter 8, on establishing a formal fitness program.

Fitness programs that are "imposed from above" by parents or other adult authorities rarely carry over to times when the child is free to choose his own activities. But when the child has been deeply involved from the outset, he's more likely to continue to pursue the program when the parent or other adult is absent.

Fourth Commandment: Get the Whole Family Involved in Fitness That's the point of strategy #3 in chapter 5, dealing with parental participation and the establishment of a weekly family fitness outing. At the end of this chapter, you'll be asked to draw up your preliminary parent-child contract and negotiate a schedule for your family activity. Remember, the more family participation, videos, and other support systems that you can marshal to back up your child's efforts, the more likely it is that the kid fitness program will succeed.

Fifth Commandment: Encourage Peer Reinforcement This commandment is similar to the last one, except that the objective is to pull in the child's peers and classmates to reinforce the fitness program. Here are some suggestions:

• Encourage sports parties, such as ice-skating outings or vigorous playground games. These events will be self-selective in that the children who like to exercise and play hard will be the ones who accept the invitations.
• Encourage your child to enroll in community sports programs. Some of the best fitness-promoting activities include basketball, soccer, lacrosse, or-

ganized "fun runs," bicycle outings, or hikes. The main idea is to find sports that involve building endurance and muscular stamina.

In the early elementary school years, say from grades one through five, parents usually have to take the initiative in signing up their children for soccer, baseball, or basketball programs. Otherwise, the deadline for enrolling passes and the opportunity to play on a team is lost.

Many of these programs provide great exercise opportunities, a chance to learn new skills, and a forum to have fun and socialize. But it usually takes some phone calls and research by the parent to find out what's available and how to join.

• Encourage friendships that will reinforce fitness goals. Sports psychologist Jim Loehr argues that one of the main reasons that young teenagers drop out of tennis programs is that they have failed to develop close friendships with other tennis players. Without a significant social bond to hold them to the activity, they quit. Conversely, those tennis players who stick with it often do so because their friends are on the courts; the key factor here is *not* winning or losing matches.

This peer issue can be a touchy point, especially with older children and teenagers who want to pick their own friends and leisure activities. On the other hand, parents often have considerable control over the peer associations of younger children. So when the opportunity arises, you should consider the benefits of including a representative percentage of active, athletic children on play dates or other outings.

Sixth Commandment: Reward the PROCESS of Fitness Rather Than the Final Product The rewards your child receives should be based on completing a certain number of exercise sessions, not on breaking a record, achieving a certain number of repetitions, or reaching another competitive goal. Hence, under the discussion of the token economy system, I suggested that you award points for the completion of the normal exercise load of sit-ups or other events—*not* that you give awards for hitting a new high in sit-ups or push-ups.

For children who are naturally competitive, there's nothing wrong with including a reward for setting a new personal record. But these achievement awards should *always* be subordinated to rewards that emphasize the process of exercise, rather than the final product.

One helpful aid to highlighting the ongoing process is the wall chart. For younger children, you might list their exercises and other fitness activities in colored pencils or crayons and then place a bright-colored star after the activity each time they complete a session. When the stars become boring or fail to get their attention, switch to an animal sticker, which can be purchased in most gift shops.

Wall charts are also challenging to older children—and adults! Everyone likes to see the broad sweep of how they've improved over the months and years. As soon as they are able, children should be encouraged to keep their own charts. This is an important way to develop systematic fitness habits that will last even through adulthood.

The universal appeal of the positive reinforcement approach is even evident at the Cooper Clinic, where we have used an award system for almost 20 years. At the conclusion of the first physical exam, the patient is given a framed certificate with his name in bold letters. He also gets a gold sticker documenting the date and walking time on the treadmill test. Each certificate has spots for five annual stickers. If the patient establishes a new personal record, a "PR" is added to the certificate along with the year and the treadmill time.

Even though our patient clientele includes men and women of all ages, of all walks of life, and usually of substantial means, I am amazed to see how most people treasure these annual stickers. They insist on correct information and train hard to get a "PR" or to keep a string of "PRs" intact. In some of the top corporate offices in America, I have been surprised to see one of those framed certificates on the wall.

Seventh Commandment: Arrange for Your Child to Lead or Teach Other Children Abe began to lose interest in soccer when he reached age 14 because he found he wasn't performing as well as many of his teammates. He had always been one of the stars when he was younger; but now the other boys were catching up to him in physical development, and he barely was able to make the team.

Then he discovered refereeing. A community soccer program needed experienced older teenagers to referee games for players of elementary age, and when Abe applied, he was accepted. Among other things, he was required to hold clinics for the younger children to teach them basic skills. He also had to learn to stand up to aggressive, pushy parents who sometimes tried to get him to change his rulings during games. The experience exhilarated Abe to the point that his interest in soccer revived, his own playing improved, and his position on his school team became more secure.

The lesson we can learn from his experience is instructive for children of all ages. By becoming involved in his sport as a coach and teacher, Abe developed new insights into the game that he had missed before. Furthermore, he discovered leadership skills he hadn't known he possessed. The overall effect was to increase his enthusiasm and performance—and prevent him from becoming another victim of the Adolescent Slump.

Eighth Commandment: Send Your Child to a Sports Camp There are thousands of camps around the country that provide kids with intensive instruction—usually for one to four weeks—in such sports as baseball, basketball, track, and tennis. The best way to find a good camp is *not* simply to respond to ads or listings but rather to get recommendations from other parents or former campers. Improvement in a sports camp can be fast and dramatic and can provide a young person with significantly greater self-confidence and motivation to pursue a fitness program. Usually the minimum recommended age for a sleep-away camp is 8, and the majority of children benefit most beginning at ages 10 or 11.

One such camp, which offered a strong track and field program, introduced 10-year-old Joey to the subtleties of broad jumping and high jumping. He found he was one of the most gifted in his age group in these events, and when he returned home after a two-week stay at camp, he immediately set up high jump and broad jump pits in his backyard. Also, he continued the regular calisthenics and strength training he had begun at camp.

Joey's response to his camp is by no means unusual. Remember, when a child is given an opportunity to improve his physical condition and learn new sports skills, he'll usually do it *naturally*. In fact, the increased sense of personal satisfaction and physical well-being would most likely make it difficult to *stop* him from participating!

During the last 13 years, our own children have spent many wonderful months at such a camp in southeastern Missouri. The skills they have developed and the friendships they have made have had a positive influence on their lives. Now, both of our children have reached the age of no longer being campers, but they continue as counselors, and they are enjoying the experience even more. (For more information regarding the one- to four-week programs offered at this Christian athletic camp, contact Kanakuk-Kanakomo Kamps, Branson, MO 65616.)

Ninth Commandment: Expose Your Child to Professional Athletes or Others Who Are Highly Proficient in Sports Just rubbing shoulders with an outstanding, well-known athlete can turn a child on to fitness activities. Here are some possibilities:

• Professional or college games in your area. Children are natural fans, and they are also quite likely to want to try out the physical skills they see displayed at a gymnastics or track-and-field meet and on the tennis court, basketball court, or baseball diamond.

• Autograph signings. A poster signed for a child personally by a top gymnast, Olympic runner, or swimmer will usually go right up on the young person's bedroom wall. There, it will serve as a reminder of the few words that may have been exchanged—and as an inspiration for the child to "go and do likewise."

A case in point: One aspiring 9-year-old tennis player went to an autograph signing by tennis great Ivan Lendl. The boy asked, "How do you keep in shape, besides playing tennis?"

Lendl's answer: "I run and do calisthenics."

"Do you use weights?"

"I used to, but I hurt my shoulder. So now I just use the weight of my own body."

This fitness message made a strong impression on the boy, who now pursues strength-training calisthenics willingly, without the token economy rewards that were once required.

• Lessons, lectures, or other opportunities to learn from a pro or other expert. Children will usually listen more intently and follow instruction more closely when the words are coming from a revered, highly accomplished athlete. "I've seen this guy play, and he knows what he's talking about!" is the typical kid's response.

Tenth Commandment: Become the Sponsor, Coach, or Helper for a Community Sports Team on Which Your Child Plays This final suggestion may require a major commitment of time and energy, especially if you volunteer to be head coach. But the potential payoffs are great. Here are some of the benefits cited by parents who have worked with their child's sports teams:

• Fitness automatically becomes a family affair because at least one and often both of the parents are present and active participants. The extensive parental involvement helps reinforce the child's commitment to and enjoyment of the activity.

• The child of the coach, assistant coach, or other volunteer will usually have at least as good a chance to play as the other kids—and often, he'll have a *better* chance. In many community leagues, there's an unspoken understanding that the coach's kid should get favored treatment. This is a kind of fringe benefit for the parent who is volunteering so much of his time.

• Other kids often look up to the coach's kid as a special person or even a leader. In other words, part of the parent's prestige rubs off on the child.

Of course, there may also be some drawbacks to being a coach's child. I've encountered several father-coaches who screamed excessively at their own children because they felt the kids weren't performing up to par. These adults felt free to give their youngsters the same rough treatment used at home. More than one of these little boys or girls has run off the playing field in tears after encountering such abuse.

But overall, most children seem to flourish in this position. They tend to develop a positive outlook toward the sport, which carries over as they grow older.

Underlying all of these commandments is this basic principle: The most compelling component of fun for a child is probably the presence of an interested and involved parent.

So whether you're supervising a calisthenics or weight-training session, playing catch, or kicking a ball around, be prepared to chat, joke, and have plenty of fun! It may sometimes seem as though you're wasting time if the activity is interrupted by a verbal interchange. But don't forget you're building a *relationship* as well as a strong young body. In the long run, that relationship will be the major factor that drives your developing youngster to get into shape.

In a similar vein, fitness advocate Bob Glover suggests in the June 1989 issue of *Runner's World* that one of the best ways to help a child focus on the enjoyment rather than the work connected with jogging is to *talk* to him throughout the activity about those topics *he* wants to discuss. Most children are eager to get mom or dad to sit in one place and listen to them for a while, and the parent is a captive audience during a 1- to 3-mile jog! Also, that keeps the parent from pushing too hard and being unable to pass the "talk test."

By this point, you should have absorbed some important principles for motivating your child *and* yourself to establish and begin a kid fitness program. So the time has arrived to sit down and write up your preliminary parent-child fitness contract—if you haven't done so already. Go ahead— I'll wait!

■   ■   ■

Now, with your preliminary agreement in hand, you're ready to move on to design a more detailed and comprehensive kid fitness program. The next step is to test the physical fitness and motor skills of your child.

CHAPTER SEVEN

Health-Related Fitness Test and Athletic Evaluation

I'm deeply committed to promoting health *and* fitness. But as you'll see in this chapter, I'm convinced that the two are not always the same.

Not every physical conditioning advocate uses the same standards I do to measure kid fitness. To enable you to understand my approach better—and also to help you apply the fitness criteria in this book more effectively—I want to devote some time at this point to the historical development of fitness testing in the United States.

THE GREAT FITNESS CONTROVERSY

The present-day concern about kid fitness was born during the 1950s, following some studies suggesting that American children were likely to perform worse on physical fitness tests than European children. As a result, President Dwight Eisenhower established the President's Council on Youth Fitness, which later became the President's Council on Physical Fitness and Sports (PCPFS).

Ironically, most of the American children in these early tests failed only because of low performance on a flexibility item. In other words, as my colleague Dr. Steven Blair has put it, "our children were labeled unfit because many could not touch their toes."

In response to the growing concern, however, the President's Council established a set of seven tests, ostensibly intended to measure fitness. In fact, these tests did more to measure *athletic* or motor skills, which were either acquired through genetic inheritance or specialized training, than they did to measure health-related fitness.

The initial council test, designed in 1958 by the American Alliance for Health, Physical Education, Recreation and Dance (AAHPERD), included these events: pull-ups, a shuttle run, a softball throw, sit-ups, a 50-yard dash, a 600-yard run or walk, and a standing long jump.

To pass this test and receive the Presidential Award, it was necessary for participants to score in approximately the 85th percentile—the top 15 percent—on *all* of the requirements. As a result, only a very small proportion, less than 1 percent, passed the test.

As you might expect, the results on this test were disheartening for many parents, educators, and politicians. The cry arose from many quarters, "Our kids are soft butterballs! They don't measure up to Western European and Soviet youth!"

But in fact, for the most part, this test didn't examine fitness at all; rather, it evaluated the child's *natural* leg power, agility, and speed. The only components of the test that measured acquired endurance or strength were the pull-ups and sit-ups. Even the 600-yard walk/run is an event that focuses on inherited sprinting speed more than the endurance that comes from regular aerobic workouts.

In response to criticism from various experts concerned with *true* fitness, the current version of the President's Council test, offered in 1986, has dropped some of the athletic skill evaluations. Present requirements are a 1-mile run or walk, a shuttle run, pull-ups, sit-ups (bent-leg curl-ups from a lying position), and a sit and reach.

But still, only the very top, highly conditioned participants—less than 1 percent of those who try out—qualify for the Presidential Physical Fitness Award. To encourage those less gifted, the council did establish a National Physical Fitness Award in 1988, which in general requires a student to achieve a 50th percentile performance on all test items. But athletic recognition seems to remain a key factor.

Because of a concern that the President's Council wasn't really testing or encouraging fitness for the majority of American youth, a number of other approaches have been tried. For example, the AAHPERD, which had designed the presidential program, proposed what in my opinion was a better basic fitness test in 1980 that included a mile run, a body fat measurement, sit-ups, and a sit-and-reach event. But the President's Council, which was apparently concerned with maintaining a continuity with past tests and statistics, elected not to include this set of evaluations in its offerings.

The widely publicized National Children and Youth Fitness Study also features fitness-oriented criteria. Specifically, this U.S. government project includes a 1-mile walk-run (or 0.5 mile for very young children, 6 to 7 years old), a body fat measurement, a sit and reach, bent-knee sit-ups in 60 seconds, and modified pull-ups, which stress stamina along with strength.

Finally, at the Institute for Aerobics Research in Dallas, we have developed the Fitnessgram,® which has been in use for nearly 10 years in many schools and communities around the country. Fitnessgram® is the first program to go nationwide with health standards that begin to answer the question, "What is the minimum fitness level needed for health?" We emphasize testing of health-related fitness rather than athletic skills, with such items as these: a 1-mile run or walk, a measurement of body fat, a sit and reach, sit-ups in 1 minute, and number of pull-ups or time in seconds for a flexed arm hang.

Our main purpose has been to establish realistic testing and to encourage acceptable health standards, which are attainable for all children.

Unfortunately, many tests are designed to find out how *good* the child is at taking a test and do not answer two questions that are considerably more important:

1. How *healthy* that youngster is
2. How *prepared* he or she is to participate at various levels of athletic activity

As I've said previously, our research at the Institute for Aerobics Research in Dallas shows clearly that only a moderate amount of exercise, such as walking a half hour a day, three days a week, can have significant benefits for health. Such minimal activity, which is sufficient to move a person out of the bottom 20th percentile, the most sedentary category of fitness, can increase longevity and provide protection against a host of illnesses, including heart attacks and cancer.

On the other hand, I always distinguish *health* from *fitness*. To put it simply, the requirements for fitness—for experiencing superior surges of personal energy and the enhanced quality of life that accompanies top conditioning—are more demanding than those for basic health. As I've told many of my audiences, I learned an important lesson when I embarked on a climb up Mt. Kilimanjaro in eastern Africa a couple of years ago with my teenage son. In short, I found it was absolutely essential that I be fit, not just healthy!

In the first part of this chapter, my Health-Related Fitness Test will provide you with five separate research-proven exams that will show whether your child is basically healthy. Also, you'll be given guidelines to determine what's required to improve fitness.

The various norms in these tests have been linked to the *chronological* ages of boys and girls because that's the easiest, most common way for researchers to report their findings. As far as the basic Health-Related Fitness Test is concerned, your child should be able to meet the minimum requirements for his chronological age level. Developmental age isn't an important consideration for this evaluation of minimal health. If your youngster can't meet these relatively undemanding standards, you should pay especially close attention to the exercise programs outlined in the following chapter.

In the second part of this chapter, the Athletic Skills, Fitness, and Physical Power Evaluation will show you at what level your child is ready to participate in sports. In contrast to the Health-Related Fitness Test, this evaluation involves some different assumptions about the meaning of your child's scores.

For one thing, I don't want you to feel discouraged if your child doesn't measure up to the highest levels of performance for his or her age. Instead, as you learned in the earlier chapters, think in terms of *developmental* age when you consider top categories of performance or acquisition of athletic skills. Also, remember that if your youngster is a little behind his age group in performance or skills, patience and commitment to improvement will often help him catch up. As we go through these various tests, I'll include reminders when developmental age is a particularly important consideration.

THE HEALTH-RELATED FITNESS TEST

There are five parts to my basic Health-Related Fitness Test—the 1-mile run or walk, the sit and reach, sit-ups, pull-ups or a flexed arm hang, and determination of the child's percent of body fat. All of these items have been researched thoroughly through our Fitnessgram® program at the Institute for Aerobics Research and also other national evaluations, such as the National Children and Youth Fitness Study.

As I've said, the emphasis in this first test will be on your child's *health*-related fitness. Then, some suggestions will follow to show you how to evaluate the higher levels of fitness associated with athletics. Your goal should first be the development of a basically healthy boy or girl; then it will be more appropriate to work on higher levels of fitness.

NOTE: Age 5 is the youngest age I've included on these tests because research results are generally unavailable or unreliable for younger children. Although fitness is a concern for children of *all* ages, testing procedures are usually ineffective for the very young because of shortness of attention span and other developmental considerations. And, of course, it's important for every child who takes the test or participates in other physical activities described in this book to undergo first a complete physical examination by a qualified physician.

Is Your Child Healthy? To answer this question, administer the following five tests to your child. The acceptable times, percentages, and repetitions are indicated in the separate tables for boys and girls. Remember, these are not superior scores; rather, they represent the level of fitness your child should have to achieve the basic benefits of good health. The descriptions of the tests are based on our Institute for Aerobics Research Fitnessgram® User's Manual and other sources.

THE HEALTH-RELATED FITNESS TEST STANDARDS FOR GIRLS

TEST ITEMS

AGE (years)	1-MILE RUN/ WALK* (minutes: seconds)	PERCENT FAT*	SIT AND REACH (inches)	SIT-UPS (number)	PULL-UPS (number)	FLEXED ARM HANG (seconds)
5	17:00	14–25	10.0	20	1	5
6	16:00	14–25	10.0	20	1	5
7	15:00	14–25	10.0	20	1	5
8	14:00	14–25	10.0	25	1	8
9	13:00	14–25	10.0	25	1	8
10	12:00	14–25	10.0	30	1	8
11	12:00	14–25	10.0	30	1	8
12	12:00	14–25	10.0	30	1	8
13	11:30	14–25	10.0	30	1	12
14	10:30	14–25	10.0	35	1	12
15	10:30	14–25	10.0	35	1	12
16	10:30	14–25	10.0	35	1	12
16+	10:30	14–25	10.0	35	1	12

*Lower scores indicate better performance.

THE HEALTH-RELATED FITNESS TEST STANDARDS FOR BOYS

TEST ITEMS

AGE (years)	1-MILE RUN/ WALK* (minutes: seconds)	PERCENT FAT*	SIT AND REACH (inches)	SIT-UPS (number)	PULL- UPS (number)	FLEXED ARM HANG (seconds)
5	16:00	10–20	10.0	20	1	5
6	15:00	10–20	10.0	20	1	5
7	14:00	10–20	10.0	20	1	5
8	13:00	10–20	10.0	25	1	10
9	12:00	10–20	10.0	25	1	10
10	11:00	10–20	10.0	30	1	10
11	11:00	10–20	10.0	30	1	10
12	10:00	10–20	10.0	35	1	10
13	9:30	10–20	10.0	35	2	10
14	8:30	10–20	10.0	40	3	15
15	8:30	10–20	10.0	40	5	25
16	8:30	10–20	10.0	40	5	25
16+	8:30	10–20	10.0	40	5	25

*Lower scores indicate better performance.

Health-Related Fitness Test #1. The 1-Mile Run/Walk The object of this exam is to see how fast the child can run or run/walk 1 mile on a flat surface. This is a test of *aerobic* fitness, that is, the person's level of endurance. As a result, the emphasis should be to run at a steady pace over the entire distance, rather than running as fast as possible at first and then experiencing "burn out."

NOTE: Aerobic activity is often contrasted to anaerobic activity, which involves short, fast bursts of speed, as in sprinting. There is a place for anaerobic ability in sports, as we'll see in the section of this chapter dealing with testing for athletic skills and preparation. But for basic health and fitness, aerobic capacity is a more important factor.

Although this test can be performed without any prior preparation, here are some suggestions to make it more enjoyable and enable the youngster to turn in his best performance:

• Spend from two to six weeks helping the child build up aerobic capacity. For example, you might take your daughter on 2- to 3-mile walks at a faster and faster pace three or more days a week. Or you might encourage your son to run back and forth continuously after balls on the playground several times a week, for 10 to 15 minutes each session.

• Instruct the child to perform at his or her pace and not to try to keep up with other children who may start off too fast.

• Teach sound running or fast-walking techniques. These include keeping the head and chest up; allowing the arms, bent at a 90-degree angle, to swing parallel to the body or slightly across the chest; having a slight forward lean to the body; using a straight back-and-forth movement of the legs; employing a longer step than a walking step; and allowing the whole foot or heel to hit the ground first (i.e., the child shouldn't run exclusively on the toes). Also, be sure the child wears well-supported running shoes.

Health-Related Fitness Test #2. Sit and Reach This event tests the flexibility of the lower back and hamstring muscles on the back of the thighs. Stiffness in this area may lead to injury. For this event, you'll need to put together a simple piece of apparatus, which can involve nothing more than a stair step, a ruler, and a piece of tape to secure the ruler to the stair. The ruler should be taped to the stair so that the 9-inch mark is exactly in line with the vertical plane of the stair. The lower numbers on the ruler should hang over the edge of the stair. A more elaborate suggestion for setting up this apparatus with a box can be found in the accompanying description and diagram.

HOW TO CONSTRUCT A SIT-AND-REACH APPARATUS TO TEST FLEXIBILITY

1. Using any sturdy wood or comparable construction material (¾-inch plywood seems to work well) cut the following pieces:

   3 pieces, 12 inches × 12 inches
   2 pieces, 12 inches × 10½ inches
   1 piece, 6 inches × 21 inches

2. Assemble the 12 × 10½-inch pieces and two of the 12 × 12-inch pieces into a box using nails or screws or wood glue. Attach the third 12 × 12-inch piece to the top of the box.

3. Inscribe the 6 × 21-inch piece with ½-inch gradations. Secure the 6 × 21-inch piece to the top of the box. It is crucial that the 9-inch mark be exactly in line with the vertical panel against which the child's feet will be placed.

4. Cover the apparatus with two coats of polyurethane sealer or shellac.
5. The measuring scale should extend from 0 to 21 inches.

TWO ALTERNATE TYPES OF FLEXIBILITY TESTING APPARATUS

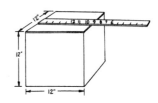

Schematic drawing of constructed sit-and-reach apparatus.

1. Find a sturdy cardboard box at least about 12 inches tall. Turn the box so that the bottom is up. Tape a yardstick to the bottom. The yardstick must be placed so that the 9-inch mark is exactly in line with the vertical plane against which the child's feet will be placed.
2. Find a bench that is about 12 inches wide. Turn the bench on its side. Tape a yardstick to the bench so that the 9-inch mark is exactly in line with the vertical plane against which the child's feet will be placed.

Now, here's the procedure for doing this sit-and-reach test.

1. Take off your shoes.
2. Take a few practice stretches by slowly touching your toes, either in a sitting or standing position.
3. Sit at the base of the box or stairs, with legs straight and feet shoulder-width apart; feet should be flat against the end of the stair or box, at a 90-degree angle to the ground, with heels on the ground.
4. Place your hands on top of each other and then put them out in front of you, toward the top of box or ruler in a comfortable position.
5. A partner, who may be a parent, should place his hands on your knees to keep them from bending.
6. Reach forward slowly with both hands along the measuring scale three times; each time, return to the starting position.
7. Now reach forward slowly with both hands a fourth time and for at least 1 second hold a position at the farthest spot you can touch on the ruler; do not bounce forward—bouncing doesn't measure flexibility.
8. Your score is the number you touched on the ruler on your fourth try, calculated to the nearest half inch; higher scores indicate better flexibility.

Health-Related Fitness Test #3. Sit-Ups This event might best be called a modified sit-up, because in line with the best thinking on performing this movement, we do *not* allow the child to put hands behind the neck. The reason is that neck injuries may result from jerking up on the head with the hands.

The purpose of this test is to check the child's abdominal strength and endurance. Here's the procedure:

1. Lie on a mat or other reasonably soft surface—but not a bed or bouncy surface—the soles of the feet should be flat on the floor with the knees bent and the heels should be approximately 15 inches from the buttocks.
2. Cross your arms and place them across your chest, with hands grasping opposite shoulders.
3. A partner should hold your feet flat on the mat.
4. Tuck your chin into your chest and curl up to a sitting position; when the elbows touch the thighs, that counts as one sit-up.
5. Using a stopwatch or watch with a second hand, the partner should say Go! and then count the number of sit-ups that the one being tested can do in 1 minute.

Some tips on achieving the best performance:

• Emphasize the importance of pacing. Sixty seconds can be a long time for this event, especially if the child goes too fast at first. A steady speed is the best pace, and establishing the optimum rate in several practice sessions for a few days before the actual test is a good idea.

• Be clear about what constitutes a complete sit-up, and stress that a failure to do a full sit-up won't count.

• Provide some training in proper technique. For example, it's much harder to do a sit-up when the heels are touching the buttocks than when they are separated by 15 inches. On the other hand, if the knees are kept straight, with the back of the knees against the floor, injury may occur to the back.

Also, inexperienced children may look up or back when doing a sit-up, rather than tucking the chin in to the chest. Looking around this way increases difficulty.

Health-Related Fitness Test #4. Pull-Up or Flexed Arm Hang This event will help you evaluate the child's upper-body strength—especially the strength of the arms, wrists, shoulders, and back. If the child can do at least one pull-up, that test should be used; otherwise, the flexed arm hang will be appropriate.

Now, here's the procedure for *pull-ups:*

1. Hang from the pull-up bar with the palms facing away from the body; feet must not be touching the floor, and the body must not swing.
2. In a smooth motion, pull the body upward until the chin is lifted over the bar; return to the full hanging position with the elbows extended.
3. Kicking, swinging, or other jerky movements aren't allowed!
4. Complete as many pull-ups as possible without dropping back to the ground to rest (although it is permissible to rest in the hanging position while holding on to the bar).

A couple of tips to improve performance:

• The bar should be wiped dry if it has become wet or sweaty from previous use.
• Chalk can be put on the bar or hands to keep the grip dry.
• It helps to practice a few days prior to the actual test to learn the proper techniques, including ways to pace yourself.

If you can't do a full pull-up, try the *flexed arm hang,* using this procedure:

1. Grasp the pull-up bar with palms facing away from the body.
2. With the help of a friend or by jumping up from the floor or from a chair, raise your body off the floor to a position where your chin is above the bar, with elbows bent. Your feet must not be touching the floor, and your body must not swing; the goal is to see how long you can hang from the bar, keeping your chin above and not touching the bar.
3. Using a stopwatch or watch with a second hand, your partner should begin timing this event as soon as you are in position, with your chin above the bar; if the head tilts backward or the chin falls to or below the bar, the clock should be stopped.
4. Your score is the number of seconds you can support your body with your chin above the bar.

Health-Related Fitness Test #5. Percent Body Fat An important part of good health is maintaining an optimum level of body fat. The more body fat you have, the more obese you are; the less you have, the less obese. Obesity has been associated with premature aging, high blood pressure, high levels of cholesterol, and a host of other medical problems.

Unfortunately, it's not possible simply to rely on the bathroom scale for this measurement. Muscle and bone tissue are more dense than fat, and so a child who is naturally muscular or who has a heavy bone structure may weigh more than another child of the same age and height—even though the heavier child may actually have a lower (and healthier) percent of body fat. You can be heavy, yet lean; light, yet fat!

So how do you measure body fat? In the past, it was necessary to go into a special sports medicine clinic or doctor's office to get this measurement. But now, with the help of simple, inexpensive plastic body fat (or skinfold) calipers, it's possible for any parent or older child to measure and calculate the percent of body fat in the privacy of their home. I've included a list of places where these calipers may be obtained.

ORGANIZATIONS THAT SELL BODY FAT CALIPERS AND RELATED EQUIPMENT

Sources of Body Fat Calipers
Lange Skinfold Calipers:
Cambridge Scientific Industries
P.O. Box 265
Cambridge, MD 21613
(800) 638–9566

Adipometers:
Fitnessgram®
Institute for Aerobics Research
12330 Preston Road
Dallas, TX 75230
(800) 635–7050

Fat Control, Inc.
P.O. Box 10117
Towson, MD 21204
(304) 825–6356

Ross Laboratories
Educational Services
Department 441
625 Cleveland Avenue
Columbus, OH 43216
(614) 227–3758

Sources of Training Films in Body Fat Measurement:
American Alliance Publications
P.O. Box 704
Waldorf, MD 20601
(703) 476–3481

Human Kinetics Publishers, Inc.
Box 5076
Champaign, IL 61820

Now, let's determine your child's percent of body fat. First, measure the skinfold (thickness of skin that can be "pinched" for measurement) on the right triceps (the muscle at the back of the right arm). Here's how:

1. Pick a spot about halfway between the shoulder and elbow at the back of the right arm, and using a marking pencil, mark that spot with an X.
2. Grasp the skinfold slightly above the mark, and using the calipers, measure the thickness of the skinfold on the mark. The skinfold should be held firmly between the fingers and lifted away from the muscle, but don't pinch too hard!
3. Read the skinfold measurement to the nearest millimeter and record that number.
4. Make two more measurements at the same spot, and record the middle score if the results are different on each of the measurements. If the measurements are the same on two or more tries, record that result.

Next, measure the skinfold on the inside of the right calf, using this approach:

1. The child should place her right foot on an elevated surface so that the knee is bent at a 90-degree angle. Using the marker, draw an X on the inside of the lower leg at the largest part of the calf muscle.
2. Grasp the skinfold slightly above the mark and measure the thickness of the skinfold on the mark with the calipers, as you did with the triceps. Again, hold the skinfold firmly between the fingers and lift it away from the muscle, but don't pinch too hard.
3. Read the skinfold thickness to the nearest millimeter on the calipers.
4. Make a total of three measurements, and record the middle score if the results are different on each of the measurements. If the results are the same on two or more measurements, take that measurement.

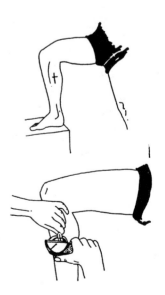

Now, for your final step, add the two measurements—those you've chosen for the triceps and the calf skinfold—and use that sum to see what the percent of body fat is according to the accompanying charts for boys and girls.

NOTE: There's typically a 3 to 4 percent error range in this mode of measurement.

Also, if you're mathematically inclined, you may be interested in the simple formulas used to calculate percent body fat for boys and girls:

> *Boys:* Multiply 0.735 times the sum of the triceps and calf skinfold measurements, and add 1.0.
>
> *Girls:* Multiply 0.61 times the sum of the triceps and calf skinfold measurements, and add 5.1.
>
> *Example:* Assume a boy measures 7 millimeters at the triceps and 11 millimeters at the calf. The sum of these two is 18. Multiply that figure by 0.735 and you get 13.2. Add 1.0 and you end up with 14.2 percent body fat—the same figure you'll find in the accompanying body composition tables.

HOW FIT IS YOUR CHILD?

There is a difference between health-related fitness and athletic fitness. Athletic fitness implies a higher degree of physical conditioning that allows the youngster to perform at superior, more efficient energy levels in daily activities and sports.

So just how fit is your child? Here are some research findings on the levels of performance in key fitness tests by boys and girls of different ages. Each of these tests should be conducted according to the procedures described under the health tests in the previous sections of this chapter.

The major difference in evaluating the results of the two tests is that with the health-related tests, you were concerned about determining whether or not your child was in good enough physical condition to derive fundamental health benefits. With these fitness tests, however, you'll be able to see just how fit your child is and the extent to which he is enjoying the *maximum* benefits of exercise, including his preparation for sports.

The results for the tests for the 1-mile run or walk, the sit-ups, the chin-ups, and the sit and reach have been taken from studies by the National Children and Youth Fitness Studies, while the percent body fat measurements come from our Fitnessgram® studies, as adapted from the widely respected work of researcher Thomas Lohman.

BODY COMPOSITION CONVERSION TABLE FOR GIRLS*

Total (millimeters)	Percent Fat	Total (millimeters)	Percent Fat	Total (millimeters)	Percent Fat	Total (millimeters)	Percent Fat	Total (millimeters)	Percent Fat
1.0	5.7	16.0	14.9	31.0	24.0	46.0	33.2	61.0	42.3
1.5	6.0	16.5	15.2	31.5	24.3	46.5	33.5	61.5	42.6
2.0	6.3	17.0	15.5	32.0	24.6	47.0	33.8	62.0	42.9
2.5	6.6	17.5	15.8	32.5	24.9	47.5	34.1	62.5	43.2
3.0	6.9	18.0	16.1	33.0	25.2	48.0	34.4	63.0	43.5
3.5	7.2	18.5	16.4	33.5	25.5	48.5	34.7	63.5	43.8
4.0	7.5	19.0	16.7	34.0	25.8	49.0	35.0	64.0	44.1
4.5	7.8	19.5	17.0	34.5	26.1	49.5	35.3	64.5	44.4
5.0	8.2	20.0	17.3	35.0	26.5	50.0	35.6	65.0	44.8
5.5	8.5	20.5	17.6	35.5	26.8	50.5	35.9	65.5	45.1
6.0	8.8	21.0	17.9	36.0	27.1	51.0	36.2	66.0	45.4
6.5	9.1	21.5	18.2	36.5	27.4	51.5	36.5	66.5	45.7
7.0	9.4	22.0	18.5	37.0	27.7	52.0	36.8	67.0	46.0
7.5	9.7	22.5	18.8	37.5	28.0	52.5	37.1	67.5	46.3
8.0	10.0	23.0	19.1	38.0	28.3	53.0	37.4	68.0	46.6
8.5	10.3	23.5	19.4	38.5	28.6	53.5	37.7	68.5	46.9
9.0	10.6	24.0	19.7	39.0	28.9	54.0	38.0	69.0	47.2
9.5	10.9	24.5	20.0	39.5	29.2	54.5	38.3	69.5	47.5
10.0	11.2	25.0	20.4	40.0	29.5	55.0	38.7	70.0	47.8
10.5	11.5	25.5	20.7	40.5	29.8	55.5	39.0	70.5	48.1
11.0	11.8	26.0	21.0	41.0	30.1	56.0	39.3	71.0	48.4
11.5	12.1	26.5	21.3	41.5	30.4	56.5	39.6	71.5	48.7
12.0	12.4	27.0	21.6	42.0	30.7	57.0	39.9	72.0	49.0
12.5	12.7	27.5	21.9	42.5	31.0	57.5	40.2	72.5	49.3
13.0	13.0	28.0	22.2	43.0	31.3	58.0	40.5	73.0	49.6
13.5	13.3	28.5	22.5	43.5	31.6	58.5	40.8	73.5	49.9
14.0	13.6	29.0	22.8	44.0	31.9	59.0	41.1	74.0	50.2
14.5	13.9	29.5	23.1	44.5	32.2	59.5	41.4	74.5	50.5
15.0	14.3	30.0	23.4	45.0	32.6	60.0	41.7	75.0	50.9
15.5	14.6	30.5	23.7	45.5	32.9	60.5	42.0	75.5	51.2

*Use this table to determine percent body fat for all girls ages 5 to 18.

BODY COMPOSITION CONVERSION TABLE FOR BOYS*

Total (millimeters)	Percent fat	Total (millimeters)	Percent fat	Total (millimeters)	Percent fat	Total (millimeters)	Percent fat	Total (millimeters)	Percent fat
1.0	1.7	16.0	12.8	31.0	23.8	46.0	34.8	61.0	45.8
1.5	2.1	16.5	13.1	31.5	24.2	46.5	35.2	61.5	46.2
2.0	2.5	17.0	13.5	32.0	24.5	47.0	35.5	62.0	46.6
2.5	2.8	17.5	13.9	32.5	24.9	47.5	35.9	62.5	46.9
3.0	3.2	18.0	14.2	33.0	25.3	48.0	36.3	63.0	47.3
3.5	3.6	18.5	14.6	33.5	25.6	48.5	36.6	63.5	47.7
4.0	3.9	19.0	15.0	34.0	26.0	49.0	37.0	64.0	48.0
4.5	4.3	19.5	15.3	34.5	26.4	49.5	37.4	64.5	48.4
5.0	4.7	20.0	15.7	35.0	26.7	50.0	37.8	65.0	48.8
5.5	5.0	20.5	16.1	35.5	27.1	50.5	38.1	65.5	49.1
6.0	5.4	21.0	16.4	36.0	27.5	51.0	38.5	66.0	49.5
6.5	5.8	21.5	16.8	36.5	27.8	51.5	38.9	66.5	49.9
7.0	6.1	22.0	17.2	37.0	28.2	52.0	39.2	67.0	50.2
7.5	6.5	22.5	17.5	37.5	28.6	52.5	39.6	67.5	50.6
8.0	6.9	23.0	17.9	38.0	28.9	53.0	40.0	68.0	51.0
8.5	7.2	23.5	18.3	38.5	29.3	53.5	40.3	68.5	51.3
9.0	7.6	24.0	18.6	39.0	29.7	54.0	40.7	69.0	51.7
9.5	8.0	24.5	19.0	39.5	30.0	54.5	41.1	69.5	52.1
10.0	8.4	25.0	19.4	40.0	30.4	55.0	41.4	70.0	52.5
10.5	8.7	25.5	19.7	40.5	30.8	55.5	41.8	70.5	52.8
11.0	9.1	26.0	20.1	41.0	31.1	56.0	42.2	71.0	53.2
11.5	9.5	26.5	20.5	41.5	31.5	56.5	42.5	71.5	53.6
12.0	9.8	27.0	20.8	42.0	31.9	57.0	42.9	72.0	53.9
12.5	10.2	27.5	21.2	42.5	32.2	57.5	43.3	72.5	54.3
13.0	10.6	28.0	21.6	43.0	32.6	58.0	43.6	73.0	54.7
13.5	10.9	28.5	21.9	43.5	33.0	58.5	44.0	73.5	55.0
14.0	11.3	29.0	22.3	44.0	33.3	59.0	44.4	74.0	55.4
14.5	11.7	29.5	22.7	44.5	33.7	59.5	44.7	74.5	55.8
15.0	12.0	30.0	23.1	45.0	34.1	60.0	45.1	75.0	56.1
15.5	12.4	30.5	23.4	45.5	34.4	60.5	45.5	75.5	56.5

*Use this table to determine percent body fat for all boys ages 5 to 18.

A WORD ABOUT PERCENTILES: A score in the 80th percentile means that your child did better than 80 percent of the children taking the test, but worse than 20 percent of the children.

Finally, a note to minimize confusion in comparing these fitness tests with the preceding health tests. These fitness tests vary slightly from the tests for basic health in two respects because the teams doing the studies used slightly different activities to measure fitness. In the first instance, chin-ups are used here instead of pull-ups. Both measure similar upper-body strength. The only difference is that with pull-ups, the hands grasp the bar with the palms *away* from the body, while with chin-ups, the hands are in a reversed position, with the palms facing *toward* the body.

Second, the sit-and-reach measurements are different because in these fitness tests, the measuring ruler was placed so that the edge of the box or stair was at 12 inches. As you'll recall, the ruler was placed with the edge at 9 inches on the preceding health tests. If you want to use the same device you used on the health tests, just add 3 inches to your results to get your percentile on the fitness tests. Or if you want to adjust your ruler so that the edge of the stair or box is at 12 inches (with the lower numbers on the ruler closer to the child), then you can use the measurements on these charts without making any adjustments. For example, if your child, using the device for the health test, reached to 11.5 inches, you'd *add* 3 inches to get 14.5 inches on the fitness scale. That would place him in the 70th percentile of fitness.

Notice, too, that data are available only for ages 10 to 18. Insufficient information has been gathered at this time for us to be able to establish reliable percentile standards for children under 10 years of age.

How to Interpret and Use the Fitness Scales Any child from ages 6 to 9 who is in the 50th percentile or higher on the majority of the fitness tests for children 10 years of age should be able to participate satisfactorily in organized play and in the team sports available in that age range.

CAUTION: Those who score lower should certainly not be barred from participation. But their parents should take their relatively low scores as a sign that they need to improve. Poor fitness can lead to a disappointing performance on the athletic field and may also make the child more vulnerable to injuries.

THE 1-MILE WALK/RUN FITNESS SCALE

NCYFS Norms by Age for the 1-Mile Walk/Run for Boys (in minutes and seconds)

Percentile	10	11	12	13	14	15	16	17	18
99	6:55	6:21	6:21	5:59	5:43	5:40	5:31	5:14	5:33
90	8:13	7:25	7:13	6:48	6:27	6:23	6:13	6:08	6:10
80	8:35	7:52	7:41	7:07	6:58	6:43	6:31	6:31	6:33
75	8:48	8:02	7:53	7:14	7:08	6:52	6:39	6:40	6:42
70	9:02	8:12	8:03	7:24	7:18	7:00	6:50	6:46	6:57
60	9:26	8:38	8:23	6:46	7:34	7:13	7:07	7:10	7:15
50	9:52	9:03	8:48	8:04	7:51	7:30	7:27	7:31	7:35
40	10:15	9:25	9:17	8:26	8:14	7:50	7:48	7:59	7:53
30	10:44	10:17	9:57	8:54	8:46	8:18	8:04	8:24	8:12
25	11:00	10:32	10:13	9:06	9:10	8:30	8:18	8:37	8:34
20	11:25	10:55	10:38	9:20	9:28	8:50	8:34	8:55	9:10
10	12:27	12:07	11:48	10:38	10:34	10:13	9:36	10:43	10:50

NCYFS Norms by Age for the 1-Mile Walk/Run for Girls (in minutes and seconds)

Percentile	10	11	12	13	14	15	16	17	18
99	7:55	7:14	7:20	7:08	7:01	6:59	7:03	6:52	6:58
90	9:09	8:45	8:34	8:27	8:11	8:23	8:28	8:20	8:22
80	9:56	9:35	9:30	9:13	8:49	9:04	9:06	9:10	9:27
75	10:09	9:56	9:52	9:30	9:16	9:28	9:25	9:26	9:31
70	10:27	10:10	10:05	9:48	9:31	9:49	9:41	9:41	9:36
60	10:51	10:35	10:32	10:22	10:04	10:20	10:15	10:16	10:08
50	11:14	11:15	10:58	10:52	10:32	10:46	10:34	10:34	10:51
40	11:54	11:46	11:26	11:22	10:58	11:20	11:08	10:59	11:27
30	12:27	12:33	12:03	11:55	11:35	11:53	11:49	11:43	11:58
25	12:52	12:54	12:33	12:17	11:49	12:18	12:10	12:03	12:14
20	13:12	13:17	12:53	12:43	12:10	12:48	12:32	12:30	12:37
10	14:20	14:35	14:07	13:45	13:13	14:07	13:42	13:46	15:18

THE SIT-UPS FITNESS SCALE

NCYFS Norms by Age for the Timed Bent-Knee Sit-Ups for Boys
(number in 60 seconds)

Percentile	10	11	12	13	14	15	16	17	18
99	60	60	61	62	64	65	65	68	67
90	47	48	50	52	52	53	55	56	54
80	43	43	46	48	49	50	51	51	50
75	40	41	44	46	47	48	49	50	50
70	38	40	43	45	45	46	48	49	48
60	36	38	40	41	43	44	45	46	44
50	34	36	38	40	41	42	43	43	43
40	32	34	35	37	39	40	41	41	40
30	30	31	33	34	37	37	39	39	38
25	28	30	32	32	35	36	38	37	36
20	26	28	30	31	34	35	36	35	35
10	22	22	25	28	30	31	32	31	31

NCYFS Norms by Age for the Timed Bent-Knee Sit-Ups for Girls
(number in 60 seconds)

Percentile	10	11	12	13	14	15	16	17	18
99	50	53	66	58	57	56	59	60	65
90	43	42	46	46	47	45	49	47	47
80	39	39	41	41	42	42	42	41	42
75	37	37	40	40	41	40	40	40	40
70	36	36	39	39	40	39	39	39	40
60	33	34	36	35	37	36	37	37	38
50	31	32	33	33	35	35	35	36	35
40	30	30	31	31	32	32	33	33	33
30	27	28	30	28	30	30	30	31	30
25	25	26	28	27	29	30	30	30	30
20	24	24	27	25	27	28	28	29	28
10	20	20	21	21	23	24	23	24	24

THE CHIN-UPS FITNESS SCALE

NCYFS Norms by Age for the Chin-Ups for Boys (number completed)

Percentile	10	11	12	13	14	15	16	17	18
99	13	12	13	17	18	18	20	20	21
90	8	8	8	10	12	14	14	15	16
80	5	5	6	8	9	11	12	13	14
75	4	5	5	7	8	10	12	12	13
70	4	4	5	7	8	10	11	12	12
60	2	3	4	5	6	8	10	10	11
50	1	2	3	4	5	7	9	9	10
40	1	1	2	3	4	6	8	8	9
30	0	0	1	1	3	5	6	6	7
25	0	0	0	1	2	4	6	5	6
20	0	0	0	0	1	3	5	4	5
10	0	0	0	0	0	1	2	2	3

NCYFS Norms by Age for the Chin-Ups for Girls (number completed)

Percentile	10	11	12	13	14	15	16	17	18
99	8	8	8	5	8	6	8	7	6
90	3	3	2	2	2	2	2	2	2
80	2	1	1	1	1	1	1	1	1
75	1	1	1	1	1	1	1	1	1
70	1	1	1	0	1	1	1	1	1
60	0	0	0	0	0	0	0	0	0
50	0	0	0	0	0	0	0	0	0
40	0	0	0	0	0	0	0	0	0
30	0	0	0	0	0	0	0	0	0
25	0	0	0	0	0	0	0	0	0
20	0	0	0	0	0	0	0	0	0
10	0	0	0	0	0	0	0	0	0

THE PERCENT BODY FAT FITNESS SCALE (for Ages 5 to 18)

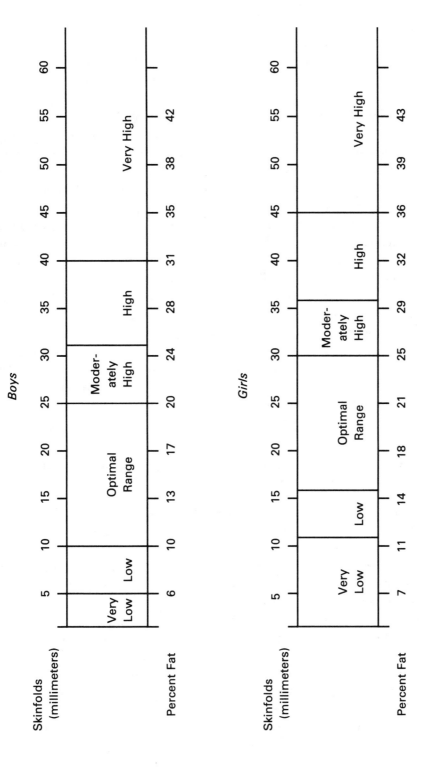

Fortunately, a child can improve his score on these five tests dramatically simply by exercising regularly, achieving optimum weight, and eating the right kinds of foods. An exercise program for this age group can be found in the following chapter, and a sound nutrition program is described in chapters 9 and 10.

Those children from ages 9 to 12 will probably find that they need to be at least in the 70th to 80th percentile on most of these tests to participate in team sports with some degree of success. But to perform at a top level, even higher scores, usually in the 90th percentile or higher, are required.

Why do fitness demands for sports increase with age? The main reason is that the competition becomes stiffer as the child gets older and stronger. Those who are in superior physical condition automatically have an edge over those who are less fit. Even boys and girls with high levels of athletic skill will fall short in competition unless they have the strength and endurance to perform at their best throughout a game or contest.

These indications of your child's level of fitness serve as a good transition to our next stage of testing, which involves an evaluation of athletic skills and preparation for sports. As you'll see, there's an overlap between being in a relatively high state of physical fitness and being in a position to do well in sports. But other factors also enter into this phase of testing. These include abilities requiring hand-to-eye coordination, throwing, agility, and explosive leg and body power.

THE ATHLETIC SKILLS, FITNESS, AND PHYSICAL POWER EVALUATION

Now, we're ready to move beyond health and fitness to athletic ability, which can always be improved but which also has an inherited or genetic component. For example, you can undoubtedly lower your running times, either over short or long distances, by regular workouts. But it takes something extra, usually an innate ability to move your body faster than most other people, to become a champion or star.

Or you can certainly become a better basketball player by getting into good shape and working hard to develop your shooting ability and other skills. But the chances are, you'll never become a pro, a college player, or probably even a member of a good high-school team unless you have some natural ability, such as above-average height or weight, exceptional jumping ability, or a superior "eye" for hitting a ball or putting one through a hoop.

The tests in this part of the book have been designed to take this natural, or genetic, component of athletics into account. At the same time, *all* young athletes, regardless of their "star" quality, can benefit from having their abilities evaluated and monitored. To this end, let me issue a couple of important and stern warnings.

WARNING #1: These tests are *not* intended to be predictive of your child's athletic ability in the future. Rather, they are just an indication of how he or she measures up *now* according to several relatively rudimentary athletic standards.

To find out more about your child's future athletic potential, you'd have to enroll him for an extensive battery of tests at a recognized sports medicine clinic. These would include laboratory evaluations of the types of muscle fibers he has and other intricate exams—and even then, you wouldn't know for sure whether or not the youngster would be a top athlete later in life. There are so many factors other than the physical that go into athletic performance, such as motivation, perseverance, and the will to win. Furthermore, those mental factors, as well as the physical capacities, change and develop with age.

WARNING #2: Remember my extensive comments in the first six chapters about the importance of focusing on your child's *developmental,* rather than chronological, age. Your child may not test that well on this athletic evaluation, but that doesn't mean that he won't come into his own in two, five, or ten years.

I'm reminded of a story that's told of the tennis star Boris Becker. Sports doctors predicted almost to the inch his eventual adult height of 6 feet, 4 inches. With this in mind, his tennis coaches began to train him as a serve-and-volley player, a tennis strategy that places a premium on height and reach.

With the heavy emphasis on rushing the net, Becker lost many matches against baseline players in his early playing days. But when he went through his adolescent growth spurt and began to outstrip his peers in height, the skills he had developed at the service line and the net gave him an edge—an edge that enabled him to win the men's singles championship at Wimbledon at age 17.

With these caveats in mind, let's turn to the tests. There are two main areas of evaluation in the following Athletic Skills, Fitness, and Physical Power Evaluation: (1) the seven-part Athletic Fitness and Physical Power Evaluation, and (2) the Athletic Skills Evaluation.

What will these events show you about the current athletic capacities of your son or daughter? They only indicate a very basic level of athletic ability, but at least you'll begin to get some idea about what your child may be capable of on the athletic field. Many sports require superior speed, agility, muscle power, and strength, and those are some of the qualities that the seven events in the first part of the test are designed to evaluate. The second part of this evaluation will explore other skills and capacities that are more specific to certain sports.

Here are a few examples of how the skills and capacities, which are covered by the test, apply to four major sports your child may play:

- *Baseball* requires flexibility (to stretch for a grounder), muscle endurance (to continue to perform at a peak in the later innings), and muscle power (to hit well), including a combination of speed and power in the muscles of the upper body. In addition, those playing this sport need fast reactions (to spear a hard-liner) and good hand-to-eye coordination (to make bat contact with pitches of different speeds), skills that will be evaluated in the second part of the Athletic Skills, Fitness, and Physical Power Evaluation.

- *Basketball* requires explosive muscle power (to jump for a rebound), running agility (to change directions at full speed), flexibility (to bend down to guard against a low dribble), overall strength (to get into position under the boards), aerobic endurance (to run back and forth on the court during the entire game), and anaerobic sprinting abilities (to execute a fast break). Also, players should have exceptional balance (to stay on the feet after body contact), and good hand-to-eye coordination (to catch passes and shoot baskets).

- *Tennis* requires muscle power (to execute a strong serve or ground stroke), muscle endurance (to continue hitting firm, accurate strokes after splitting sets with an opponent), running agility (to scramble after difficult crosscourt shots), anaerobic sprinting ability (to reach drop shots or lobs that make it over your head), and aerobic endurance (to stay reasonably fresh in the later stages of a long match). In addition, superior players need fast reactions (to stab sizzling volleys) and good hand-to-eye coordination (to hit the ball consistently in the "sweet spot" on the racket).

- *Football* requires anaerobic sprinting speed (to run or to catch an elusive running back), overall muscle power (to get off to an explosive start when you receive a handoff), muscle strength (to get that extra half yard at the goal line or to make an effective goal-line stand), flexibility (to get down low for a block or tackle), and a good aerobic or endurance capacity (to reduce injuries by delaying the onset of fatigue, and to play more effectively in the final part of the game). Other important skills include good balance (to stay on your feet after a hard hit), quick reactions (to respond effectively to a fake), and hand-to-eye coordination (to catch a pass).

Any other activity can be analyzed the same way. I'll indicate how these evaluations apply to some other sports as we go along.

I. The Athletic Fitness and Physical Power Evaluation The first part of this evaluation, the Athletic Fitness and Physical Power Evaluation, contains these seven events:

- A 50-yard dash to test running speed
- A shuttle run to test running agility
- A vertical jump to test explosive power (many experts consider this test to be the key indication of athletic ability)
- Chin-ups to test upper-body strength; serious fitness training of the type described in the following chapter can do wonders to improve the child's performance on this event
- Sit-ups to test abdominal strength; again, fitness training can help greatly
- The sit and reach to check hamstring and lower-back flexibility—flexibility is another athletic capacity that can be improved significantly with a fitness program
- The 1-mile run to test aerobic capacity; endurance workouts will lower this score but, obviously, at some point natural athletic ability takes over—4-minute milers are primarily born, not made

The Meaning of the Evaluations. It's important not to become discouraged or to give up if your child performs poorly on one or more of these events. After all, some sports place a premium on upper-body strength, while others don't; and great sprinting speed helps with some athletic endeavors more than with others.

Use this guideline as you do your evaluations: You can assume that if your child scores at the "athletic level" on two or more of these tests, he or she should be in a position to do quite well in at least one sport. An athletic level score on four or more events indicates outstanding athletic ability.

Now, it's time to check your child's performance on each of the seven events.

NOTE: The "athletic scores" on these events often aren't presented below age 10, simply because they aren't available. Or if they are available, they don't, in my opinion, represent a helpful tool in athletic evaluation. The reason is that good performance on these tests depends on the child's having reached a minimum degree of physical and cognitive development. He simply must have certain basic muscular and neurological abilities, and a certain level of understanding, to do well. Most children aren't prepared for this sort of an evaluation until they are at least 9 or 10. Of course, it's acceptable to test a younger child just for fun, but don't put too much credibility in the results.

Event #1. The 50-Yard Dash.

AREA AND EQUIPMENT: Mark off a straight, level 50-yard stretch on a playground, sidewalk, or other hard surface, with a starting line and a finish line. Use a stopwatch that will at least time the event to one-tenth of a second.

PROCEDURE:

1. The timer (usually a parent) should stand at the finish line with the stopwatch. The runner stands just behind the starting line.
2. The timer raises his hand and shouts, "Get ready!" Then he shouts, "Go!" and simultaneously lowers his raised hand and starts the stopwatch.
3. When the child crosses the finish line, stop the watch. The child's time for the dash should be calculated to the nearest tenth of a second.

The "athletic times" for this event—that is, the times that will be turned in by a youngster with some natural speed—are indicated below in seconds:

Age:	9–10	11	12	13	14	15	16	17
Girls:	7.5	7.5	7.2	7.0	7.0	7.0	7.1	7.0
Boys:	7.5	7.2	7.0	6.7	6.4	6.2	6.2	6.0

These times represent the 90th percentile of those taking the test administered by the American Alliance for Health, Physical Education, Recreation and Dance.

NOTE: The increase in time for girls between ages 15 and 16 may be just a statistical quirk or it may reflect a decrease in activity by teenage girls. Because the same phenomenon can be observed in other fitness tests, I'm inclined to attribute the variation to a decrease in activity triggered both by an increase in fitness dropouts and hormonal changes in teenage girls.

Event #2. The Shuttle Run.

AREA AND EQUIPMENT: You'll need two blocks of wood, 2 inches by 2 inches by 4 inches and a stopwatch.

Mark two parallel lines on the ground 30 feet apart. Then put the blocks of wood behind one of these lines. The child will start from behind the other line.

PROCEDURE:

1. The timer should raise his arm and say, "Get ready!"
2. Then the timer simultaneously says "Go!" lowers his arm, and starts the stopwatch.
3. The child runs from the starting line to the blocks, which have been placed just behind the second line. She picks up one of the blocks, runs back with it to the starting line, and places the block behind the line. The block must be placed, not thrown, on the ground.
4. Then the child runs back to the other line, picks up the other block, and carries it back across the starting line.
5. As the child crosses the starting line with the second block, the timer should stop the stopwatch. The child's time should be calculated to the nearest tenth of a second.
6. The child should then be given a chance to do the event again. The better of the two times will become her time for the shuttle run.

The "athletic times" for this event for girls and boys are as follows:

Age:	9–10	11	12	13	14	15	16	17
Girls:	10.5	10.3	10.2	10.0	10.0	10.0	10.2	10.0
Boys:	10.2	9.9	9.8	9.5	9.2	9.1	8.9	8.9

30'

These times represent the 90th percentile of those taking the test administered by the AAHPERD.

Event #3. Vertical Jump.

AREA AND EQUIPMENT: You'll need a fairly high, smooth wall surface that will take a chalk mark easily, a piece of blackboard chalk, and a yardstick.

PROCEDURE:

1. The child should stand with one side to the wall, usually the side with his dominant hand. Heels should be together and flat on the floor. He should hold a 1-inch piece of chalk in the hand nearest to the wall.
2. Keeping his heels together and on the floor, he should reach up as high as possible and make a mark on the wall with the chalk.
3. Finally, he should jump up as high as possible, driving himself with both his legs, and make a mark on the wall at the peak of his jump.
4. The scorer should measure the distance between the reach mark and the jump mark to the nearest half inch. That will be the child's score.
5. It's recommended that the child try the jump four or five times to get used to this event, and then the best of the jumps should be recorded as the final score.

CAUTION: Double jumps aren't permitted. The child must keep his two feet in place before he jumps, but of course, it's acceptable to bend the legs before the jump.

Also, the scorer should instruct the child to keep the chalk at the same place in his hand when he jumps as when he reached. This way, the accuracy of the test will be enhanced.

The athletic scores for the vertical jump, in inches, are as follows for girls and boys:

Age:	9–11	12–14	15–17
Girls:	15	15	16
Boys:	15	18	24

These scores represent the 90th percentile from a study done by Barry L. Johnson and Jack K. Nelson, which was reported in *Practical Measurements for Evaluation in Physical Education* (Burgess Publishing Co., Minneapolis).

The next four events should be performed according to the instructions in the preceding Health-Related Fitness Test. I'll just provide the athletic scores for each test, which represent the 90th percentile by the NCYFS evaluations.

Event #4. Chin-Ups. The athletic scores for this event, in number of repetitions, are as follows:

Age:	10	11	12	13	14	15	16	17	18
Girls:	3	3	2	2	2	2	2	2	2
Boys:	8	8	8	10	12	14	14	15	16

Event #5. Sit-Ups. The athletic scores for this event, in number of repetitions during 1 minute, are as follows:

Age:	10	11	12	13	14	15	16	17	18
Girls:	43	42	46	46	47	45	49	47	47
Boys:	47	48	50	52	52	53	55	56	54

Event #6. Sit and Reach. The athletic scores for this event, in inches reached according to the NCYFS scale (with the edge of the stair or box at 12 inches), are as follows:

Age:	10	11	12	13	14	15	16	17	18
Girls:	17.5	18.0	19.0	20.0	19.5	20.0	20.5	20.5	20.5
Boys:	16.0	16.5	16.0	16.5	17.5	18.0	19.0	19.5	19.5

Event #7. 1-Mile Run. The athletic scores for this event, in minutes and seconds, are as follows:

Age:	10	11	12	13	14	15	16	17	18
Girls:	9:09	8:45	8:34	8:27	8:11	8:23	8:28	8:20	8:22
Boys:	8:13	7:25	7:13	6:48	6:27	6:23	6:13	6:08	6:10

II. The Athletic Skills Evaluation This second and final part of the Athletic Skills, Fitness, and Physical Power Evaluation has been designed to help parents identify and evaluate specific athletic skills not covered by the seven-part Athletic Fitness and Physical Power Evaluation. Again, you shouldn't look on the suggestions in this section as a means to predict how athletic your child will be in the future. Rather, these are just tools to help you determine your child's current stage of athletic development and to help you pinpoint areas where he or she needs improvement. Athletic skills can always be improved, and if you learn how your child stands with a given movement or ability, you'll know where the most practice will be helpful and where parental training should be focused.

In chapter 2, I referred to 21 basic physical skills that many experts feel children should master during what I've called the second major phase of development, the First Skills Phase. The average child will finish this phase by about age 5, while others will take a little longer, and still others will go faster. In any case, parents should help their children to learn these skills by the time they are in the third stage of development, the Basic Fitness Phase, which ends on average at about age 8.

In some cases, skills like catching or striking a ball, which require advanced hand-to-eye coordination, may come a little later for a particular child. But many times, parents can help speed up the process by taking the child out to practice various skills.

The reason for developing these skills early becomes increasingly important as the child moves into stage four of fitness development, the Early Team Phase, which typically occurs among those aged 8 to 10. At that point, sports skills begin to play a major role in promoting self-confidence. An ability to play well, or at least adequately, also helps motivate children to participate in games and sports, which keep them fit.

Now, here is a more detailed list of three types of sports-related skill and the average ages when children should develop them. They are divided into (1) locomotor skills, which require displacing the body from one location to another; (2) manipulative skills, which involve handling, controlling, or maneuvering objects like balls and bats; and (3) balancing skills.

The following 55-item list includes the 21 skills listed earlier as well as additional ones, but in this case, they are divided according to specific age ranges. Again, though, don't get nervous or panicky if your child hasn't developed one of these skills by the indicated age. The ages merely represent general guidelines that will apply to the average child.

LOCOMOTOR SKILLS:

1.	Creeping (dragging body along floor)	7 months
2.	Crawling (abdomen clear)	8–10 months
3.	Climbing stairs (on hands, knees, and feet)	8–10 months
4.	Descending stairs	2–3 years
5.	Standing (pulling self up)	8–9 months
6.	Standing (no support)	9–12 months
7.	Walking forward unassisted	9–15 months
8.	Walking backward unassisted	16–19 months
9.	Walking up steps	18–21 months

10. Running attempts	18 months
11. Running consistently, rough movement	2–3 years
12. Running smoothly	4–5 years
13. Jumping, one-foot takeoff	1.5–2 years
14. Jumping, two-foot takeoff	2–2.5 years
15. Jumping, overall skillful execution	5 years
16. Hopping (one foot), rudimentary	3 years
17. Hopping (one foot), skillful	6 years
18. Rolling forward (somersault)	3–4 years
19. Rolling backward (backward somersault)	4–5 years
20. Gallop, rudimentary	4 years
21. Gallop, skillful	6.5 years
22. Slide (sideward, on feet), rudimentary	4 years
23. Slide, skillful	6.5 years
24. Skip, rudimentary	4 years
25. Skip, skillful	6.5 years

MANIPULATIVE SKILLS:

26. Rolling a ball	2–4 years
27. Throwing, underarm (one or two hands)	3–4 years
28. Throwing, elementary overarm pattern, without leading with opposite foot (see illustrations, p. 130)	4–5 years
29. Throwing, mature overarm pattern, leading with opposite foot, trunk rotation (see illustrations, p. 131))	6–8 years
30. Catching, trapping ball to chest	4 years
31. Catching, use of hands to grasp ball	5 years
32. Catching, mature pattern for large balls	6.5 years
33. Catching, judging flight projection of smaller balls from various distances and angles (as with baseball fly ball)	10–11 years
34. Kicking, stationary ball	3 years
35. Kicking, rolled ball (as in soccer or kick-ball game)	5–6 years
36. Dribbling a ball with feet	6+ years
37. Punting (dropping a ball and kicking it before it touches the ground)	5–6 years
38. Dribbling ball with two hands	2–4 years
39. Dribbling a ball with one hand	5–6 years

(Continued on page 132)

DIAGRAMS SHOWING PRO-
GRESSIVE DEVELOPMENT
OF OVERARM THROWING
MOTION. *

1.

2.

3.

*From George Graham et al., *Children Moving: A Teacher's Guide to Successful Physical Education Program,* Mountain View, California: Mayfield Publishing Co., second edition, 1987; and adapted from V. Seefeldt and J. Haubenstricker, *Developmental Sequences of Throwing,* Athens: University of Georgia, 1978; and R. L. Wickstrom, *Fundamental Motor Patterns,* Philadelphia: Lea & Febiger, second edition, 1977.

4.

5.

40. Striking an object with hand, overarm or
    sidearm, depending on target   3 years
41. Striking an object sidearm with an imple-
    ment, such as a stick or racket   4 years
42. Striking an object, using an implement
    like a stick or bat and a two-arm batting
    motion   4–5 years

NOTE: Expertise in striking *moving* objects usually comes later, as the child moves through the Basic Fitness Phase, roughly ages 6 to 8. But some well-coordinated or well-trained 3- to 4-year-old children can make contact with moving balls when they use a racket or oversize bat.

43. Pushing a person or object   2–3 years
44. Pulling a person or object   2–3 years
45. Lifting, rudimentary   2 years
46. Lifting, advanced, keeping back straight,
    head up, and using legs to exert power   4–5 years

BALANCE (STATIC):

47. Balance on one foot for 3 to 4 seconds   3 years
48. Balance on one foot for 10 seconds   4 years
49. Support body in basic inverted position,
    as in rudimentary headstand, with feet off
    floor and knees on elbows   6 years

BALANCE (DYNAMIC):

50. Walk several steps on a 1-inch-wide
    straight line   3 years
51. Walk on a 4-inch-wide beam, using foot-
    over-foot, alternating steps   3 years
52. Walk along a 1-inch-wide circular line   4 years
53. Walk on a 2- or 3-inch beam, using foot-
    over-foot, alternating steps   4.5 years
54. Hop on one foot proficiently   6 years
55. Ride a two-wheel bike   5–6 years

A FURTHER WORD ON INTERPRETING THESE TESTS

The main purpose in testing and evaluating your child in this section of the book has been to determine more precisely where he or she stands in health, fitness, and athletic development. Remember these important points about each test:

The Health-Related Fitness Test. As you've seen from my description of this first set of tests, a child's health status and fitness level can *always* be improved.

Systematic exercise, weight control, and nutrition programs, of the type described later in this book, can *definitely* raise your child to the healthy level of physical well-being. Also, more intense workouts can *definitely* push him beyond a healthy state to a high level of conditioning. The items in this first test have been designed to show you where your child stands now by generally accepted health and fitness standards, and on what areas you need to concentrate more.

The Athletic Skills, Fitness, and Physical Power Evaluation. This second set of evaluations, although similar to the Health-Related Fitness Test, has a somewhat different purpose. With the first tests, we were concerned about basic health-related fitness; with this group of evaluations, we zeroed in on specific athletic capacities and skills that will enable your child to play sports and enjoy his or her fitness to the maximum.

A score at the athletic level of four or more of the seven events in the Athletic Fitness and Physical Power Evaluation will indicate that you may have a very good young athlete on your hands. Also, achieving or bettering the suggested age levels on the Athletic Skills Evaluation suggests that your child could do well in at least one or more sports.

But there are no right or wrong answers, no pass or fail considerations in this athletic evaluation. Rather the objective is just to identify your child's current athletic status. That will show you where the youngster's present strengths lie, and also where extra parental involvement and training may help overcome weaknesses and enhance lagging skills.

Remember, too, that there are few who can reach the top level of excellence in even one sport, much less two. Bo Jackson may play both pro baseball and pro football, but almost everyone else must specialize to some extent. Most of us tend to be stronger in one set of skills than another.

Probably, your child will naturally gravitate toward those activities that he does best. If not, it will be up to you to nudge him gently in the most productive direction—and this test will give you some idea about what that direction may be.

Furthermore, the scores on this test aren't written in stone. As with the Health-Related Fitness Test, the events in the Athletic Skills, Fitness, and Physical Power Evaluation can always be improved. If your son can't execute a mature overarm throw at age 8, he can learn; likewise, if your daughter can't catch a large ball in a mature fashion with her hands at age 6.5, she can learn.

To be sure, your child may not reach the top athletic level on any of the evaluations—but really that isn't so important, and it's certainly nothing to worry about. Usually, there are clear reasons for relative slowness or inability. Some possibilities:

- Your child hasn't been taught certain skills.
- He's unfit—that is, he can't "max" the sit-up test because he never does sit-ups at home!
- Her physical or cognitive development may be slightly behind those of the same chronological age; in this case, it's simply necessary to be patient, continue to work with her on fitness and athletic skills, and wait for her to catch up.
- She is not particularly interested; for more on motivation, see chapter 6.
- He lacks a high level of natural athletic ability.

Most people fit into this final category. Remember, those in the 90th percentile in the seven events described in the Athletic Fitness and Physical Power Evaluation tend to be the best athletes. But that means 9 out of 10 people score worse than these exceptional athletes in the top 10 percent!

On the other hand, there are still plenty of average folks who run adequately, swim strongly, play a mean game of tennis, or otherwise perform well on the playing fields because they've been willing to work at it. Even more important, their level of skill, although not of championship or professional caliber, enables them to have fun and motivates them to keep active and fit. In the long run, an active, fit lifestyle is far more important than achievements or accolades on the school or professional playing fields.

But how do you translate the results from these tests to a regular fitness regimen for your child? The next chapter will suggest some specific ways that your boy or girl can build a great body from birth.

CHAPTER EIGHT

Building a Great Body from Birth

N ow that you've determined your child's health, fitness, and athletic status, it's time to embark on an exercise program. You want to put that boy or girl into the best shape possible, or maintain a fit condition if he or she is already there.

Physical well-being and superior sports performance depend heavily on endurance, or aerobic capacity, and well-conditioned, well-developed muscles. The earlier you get started, the better, and so my philosophy has been to *Build a great body from birth!*

How do you achieve this goal? In a nutshell, your children should begin a systematic aerobic and strength-training program at a young age. Then they stick with it over the years so that it becomes a firmly entrenched habit, one that is likely to remain with them for life.

A basic exercise session for children who are involved in an exercise program should be organized along these lines:

The Warm-Up. The child should spend 2 to 5 minutes in light activity, including such things as fast walking, jumping jacks, calisthenics, and stretching, to get the muscles ready to do the more strenuous activity that follows.

The Aerobic Phase. This is the main endurance segment of the activity, which will typically last for 15 to 40 minutes. The child might walk fast, run, swim, cycle, jump rope, play soccer, or participate in other activities that have an endurance component.

The idea is to keep moving, but *not* to move as fast as possible all the time. Moving at top speed soon becomes an "anaerobic" activity, one that quickly exceeds the body's capacity to utilize oxygen and leads to exhaustion. Rather, the emphasis should be on slower, although still demanding, movement that produces endurance. (In other words, pedaling a bike at a steady pace may produce endurance, but coasting on the bike won't!)

The Cool-Down. After the vigorous aerobic workout, it's time to bring the body back to a slower rhythm. That's the purpose of the cool-down, which should last for at least 5 minutes. The best approach is walking slowly for about 5 minutes and then engaging in flexibility exercises that stretch the calves, thighs, lower back, and upper body.

The Strength-Training Phase. This final stage of training should involve exercises that will increase the strength and power of all the major muscle groups, from legs to trunk to arms. Strength training can be done immediately after the cool-down stage, or it can be scheduled for alternate days.

A visual representation of the four phases of an effective workout can be seen in the accompanying illustrations on pages 138–141.

This basic four-part sequence of exercise should always be observed when you're planning your child's specific exercise program. This way, you'll get the maximum benefits from your exercise sessions and also reduce the chances of injury.

You'll be able to plug in particular exercises after you consider the exercise suggestions in the following pages. Usually, the child should go through this routine at least three to four times a week to get the maximum fitness benefits. Now, let's turn to specific exercises for different age groups.

EXERCISES FOR CHILDREN 7 YEARS OLD AND YOUNGER

How young can a child start a fitness program? Physical conditioning does begin, quite literally, at birth. But obviously, there are limits to how structured or systematic parents should make fitness regimens for very young children.

Although I'm a great advocate of kid fitness, I'm also a great *opponent* of rushing very young children into exercises or sports for which they are ill-suited, either physically or emotionally. As far as infants are concerned, I agree wholeheartedly with the policy statement by the American Academy of Pediatrics, which says in effect that structured infant exercise programs shouldn't be promoted. Instead, the academy recommends that parents should provide a "safe, nurturing, and minimally structured play environment for their infant."

Older children, up to about age 7, should be encouraged to participate in vigorous aerobic play activities. These may include tag, chase, random running, racing, swimming, cycling, and walking.

Rope jumping, climbing trees, and playing on playground apparatus are also useful, primarily for building muscle strength and stamina. For some further ideas about unstructured strength training, see the cartoons under the heading "Strength Development Activities" in the illustration of a kid fitness workout. The main idea here is to keep it fun and avoid heavy lifting that might hurt the child or damage growth plates. Strength activities that require constant movement, high repetitions, and stamina, such as climbing on a jungle gym or hanging as long as possible on a bar, are best.

Those parents who want more specific guidelines for aerobic activities, such as fast walking, running, swimming, or cycling, may prefer to schedule regular play sessions five to seven days a week. Here's a suggested program for children up to about age 7 that involves increasing the time *each day* in aerobic exercise from 5 minutes to 30 minutes over a 10-week period. N O T E : To make the program more effective, at least one parent should plan on exercising with the child.

Week	Play Session (minutes)	Days/Week
1	5	7
2	7	7
3	9	7
4	12	6
5	15	6
6	18	6
7	20	5
8	23	5
9	26	5
10	30	5

THE FOUR BASIC AEROBICS PROGRAMS FOR YOUNG PEOPLE 8 TO 18 YEARS OLD

When children reach the Early Team Phase of fitness development, which typically includes those 8 to 10 years old, they are more ready for a structured exercise program.

In fact, it's *essential* that parents get children involved in some sort of structured aerobics program by this age because fitness begins to decline

FITNESS PROGRAM—GET FIT EXERCISES

Warm-Up Activities

Side Bend   *Trunk Twist*   *Knee Lift*   *Calf Stretch*

Aerobic Activities

Jogging   *Cycling*   *Swimming*

Brisk Walking   *Rope Jumping*   *Soccer*   *Basketball*

Cool-Down Activities

Slow Walking   *Calf Stretch*   *Thigh Stretch*   *Sitting Toe Touch*

Arm Circles   *Jumping Jacks*   *Brisk Walking*

Knee Hug   *Arm/Shoulder Stretch*   *Arm/Side Stretch*

Strength Development Activities

Crunch

Curl-Ups

Sit-Ups

Single Leg Lift

Arm Curls

Military Press

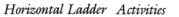

Horizontal Ladder Activities

Push-Ups

Back Arch

Wall Sit

Lunges

Modified Pull-Ups

Climbing Activities

rapidly in many children after age 10 for several possible reasons. One is that many children don't develop good exercise habits. Another is that the drop-out rate increases as both boys and girls become discouraged with or uninterested in team sports.

Here are four basic aerobics programs for children—walking, running/jogging, cycling, and swimming—that are easy to understand and put into practice. After consulting with your child and reaching an agreement, choose one and begin to implement it immediately. And remember, even at this age, the best way to motivate your children is to participate with them.

As with the suggestions for younger children, these 10-week programs are progressive, in that they involve a gradual increase in distance, time, and frequency. The purpose here is to build up cardiovascular endurance, a key factor in lowering the risk for heart disease and many other illnesses.

When your girl or boy can maintain the level of activity indicated at the 10th week, she or he will have reached a good state of aerobic fitness. Then, if the "exercise bug" catches on, he may want to try other sports or intensify his involvement in athletics, as indicated in chapter 16, which discusses the Elite Child Athlete. Also, the charts and explanations contained in my book *The Aerobics Program for Total Well-Being* will be helpful for those people of any age who want to forge ahead toward more demanding levels of aerobic fitness training.

AN AEROBICS VARIATION:
THE MISSOURI EXPERIENCE

The Missouri Governor's Council on Physical Fitness and Health decided that its state's junior-high and high-school students needed to get in better shape. So it is using the following simplified version of a number of activities in my aerobics point system to encourage its kids to improve their conditioning.

To keep your own child's interest up, you may want to consider plugging one or more of these activities into your child's exercise schedule. Use this approach: when your child finishes one of the previously described basic 10-week programs, substitute one of the activities listed below, such as rope skipping or roller-skating, for one of the regular workout sessions. Or if you have time, you might *add* one of these activities to the exercise program. That way, your youngster will get even more beneficial fitness training.

Encourage your child to participate at the level that he feels comfortable, yet challenged. Then as he pursues the sport over a period of weeks, encourage him to do what's necessary to earn additional points.

In Missouri, students who earn 30 points per week for 18 weeks receive an award. You might consider the same incentive for your child, although perhaps you'll want to reduce the time period for earning the reward. Refer back to the discussion on token economies, contracts, and other motivational techniques in chapter 4.

N O T E : Our four basic aerobic activities—walking, running/jogging, cycling, and swimming—are included in this list in a slightly different way. It may be that relating these activities to points and rewards will capture your child's interest more than using a straight 10-week program. Either approach is perfectly acceptable. Just use what works!

THE FOUR BASIC KID FITNESS AEROBICS PROGRAMS: WALKING, RUNNING/JOGGING, CYCLING, AND SWIMMING

WALKING PROGRAM

WEEK	DISTANCE (miles)	TIME GOAL (minutes)		FREQUENCY/WEEK
8 to 9 Years		Girls	Boys	
1	†	15:00	15:00	3
2	†	15:00	15:00	3
3	†	20:00	20:00	4
4	†	20:00	20:00	4
5	1.0	20:00	20:00	4
6	1.0	20:00	18:00	4
7	1.5	30:00	28:00	4
8	1.5	28:00	27:00	4
9	2.0	40:00	36:00	4
10	2.0	<40:00*	<34:00	4

WEEK	DISTANCE (miles)	TIME GOAL (minutes)		FREQUENCY/WEEK
10 to 11 Years		Girls	Boys	
1	†	15:00	15:00	3
2	†	20:00	20:00	3
3	†	20:00	20:00	4
4	†	25:00	25:00	4
5	1.5	30:00	27:00	4
6	1.5	30:00	26:00	4
7	2.0	40:00	35:00	4
8	2.0	38:00	34:00	4
9	2.5	48:00	43:00	4
10	2.5	<45:00	<42:00	4

* < means less than.

† Emphasis should be placed on continuous activity during time period, not on covering distance.

WEEK	DISTANCE (miles)	TIME GOAL (minutes)		FREQUENCY/WEEK
		Girls	Boys	
12 to 13 Years				
1	†	20:00	20:00	3
2	†	25:00	25:00	3
3	†	25:00	25:00	4
4	†	30:00	30:00	4
5	2.0	36:00	35:00	4
6	2.0	36:00	33:00	4
7	2.5	45:00	42:00	4
8	2.5	42:00	40:00	4
9	3.0	52:00	47:30	4
10	3.0	<50:00	<45:00	4

WEEK	DISTANCE (miles)	TIME GOAL (minutes)		FREQUENCY/WEEK
		Girls	Boys	
14 to 18 Years				
1	†	20:00	20:00	3
2	†	25:00	25:00	3
3	†	30:00	30:00	4
4	†	30:00	30:00	4
5	2.0	32:00	32:00	4
6	2.0	32:00	30:00	4
7	2.5	41:00	38:00	4
8	2.5	39:00	37:00	4
9	3.0	47:00	45:00	4
10	3.0	<45:00	<43:00	4

* < means less than.

† Emphasis should be placed on continuous activity during time period, not on covering distance.

RUNNING/JOGGING PROGRAM

WEEK	ACTIVITY	DISTANCE (miles)	TIME GOAL (minutes)		FREQUENCY/WEEK
			Girls	Boys	
8 to 9 Years					
1	W†	1.0	20:00	20:00	3
2	W	1.5	30:00	30:00	3
3	W	2.0	40:00	40:00	3
4	W	1.5	27:00	27:00	4
5	W/J	1.5	26:00	23:00	4
6	W/J	1.5	24:00	21:00	4
7	J	1.5	23:00	20:00	4
8	J	2.0	30:00	27:00	4
9	J	2.0	28:00	26:00	4
10	J	2.0	<28:00*	<25:00	4

WEEK	ACTIVITY	DISTANCE (miles)	TIME GOAL (minutes)		FREQUENCY/WEEK
			Girls	Boys	
10 to 11 Years					
1	W	1.5	27:00	27:00	3
2	W	1.5	25:00	24:00	3
3	W/J	1.5	22:00	21:00	4
4	W/J	1.5	20:00	19:00	4
5	J	1.5	19:00	17:00	4
6	J	1.5	17:00	15:00	4
7	J	2.0	23:00	21:00	4
8	J	2.0	22:00	19:00	4
9	J	2.5	28:00	26:00	4
10	J	2.5	<26:00	<24:00	4

† W = walk, J = jog.
* < means less than.

WEEK	ACTIVITY	DISTANCE (miles)	TIME GOAL (minutes)		FREQUENCY/WEEK
			Girls	Boys	
12 to 13 Years					
1	W	2.0	34:00	32:00	3
2	W	2.5	42:00	40:00	3
3	W/J	2.0	28:00	26:00	4
4	W/J	2.0	26:00	24:00	4
5	J	2.0	24:00	22:00	4
6	J	2.0	22:00	20:00	4
7	J	2.5	27:00	25:00	4
8	J	2.5	25:00	23:00	4
9	J	3.0	33:00	30:00	4
10	J	3.0	<30:00	<27:00	4

WEEK	ACTIVITY	DISTANCE (miles)	TIME GOAL (minutes)		FREQUENCY/WEEK
			Girls	Boys	
14 to 18 Years					
1	W	2.0	32:00	30:00	3
2	W	3.0	48:00	45:00	3
3	W/J	2.0	26:00	24:00	4
4	W/J	2.0	24:00	22:00	4
5	J	2.0	22:00	20:00	4
6	J	2.0	20:00	18:00	4
7	J	2.5	25:00	23:00	4
8	J	2.5	23:00	21:00	4
9	J	3.0	29:00	26:30	4
10	J	3.0	<27:00	<24:00	4

† W = walk, J = jog.
*< means less than.

CYCLING PROGRAM

WEEK	DISTANCE (miles)	TIME GOAL (minutes)		FREQUENCY/WEEK
8 to 9 Years†		Girls	Boys	
1	3.0	26:00	24:00	3
2	3.5	28:00	26:00	3
3	3.5	25:00	24:00	4
4	4.0	28:00	26:00	4
5	4.5	32:00	29:00	4
6	5.0	35:00	33:30	4
7	5.0	34:00	31:30	4
8	5.0	33:00	30:00	4
9	5.5	36:00	33:00	4
10	6.0	<39:00*	<36:00	4

WEEK	DISTANCE (miles)	TIME GOAL (minutes)		FREQUENCY/WEEK
10 to 11 Years*		Girls	Boys	
1	4.0	30:00	28:00	3
2	4.0	26:00	24:00	3
3	5.0	33:00	30:00	4
4	5.0	30:00	27:00	4
5	6.0	39:00	36:00	4
6	6.0	36:00	33:00	4
7	7.0	46:00	43:00	4
8	7.0	42:00	38:00	4
9	8.0	52:00	48:00	3
10	8.0	<48:00	<44:00	3

†Single-speed bicycle; for geared bikes, subtract 1 minute.
*< means less than.
‡Standard 3- to 10-speed bicycle, including mountain bikes.

WEEK	DISTANCE (miles)	TIME GOAL (minutes)		FREQUENCY/WEEK
12 to 13 Years‡		Girls	Boys	
1	5.0	32:00	30:00	3
2	5.0	30:00	27:00	3
3	5.0	28:00	25:00	4
4	6.0	37:00	34:00	4
5	6.0	34:00	30:00	4
6	7.0	42:00	39:00	4
7	7.0	38:00	35:00	4
8	8.0	48:00	45:00	3
9	8.0	47:00	43:00	3
10	8.0	<44:00	<40:00	3

WEEK	DISTANCE (miles)	TIME GOAL (minutes)		FREQUENCY/WEEK
14 to 18 Years‡		Girls	Boys	
1	5.0	30:00	28:00	3
2	5.0	28:00	25:00	3
3	5.0	27:00	23:00	4
4	6.0	34:00	26:00	4
5	6.0	30:00	24:00	4
6	7.0	38:00	30:00	4
7	7.0	35:00	28:00	4
8	8.0	48:00	35:00	3
9	8.0	44:00	34:00	3
10	8.0	<40:00	<32:00	3

†Single-speed bicycle; for geared bikes, subtract 1 minute.
*< means less than.
‡Standard 3- to 10-speed bicycle, including mountain bikes.

SWIMMING PROGRAM†

WEEK 8 to 9 Years	DISTANCE (yards)	TIME GOAL (minutes) Girls	Boys	FREQUENCY/WEEK
1	200	12:00	11:00	3
2	200	10:00	9:00	3
3	300	16:00	15:00	4
4	300	14:00	13:00	4
5	400	20:00	19:00	4
6	400	18:00	17:00	4
7	500	24:00	23:00	4
8	500	22:00	21:00	4
9	600	28:00	27:00	4
10	600	<25:00*	<24:00	4

WEEK 10 to 11 Years	DISTANCE (yards)	TIME GOAL (minutes) Girls	Boys	FREQUENCY/WEEK
1	200	10:00	9:00	3
2	200	8:00	7:00	3
3	300	14:00	13:00	4
4	300	12:00	12:30	4
5	400	18:00	17:00	4
6	400	16:00	16:30	4
7	500	22:00	21:00	4
8	500	20:00	20:00	4
9	600	25:00	24:00	4
10	600	<22:00	<23:00	4

†Overhand crawl or a combination of strokes enabling the swimmer to cover the required distance in the allotted time.

*< means less than.

WEEK	DISTANCE (yards)	TIME GOAL (minutes)		FREQUENCY/WEEK
12 to 13 Years		Girls	Boys	
1	300	14:00	13:00	3
2	300	12:00	11:00	3
3	400	17:00	16:00	4
4	400	15:00	14:00	4
5	500	20:00	19:00	4
6	500	18:00	17:00	4
7	600	23:00	22:00	4
8	600	21:00	20:00	4
9	700	26:00	25:00	4
10	800	<29:00	<28:00	4

WEEK	DISTANCE (yards)	TIME GOAL (minutes)		FREQUENCY/WEEK
14 to 18 Years		Girls	Boys	
1	400	15:00	14:00	3
2	400	13:00	12:00	3
3	500	15:00	14:00	4
4	500	13:00	12:00	4
5	600	18:00	17:00	4
6	600	16:00	15:00	4
7	700	19:00	18:00	4
8	800	21:00	20:00	4
9	900	23:00	22:00	4
10	1,000	<25:00	<24:00	4

†Overhand crawl or a combination of strokes enabling the swimmer to cover the required distance in the allotted time.

*< means less than.

The Aerobics Variation: Sports with Points*

AEROBICS AND OTHER EXERCISE PROGRAMS CONDUCTED TO MUSIC

TIME (MIN:SEC)	POINT VALUE†
30:00	6.0
45:00	9.0
60:00	12.0

OR 1 point/5 minutes

CIRCUIT WEIGHT TRAINING

TIME (MIN:SEC)	POINT VALUE
15:00	2.5
30:00	5.0
45:00	7.5
60:00	10.0

ROPE SKIPPING

TIME (MIN:SEC)	POINT VALUE
5:00	2.0
10:00	4.0
15:00	7.0
20:00	10.0
25:00	13.0
30:00	16.0

NOTE: Skip with both feet together or step over the rope, alternating feet; must be 90 to 110 steps/minute.

CROSS-COUNTRY SKIING

TIME (MIN:SEC)	POINT VALUE
15:00	4.0
30:00	9.0
45:00	13.0
60:00	18.0

*To obtain the Missouri Fitness and Sports Award, children must maintain an average of 30 points per week for 18 weeks. No more than 15 points may be awarded on any one day. Points should be spread out over at least three days per week. Points can be earned from any activity listed.

†For more detailed point values, including additional sports and activities, refer to the point charts found in Kenneth H. Cooper, M.D., *The Aerobics Program for Total Well-Being* (New York: Bantam Books, 1980).

WATERSKIING OR DOWNHILL SNOW SKIING

TIME (HR:MIN:SEC)	POINT VALUE
30:00	3.0
1:00:00	6.0
1:30:00	9.0
2:00:00	12.0

OR 3 points/30 minutes

NOTE: For downhill skiing, it requires 3 hours on the slopes to accumulate 1 hour of actual skiing.

FOOTBALL

TIME (HR:MIN:SEC)	POINT VALUE
30:00	3.0
1:00:00	6.0
1:30:00	9.0
2:00:00	12.0

OR 1 point/10 minutes

NOTE: Count only the time you are actively participating.

ROWING

TIME (MIN:SEC)	POINT VALUE
15:00	3.5
30:00	7.0
45:00	10.5
60:00	14.0

NOTE: Two oars, 20 strokes/minute, continuous rowing.

ICE- OR ROLLER-SKATING

TIME (HR:MIN:SEC)	POINT VALUE
30:00	2.25
1:00:00	4.50
1:30:00	6.75
2:00:00	9.00

OR 2 points/30 minutes

NOTE: For speed skating triple the point value.

WALKING/RUNNING			WALKING/RUNNING		
TIME (HR:MIN:SEC)		POINT VALUE	TIME (HR:MIN:SEC)		POINT VALUE
1.0 Mile			4.0 Miles		
20:00–15:01		1.0	over 1:20:01		3.0
15:00–12:01		2.0	1:20:00–1:00:01		7.0
12:00–10:01		3.0	1:00:00– 48:01		11.0
10:00– 8:01		4.0	48:00– 40:01		15.0
8:00– 6:41		5.0	40:00– 32:01		19.0
6:40– 5:44		6.0	5.0 Miles		
under 5:43		7.0	over 1:40:01		4.0
2.0 Miles			1:40:00–1:15:01		9.0
over 40:01		1.0	1:15:00–1:00:01		14.0
40:00–30:01		3.0	1:00:00– 50:01		19.0
30:00–24:01		5.0	6.0 Miles		
24:00–20:01		7.0	over 2:00:01		5.0
20:00–16:01		9.0	2:00:00–1:30:01		11.0
16:00–13:21		11.0	1:30:00–1:12:01		17.0
13:20–11:27		13.0	7.0 Miles		
under 11:26		15.0	over 2:20:01		6.0
3.0 Miles			2:20:00–1:45:01		13.0
over 1:00:01		2.0	1:45:00–1:24:01		20.0
1:00:00– 45:01		5.0			
45:00– 36:01		8.0			
36:00– 30:01		11.0			
30:00– 24:01		14.0			
24:00– 20:01		17.0			

HANDBALL/RACKETBALL/SQUASH/BASKETBALL/ SOCCER/HOCKEY/LACROSSE

TIME (HR:MIN:SEC)	POINT VALUE
30:00	4.50
1:00:00	9.00
1:30:00	13.50

NOTE: Continuous exercise—do not count breaks, time-outs, etc.

WRESTLING AND BOXING

TIME (MIN:SEC)	POINT VALUE
5:00	2.0
10:00	4.0
15:00	6.0
20:00	8.0
25:00	10.0
30:00	12.0
35:00	14.0

TENNIS/BADMINTON/AERIAL TENNIS

TIME (HR:MIN:SEC)	DOUBLES POINT VALUE	SINGLES POINT VALUE
45:00	1.0	3.0
1:30:00	2.25	6.0
2:00:00	3.0	8.0

OR 1 point/45 minutes

GOLF

HOLES	POINT VALUE
9	1.5
18	3.0
27	4.5
36	6.0

VOLLEYBALL

TIME (MIN:SEC)	POINT VALUE
30:00	2.0
45:00	3.0
60:00	4.0

NOTE: For times greater than 1 hour, compute points at a rate of 1 point/15 minutes.

SWIMMING

TIME (MIN:SEC) *200 Yards*	POINT VALUE
6:40–5:01	1.25
:00–3:21	1.67
under 3:20	2.50

500 Yards	
16:40–12:31	3.12
2:30– 8:21	4.17
under 8:20	6.25

900 Yards	
30:00–22:31	7.13
2:30–15:01	9.00
under 15:00	12.75

CYCLING

TIME (HR:MIN:SEC) *5.0 Miles*	POINT VALUE
over 30:01	2.0
30:00–20:01	3.5
20:00–15:01	6.0
under 15:00	8.5

10.0 Miles	
over 1:00:01	5.5
1:00:00– 40:01	8.5
40:00– 30:01	13.5

15.0 Miles	
over 1:30:01	9.0
1:30:00–1:00:01	13.5

20.0 Miles	
over 2:00:01	12.5

CALISTHENICS

TIME (MIN:SEC) 10:00	POINT VALUE 0.25
20:00	0.50
30:00	0.75
40:00	1.00
50:00	1.25
60:00	1.50

NOTE: These are continuous, repetitive calisthenics that are more stretching than muscle strengthening.

A NOTE ON OVERHEATING

Whenever I prescribe an aerobics program, I always feel compelled to inject a cautionary word about overheating, especially when children are involved. Heat exhaustion and even heatstroke may become threats during hot weather or even in relatively cool weather if the humidity is high and the child is exercising hard and has failed to drink sufficient liquids.

In general, children who haven't yet attained puberty—that is, those in the Early Team Phase of fitness development or younger—are at higher risk for "hyperthermia," or dangerous rises in body temperature during exercise. There are several important reasons for this phenomenon, including the following points made by Dr. Oded Bar-Or, of the department of pediatrics of McMaster University in Hamilton, Ontario, Canada.

• Small children have a larger ratio of surface area of the body to body mass than do adults. For example, a 6-year-old child has a ratio that is about 50 percent larger than that of an adult. Because they have relatively more surface area, small children absorb heat from the outside faster in hot climates (and they also lose heat faster in cold weather).

• Prepubescent children have a lower sweating rate during exercise than do adults. This is because each of their sweat glands produces only about 40 percent as much sweat as an adult sweat gland.

• The bodies of younger children become acclimatized to hot conditions slower than those of adults. So if you live in the north and are taking a vacation in the south or on a tropical island, you can expect that your small boy or girl will be more affected by the heat than you will (see Oded Bar-Or, "Temperature Regulation During Exercise in Children and Adolescents," *Perspectives in Exercise Science and Sports Medicine, Volume 2: Youth, Exercise, and Sport*. Indianapolis, Indiana: Benchmark Press, Inc., 1989).

My conclusions from these and related findings:

#1. Be sure that all children who plan to exercise strenuously, especially during hot weather, drink plenty of water before their activity. This means at least one to two 8-ounce glasses of water about an hour prior to competition.

During the event, they should be allowed to drink water freely and, in fact, encouraged to drink more than they think they want. Forget the old fear about becoming "waterlogged," cramping, or otherwise debilitated by drinking too much water.

NOTE: Usually electrolyte-based drinks should be diluted by 50 percent with water to provide their maximum effect. These drinks provide salts and other nutrients to replace those lost through perspiration, but you get all you need with "half a dose" and the most important thing to take in is the extra water.

#2. All children who have not yet reached puberty should be watched closely if they are engaging in continuous aerobic activity for more than about 30 to 40 minutes. Parental monitoring becomes especially crucial during hot, humid weather when heat stress is more of a problem.

Signs of heat exhaustion: profuse perspiration, dizziness, nausea, and weakness. Antidote: get out of the heat and into the shade or an air-conditioned room, if possible. Immediately begin to drink liquids and rest until the symptoms disappear. Generally, no other exercise should be performed on the day the heat exhaustion occurs.

Signs of heatstroke: hot, dry skin; headaches; sharp rise in body temperature; rapid pulse; faintness; flushing of the skin. Antidote: put the person into cold water or rub him down with ice until the body temperature drops. This condition can be life-threatening and should be treated without delay by a medically qualified person.

#3. To minimize the possibility of overheating or other physical problems, I recommend the following limits on runs or races for children of different ages:

• Below age 5: no formal distance racing (although with close parental supervision lengthy aerobic play sessions are fine)
• Ages 5 to 10: races up to 3 miles, or 5 kilometers
• Ages 10 to 12: races up to 6 miles, or 10 kilometers
• Above age 12, or after puberty: longer races are permissible (but I discourage marathons—runs of 26.2 miles, or 42 kilometers—until 18 years of age)

NOTE: Anytime the humidity added to the temperature in degrees Fahrenheit equals or exceeds 150, racing and vigorous outdoor physical activity should be avoided by people of any age, but particularly children.

Although I've inserted these comments about overheating along with the suggested aerobics program for kids, the principles also apply to strength and flexibility training, which may cause considerable sweating and dehydration. So keep these cautionary words in mind as we move on to our next topic.

THE KID FITNESS STRENGTH AND FLEXIBILITY PROGRAMS

The strength exercises in this section may be performed as the fourth phase of a daily workout session, after the cool-down, or they may be done on alternate days, when your child isn't engaging in an aerobic activity. The flexibility exercises may be done as part of the warm-up for the aerobic phase, part of the cool-down, or part of the strength-training routine.

First, let's deal with strength training. A formal program of this type is usually best suited for children 8 years of age or older. Younger children tend to lack the emotional development and attention span to complete one of these sessions. Too often, they become bored or turned off and may lose interest in exercise for the future. As one of my colleagues has said, exercise for children 7 and younger must be "camouflaged with fun" and, above all, must *not* seem like work.

The basic strength-training program I recommend focuses on just three types of calisthenics: push-ups, sit-ups, and chin-ups (or variations on these if initially a child can't perform a complete exercise). For those who want to try a more comprehensive program, I've also included several additional exercises.

A NOTE ON TRAINING WITH APPARATUS: I don't recommend the use of weights or other apparatus by a child until at least age 10, and in most cases after age 12.

Recent research has shown that strength training with free weights or similar equipment can produce significant increases in strength for prepubescent children, even though there isn't much of an increase in muscle mass. But I worry that in the years just before and during puberty, children may not have the good judgment to use such apparatus safely. It's clear, for example, that heavy lifting for young children is dangerous and definitely *not* recommended.

We'll explore this more advanced type of strength training in greater detail in chapter 16 for the Elite Child Athlete. For now, however, let's stick to the more fundamental issue of getting your child into better shape with a simple and safe calisthenics program.

The routine for doing these exercises involves first giving the child a "test" to see how many repetitions of each exercise he can do. Then when you determine the maximum, you take 50 percent of the number for the exercise, divide the exercises into "sets," and organize the overall routine according to what is called a "circuit training" program. Here's how it works:

Say your son can do eight push-ups. Half of that number would be four, or the number he should do during his exercise session. To put this another way, four "repetitions" constitutes one "set." In a similar manner, he should be tested on each of the other exercises. So, if he can do a maximum of 30 sit-ups, his exercise number would be 15. And if he can do a maximum of four chin-ups, his exercise number would be two.

Having identified the exercise repetitions that constitute one set, you then set up a "circuit" for the child's workout. Specifically, he does one set of push-ups, and rests for about 30 seconds. Then he goes on to one set of sit-ups and rests for another 30 seconds. Finally, he does the chin-ups.

When this routine becomes relatively easy, you should add one extra "circuit," or a separate set of each exercise, again, with a rest of about 30 seconds between sets. In other words, the boy would do one set of push-ups, one of sit-ups, and one of chin-ups. Then he would begin again with one set of each exercise.

When two sets become easy, he should add a third set of each exercise, with an appropriate rest period between sets. Finally, when three sets becomes easy, he should be retested, to see what his maximums are on each exercise. Now, he may be able to do a "max" of 14 push-ups at a time instead of 6. Half of that would be 7, or the number he should now use for his exercise sessions. He can begin again with one set and work up to three with the push-ups and other events. Now, here's a more detailed description of the exercises for a complete strength-training routine.

Basic Strength Exercise #1. The Push-Up The old-fashioned push-up is one of the best exercises for strengthening many of the muscles of the upper body, as well as those of the lower trunk, back, and legs. In fact, the great football running back Hershel Walker uses push-ups as his premier strength builder! Here's how you do it:

The Full Push-Up. With toes on the ground, lean forward and put your hands on the ground about shoulder width apart. Keeping your back straight, lower your upper body to the ground and "push" yourself back up again.

The Modified Push-Up. This exercise, for those who can't do one full push-up, involves many of the same basic techniques as above. The only difference is that you keep your knees on the ground. Also, it's important to keep the back straight and do the repetitions carefully because some exercise experts have cautioned that improper execution of this event *may* cause injuries from hyperextension (back-bending) of the lower back.

Basic Strength Exercise #2. The Modified Sit-Up The modified sit-up, like the old-fashioned sit-up, strengthens the abdominal muscles. But this exercise has been changed because various studies have revealed that the old way of doing sit-ups—with knees flat against the floor, legs straight, and arms clasped behind the head—can put undue pressure on the lower back and neck. Here's the new procedure:

Lie flat on your back with knees *bent* and the back of the heels about 15 inches from the edge of the buttocks. The arms should be crossed in front of the chest, with hands grasping the opposite shoulders.

Raise your head, shoulders, and trunk off the ground until you touch your thighs with your elbows. One repetition is completed when your trunk returns to the floor.

Basic Strength Exercise #3. Pull-Ups or Chin-Ups As we've already seen, the difference between a chin-up and pull-up is that the former is done with the palms of the hands facing inward, toward the body, as they grasp the bar; the latter is executed with the palms facing away from the body. I prefer pull-ups because in employing their arm and upper-body strength, children and adults most often grasp things with the overhand grip (e.g., climbing up rocks, holding bicycle handlebars, and water-skiing). But essentially the same muscles—those of the arms and upper body—will be developed with either grip.

This classic exercise is done by jumping up onto a bar and hanging with arms extended so that the feet are off the floor. Simple bars can be purchased in any sporting goods store and then set up in the garage, in the backyard, or in a doorway in the home.

N O T E : If you choose the doorway method, older children will usually have to bend their legs so that their feet don't touch the floor as they do repetitions.

As described under the chin-up tests in the previous chapter, the exercise begins with the child hanging with arms extended, feet off the ground. Then he pulls himself up so that the chin is slightly above the bar. Finally, he lowers himself to the arms-extended position to complete one repetition.

I realize, however, that it's not so easy for many children to execute even one repetition. In fact, a number of studies have indicated that 70 percent of American girls can't even do one chin-up! To help those who can't do any chin-ups, or who can only do one or two, here's a modified chin-up

routine to help strengthen the same upper-body and arm muscles helped by the regular pull-up or chin-up.

The Modified Pull-Up or Chin-Up. The child should stand on a sturdy chair or other raised area so that he can reach the bar with arms slightly bent at more than a 90-degree angle. It's even better to use a lower bar that allows the youngster to stand on the ground, with arms bent at that angle.

The child should then jump up and simultaneously pull himself up with his arms until his chin rises above the bar. Then he should lower himself as slowly as possible until he's on his feet once again. This completes one repetition. The movement should be repeated immediately without any rest until the child has completed the required number of repetitions in the set.

Another variation consists of lying flat on the floor under a low horizontal bar that can be grasped at arm's length. (Many playgrounds and exercise facilities now have this equipment.) Reach up and grab the bar, with the palms facing either in or out. With the body straight, lift the chin up to the bar, at the same time keeping the heels on the floor. Then lower the body to the arms-extended position to complete the repetitions. Repeat the movement until the required number of repetitions in the set have been completed.

N O T E : If a child has trouble even with one of these modified methods, he should do a flexed-arm hang from the bar for an increasing number of seconds over a period of a couple of weeks and then graduate to the modified chin-up.

After doing these modified chin-ups for a few weeks, or at the most a few months, most children should be able to execute at least one complete regular chin-up. When he can do a maximum of at least four regular chin-ups and can exercise with at least two to a set, then he can switch from the modified chin-ups to the regular chin-ups.

The Extra Strength Prescription Most young people who follow a regular circuit-training program three to four days a week using these three basic exercises will experience a dramatic increase in muscular strength in two to three months. After a foundation of strength has been laid, you should consider adding on these additional exercises, either all at once or one or two at a time until your boy or girl is doing all of them.

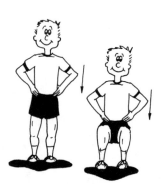

Additional Strength Exercise #1. Half-Knee Bends This exercise, which strengthens the thighs, should be started with the feet placed shoulder-width apart, hands on the hips or straight out in front of the body. Squat until the thighs are parallel to the ground and then return to a full standing position. Do *not* bend all the way down—full squats put too much stress on the knees.

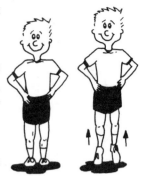

Additional Strength Exercise #2. Heel Raises To build up the calf muscles and ankles, place the feet shoulder width apart, hands on hips. Stand erect. Raise up on the toes as far as possible and then lower the body back down until the heels touch.

Additional Strength Exercise #3. Straight Leg Lifts The outer thighs and hips can be strengthened with this exercise. Lie on your right side and support yourself on your elbows, or with the right elbow and the left hand. Keep the lower leg straight or bend it slightly behind you. Lift and lower the top leg (the left leg), keeping the body facing straight ahead at all times. Repeat the same number of repetitions using the opposite leg (the right leg).

Additional Strength Exercise #4. Hip Raises To build up the back of the arms (triceps) and chest muscles, sit on the floor with your hands flat on the floor next to your hips and pointed outward. Keeping your elbows straight, raise your hips off the floor until your body is straight and at a 45-degree angle from the floor. The only parts of your body touching the floor should be the heels and hands. Lower the buttocks toward the floor keeping your arms straight. Repeat for the desired number of repetitions.

The final essential part of any effective kid fitness workout is the flexibility program. As with the strength program, I've included basic flexibility exercises and several additional exercises, which are optional. Remember, these flexibility events may be included in the warm-up, the cool-down, or the strength phase of your program, or in all three.

Basic Flexibility Exercise #1. Lower Back Stretch Lie on your back and clasp hands around right knee. Pull right knee to the chest, and at the same time, keep the lower back on the ground. Hold that position for 10 to 15 seconds and repeat with left knee. Now clasp hands around *both* knees and pull them up to the chest. You should experience a feeling of stretching in the lower back and the hamstrings (the muscles at the back of the upper leg).

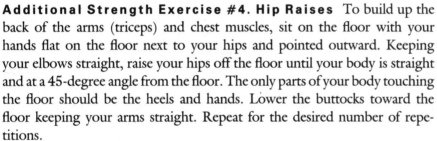

Basic Flexibility Exercise #2. Calf Stretch Stand about 12 inches away from the wall. With your hands against the wall lean forward and extend your left leg back. With both heels remaining flat on the ground, bend the front (right) knee, while keeping the back knee straight. As the front knee bends, a stretching pressure will be felt in the Achilles tendon (at the back of the heel) in the left leg, which is farthest from the wall. Bend slightly and release the pressure on the left Achilles tendon about 10 times and then switch legs and repeat, stretching the right leg.

Basic Flexibility Exercise #3. Hamstring Stretch with Leg Up Stand facing a platform railing or chair that is slightly less than waist high. Raise the left leg in front of your body, and rest the left foot on the railing. Lean the upper torso toward the raised leg, bending at the hips, and hold the body in that position for a second or two. Repeat 10 times. The stretch should be felt in the hamstring (the back of the thigh) of the raised leg, and in the lower back. Repeat these movements and repetitions with the right leg.

Additional Flexibility Exercise #1. Hip Stretch Place your right knee on the floor behind the left foot. Move the left knee forward so that it is positioned over the left toes. Place the palms on the left knee. Without changing the position of the left knee, push your hips down and toward the floor. Be sure that the left knee and toes are pointing forward and not to the side. The stretch should be felt in the front of the hip of the back leg and possibly in the groin and hamstring. Repeat this motion 10 times. Now, switch positions and repeat with the right leg forward and left knee on the ground.

Additional Flexibility Exercise #2. Groin Stretch (also known as the Butterfly) Sitting on the floor, place the soles of your feet together, and holding your feet with both hands, pull your feet in toward your body as far as you can. Your elbows should rest against the inside of your knees as you grasp your feet. Pull up on your toes as you push down with your knees. Then, relax. Repeat about 10 times.

Additional Flexibility Exercise #3. Thigh Stretch Lie on your stomach with your head down. With your right hand, pull the right foot toward the buttocks. The stretch should be felt in the front of the thigh (the quadriceps muscles). Relax, and repeat 10 times. Now, switch positions, with your left hand on your left foot, and repeat the repetitions.

HOW LARRY PUT THE PROGRAM INTO PRACTICE

Now that you understand the basic ingredients that go into a comprehensive kid fitness program, it's time to put the principles into practice. As described in chapter 4, you may have to take some steps to motivate your youngster to start a program and maintain it. Possible inducements include offering rewards for participation and achievement, establishing a token economy system, or simply participating with your youngster. Here's how the program worked with Larry, an 11-year-old:

Larry had been gaining extra weight and was finding he had trouble keeping up with classmates in sports. As a result, his self-confidence had declined, and he seemed to be becoming a TV and video game addict. His parents felt that his health was declining—and their fears were confirmed after he took the health and fitness test in the previous chapter and did poorly on it. The answer seemed to be a systematic fitness program.

First, Larry's parents selected the aerobics walking program for 11-year-olds, described earlier in this chapter. They began with week one, involving a 15-minute walk, three times a week. They also selected the three basic strength exercises and the three basic flexibility exercises. Larry was able to start out doing sets of 8 push-ups and 15 sit-ups, but he couldn't do a complete chin-up. Consequently, his parents used the modified chin-up approach, with 6 repetitions jumping from the ground and pulling his chin up over the bar.

To make the activity more attractive to Larry, his parents resolved to participate themselves. They also used a simple token economy system, awarding him 5 points every time he completed the aerobics segment of his workout and 1 point every time he successfully completed one set of strength or flexibility exercises. In this way, he could earn a total of 11 points for every complete workout (5 for the aerobics, 3 for strength, and 3 for flexibility).

According to an informal agreement between parents and son, the points could be turned in for small increases in his allowance, movies, and other rewards. The family adjusted the point exchange to fit their limited budget and soon discovered that the benefits far outweighed the costs.

After about a week, the family realized that it was too hard to fit the entire workout into one session. Consequently, they did the flexibility and walking events on one day, and on alternate days, they did the strength workout.

The combination of parental participation and concrete rewards quickly helped Larry get into much better physical condition. After only about three months, he could do two complete pull-ups and he graduated to jogging instead of walking with his parents. Also, he was able to keep up with the other kids in a basketball league sponsored by a community organization.

Within another month or two, Larry's parents found that they no longer had to offer him prizes or rewards for his efforts. Now, he was motivated internally by wanting to stay in shape and perform well with his peers. Even parental participation became less important as he engaged more in team athletics, although the enhanced relationships he had experienced during the workouts, especially with his father, were something he indicated he wanted to continue.

A typical comment: "No matter what teams I play on, I still want to keep running with *you*, Dad."

We'll continue to explore the benefits of exercise in later chapters, such as in chapter 16 on the Elite Child Athlete. For the present, however, you have plenty to get started. Also, it's important at this point to turn to an equally important issue—smart eating for the fast-food generation.

CHAPTER NINE

Smart Eating for the Fast-Food Generation

Kids today seem to move at the speed of light compared with those of generations past, and sometimes flitting from activity to activity, appointment to appointment, they leave the basics of good nutrition far behind. Two cases in point:

Danny. Ten-year-old Danny's daily schedule was so packed that he barely had time to take a deep breath from the time he left for school to the moment he sat down to eat dinner. He often skipped breakfast and barely touched lunch at school because he hated the flat, institutional fare. As a result he was starving when he finished his last class in midafternoon and headed toward a piano lesson or soccer practice.

Danny's solution to his hunger pangs, assented to by his equally rushed mother who was trying to get him to his activities on time, was to grab a hot dog, hamburger, or ice cream cone from the local fast-food restaurant. Then when he reached home he was exhausted and had little appetite. He would just nibble at his food and then consume a piece of pie or other high-calorie dessert, and finally he would plop down in front of the TV set until time for bed.

Danny's parents finally realized that their son had a major nutritional problem when a blood test revealed that his total cholesterol was 192 mg/dl, a figure high enough to increase his risk of heart disease in the future.

Rachel. Fourteen-year-old Rachel was worried about her looks because she was afraid that she was getting too fat. So she refused to eat more than a few bites of the meals served to her, either at home or at school. She was a promising member of the school tennis team, but found when she reported for practice immediately after school, she felt weak and ravenous. To satisfy her hunger, she carried several high-fat, high-calorie candy bars—for "quick energy," she rationalized.

After practice, Rachel would usually drop into an ice-cream parlor with friends on the way home and consume a chocolate sundae. Like Danny, when she finally got home, she wasn't particularly interested in eating her home-prepared evening meal. But *also* like Danny, later at night she *was* ready to eat whatever dessert had been prepared—and have a bedtime snack.

With such eating habits, Rachel continued to gain unwanted pounds. Also, she found she chronically lacked energy to play her best tennis, to study effectively, or to carry on other important activities in her life.

Danny and Rachel are typical of many contemporary children, and frequently they turn in subpar performances in many areas of life because they are not properly nourished. So how can such members of the fast-food generation overcome this problem? To put it another way, how can they become "smart eaters"?

There are two major challenges in getting young people to eat properly:

Challenge #1. The basic principles of good nutrition must be learned by both parents *and* children.

Challenge #2. Both children *and* parents must be motivated to incorporate these principles into their lives.

In short, it takes a partnership between the parent and child to establish an effective kid fitness smart eating program.

In showing you how to meet these challenges successfully, I'll be discussing such issues as these:

• Why various foods are essential to ensure maximum growth and development at different stages of childhood
• Strategies to motivate the entire family to eat smart
• A program to overcome obesity in children—including two weeks of sample weight-loss management
• Insights into some adolescent eating disorders
• The special problems posed by vegetarianism
• Guidelines for good nutrition for infants and toddlers
• How to feed young athletes to promote maximum performance
• Sample menus to enable boys and girls of different ages to obtain the nutrients they need for proper growth and development

GOING FOR MAXIMUM GROWTH

Exercise will help to build strong muscles and bones and will increase the body's endurance capacity—but *only* if that exercise is backed up by sound nutrition. Proper food is the fuel that enables the child to achieve real fitness. In fact, the right kinds of foods are *absolutely necessary* for each youngster to move successfully through the six phases of development discussed earlier in this book.

To get a general idea about how much food a growing child needs, some find it helpful to think in terms of that common but much-maligned measure of food energy, the heat unit that we call the calorie. I'm not an advocate of calorie-counting for most people, including children. As a matter of fact, as we'll see shortly in our discussion of effective eating strategies, a heavy emphasis on calories can make a child focus on the negatives of nutrition, i.e., on what he *shouldn't* eat, rather than what he *should* eat.

At the same time, however, I've always included calorie values in the menus in my books. Furthermore, the menus and recipes in this book have been designed with an eye to calories. The reason? It's necessary to have some means of measuring the amount of food that the child should be consuming.

In general, nutritionists say that to develop maximum physical potential—for every kilogram, or 2.2 pounds, of body weight—children should be consuming these levels of calories each day:

Infants: 120 calories
Ages 1 to 2 years: 100 calories
Ages 3 to 5 years: 90 calories
Ages 6 to 8 years: 85 calories

For example, a 12-pound infant should be consuming 654 calories per day. The calculation goes like this: 12 pounds ÷ 2.2 pounds = 5.45. 5.45 × 120 calories = 654 calories per day.

From about ages 9 to 12, the requirements range from about 55 to 65 calories for every kilogram, or 2.2 pounds, of body weight. But at this age and older ages, the individual needs vary greatly, depending on the child's activity levels, developmental stage, and natural metabolism. Probably the best guidelines for older children and adolescents are body fat measurements, as described in chapter 7.

Parents can expect infants to 12 months to gain about two-thirds of an ounce per day and children 1 to 2 years of age to increase their poundage by about 5.5 pounds a year. Those 3 to 5 years of age will put on about 4.5 pounds a year, and those 6 to 8 will gain 6.5 pounds a year.

Boys from about ages 9 to 12 will put on about 6 to 7 pounds a year on average. Then beginning at age 12, most boys start gaining about 10 to 12 pounds per year until they begin to approach their adult weight in their late teenage years. Girls, in contrast, will average about a 6.5-pound weight increase from ages 9 to 10, and then they'll increase their poundage at a faster rate of about 9 to 10 pounds per year from ages 10 to 14. At that time, their weight gain will gradually level off to their adult weight.

At the same time that a child is putting on the pounds, his or her height will be increasing as well. As a very broad rule, parents can expect children 1 to 2 years old to grow about 4.75 inches each year, those 3 to 5 years to increase by 2.75 inches a year, and those 6 to 8 years of age to increase by about 2.25 inches per year. From age 9 and older, height increases vary widely because of the different growth spurts children experience.

As we've already seen in chapter 3, girls usually mature and grow earlier than boys. Also, children of *either* sex may undergo early *or* late bursts of height and weight, depending on the particular genetic programming. CAUTION: Remember that all these weight and growth figures represent averages, not what every parent should expect for every child. So don't worry if your child seems to be ahead or behind any of these guidelines. Regular check-ups by your physician or pediatrician will show you exactly where your child stands and also whether or not there is any cause for concern.

If at any time between about ages 10 and 12 a certain calorie intake seems to be putting on excess pounds and body fat, it may be advisable to increase exercise levels and cut back on the consumption of food. I don't advise very low calorie diets for younger children because of the possibility that a restricted eating plan may deprive the child of essential nutrients for growth. In fact, any weight-loss program for children, especially those who haven't reached puberty, should be closely supervised by a physician and should focus on good nutrition, healthy eating habits, and more physical activity.

On the other hand, if a child's weight is declining or staying at levels that the parents and physician feel are too low, a higher-calorie diet may be in order. Your doctor will be able to advise you about the course of action that's best to take. In any event, the menus and recipes included later in this chapter have been designed with these special needs in mind.

Poor nutrition—including an unhealthy balance of protein, carbohydrates, fats, vitamins, minerals, and water—may cause a child to tire easily, have a poor appetite, experience slower growth, or lag in muscle coordination. Also, poor nutrition can cause a kid to become sick more easily because of an inability to ward off infections and viruses. Here is a sampling of what some key foods will do for your growing child.

Milk and Dairy Products. These include foods such as milk, yogurt, cheese, ice cream, cottage cheese, and some puddings. The principal nutrients in them are calcium, phosphorus, magnesium, protein, riboflavin, and vitamins A, D (in fortified products), B_6, and B_{12}.

What do these nutrients do for a child? They promote growth and development; they help build and maintain healthy bones and teeth; they build and repair body tissues; and they help nerves, muscles, and the heart to function properly.

All children, of every age, need milk and dairy products, although I recommend that the fat content of these foods be reduced in the later years. In general, children up to age 2 should consume whole milk, those from ages 2 to 6 may lower the fat content to 2 percent, and those in the older ages should use only low-fat or skim milk products.

N O T E : Those in the 2- to 6-year age range may consume 1 percent milk products if their weight is appropriate and development is on track. But children who are underweight, are poor eaters, or seem to have a growth problem should probably stick to 2 percent milk or even whole milk. A physician or qualified nutritionist should be consulted in this situation.

High-Protein Foods, Including Meats. Protein provides the nutrients needed to build the structures for the body's cells, including those in the muscles, blood, bones, and skin. All bodily growth and development in the younger years, along with hormone and antibody production, depends on the intake of protein. Those children who receive inadequate amounts not only can suffer lags in growth but may also become anemic, a condition that lowers their immunity by making them more susceptible to disease.

Foods that typically contain a lot of protein include beef, lamb, pork, veal, poultry, liver, fish and shellfish, peanut butter (I recommend *only* the natural, nonhydrogenated kind), eggs (primarily the egg whites), dried beans (e.g., soy, navy, pinto, kidney), dried peas, lentils, tofu, cheese, milk, yogurt, and vegetable protein.

A F U R T H E R N O T E O N P E A N U T B U T T E R : You'll find peanut butter in moderate amounts suggested as an ingredient in some of the recipes in this book. But be aware that any reference to this food assumes the use of *natural, nonhydrogenated peanut butter.*

I'm well aware that certain studies, especially animal studies, have indicated that the consumption of *hydrogenated* peanut butter will increase the clogging of the arteries with fatty deposits (atherosclerosis). Hydrogenation, by the way, refers to the process by which fats become more saturated and potentially more damaging. Natural, *non*hydrogenated peanut butter can be made from crushed nuts at home or can be bought in many groceries or health food stores.

Protein derived from animal products are known as complete proteins. Vegetable proteins, in contrast, are known as incomplete proteins. When we say that a protein is incomplete, it means that the body doesn't use it sufficiently unless it's combined with another specific group of vegetable proteins or with an animal protein. The process of combining creates a complete protein.

So when we include incomplete vegetable proteins in our menus and recipes in this book, we've always tried to "complete" them so that the body can make use of all their nutritional potential. Here are a couple of examples of how vegetable proteins can be linked to produce a complete protein:

- Combine a legume (e.g., natural, nonhydrogenated peanut butter) with a grain (wheat bread)
- Combine dried beans (pinto beans) with a grain (flour tortilla)

Any of the above incomplete proteins can be combined with a complete protein from an animal product, such as chicken or milk, to produce a complete protein meal.

Complex Carbohydrates Such as Fruits and Vegetables. Complex carbohydrates, which are typically found in fruits, vegetables, and starches, provide the body with easy-to-burn energy necessary to keep the young, growing body functioning at a good pace. Carbohydrates tend to be used by the body before protein, and so adequate carbohydrate foods are necessary to "spare" or "save" the dietary protein for other uses, such as growth and tissue repair. The more active a young person is, the more carbohydrates he or she needs to function efficiently.

At this point, I want to distinguish between "sugary" carbohydrates and "nutritive" carbohydrates. The term *complex carbohydrates* refers to those foods with slower-burning sugars and with important nutrients such as minerals, vitamins, and fiber. In contrast, desserts, candies, soft drinks, and other such sweets contain primarily simple, fast-burning sugars, with few, if any, nutritive ingredients. For this reason, commercially produced sugary, simple carbohydrates are said to provide "empty calories." These are calories that, if not used for instant fuel, are converted to fat and add unwanted pounds without other benefits.

To be sure, foods such as fruits, fruit juices, and milk often contain natural simple sugars, but they also provide important vitamins and minerals that a commercial candy bar doesn't contain. In particular, a diet consisting of a proper balance of vegetables, fruits, whole grain products, milk, or milk substitutes will provide various vitamins, such as A, C, thiamine, niacin, and folic acid and minerals such as iron, magnesium, and copper. These foods also contain soluble and insoluble fibers, which promote regular bowel movements. Among other things, these simple and complex carbohydrates provide a source of energy, help maintain healthy body tissues, increase the child's resistance to infections, strengthen growing blood vessels, promote healthy vision, and enhance the development of the youngster's nervous system.

Fats and Oils. Despite the bad press they have received for adult diets, fats and oils are important elements in the growing child's nutritional plan— so long as they aren't consumed in excess. Fats are necessary for a number of reasons.

• They provide a high-energy source that is used up by the body at a slower rate than many carbohydrates. As a result, most highly energetic children need fats to continue functioning at an efficient rate throughout the day.

• Fats carry fat-soluble vitamins such as A, D, E, and K into the bloodstream so that they can perform their missions throughout the body. Without adequate fats, these nutrients wouldn't make it to their final destinations.

• Ingredients in many fats, such as cholesterol, are necessary for cell building and the sheathing process (known as "myelination") that occurs in nerve and brain cells. The body produces many of the nutrients necessary for these growth and maintenance functions, but diet is also a factor.

Because fats are so important to the growing child, I have recommended that children up to age 2 drink and eat whole-milk dairy products and those up to age 5 scale back on these products gradually. Certainly, as a child grows older, it's important to learn low-fat eating habits and strategies that will carry over to adulthood. But during the earliest years, it's not necessary or advisable to recommend extremely low-fat or no-fat dishes unless the child has a cholesterol or other blood lipid problem.

CAUTION: I'm *not* saying that it's acceptable at any time to load up on high-fat foods. Too many fatty foods at *any* age will cut the child's hunger for other, more nutritious dishes and will also tend to promote obesity and lay the groundwork for atherosclerosis (hardening of the arteries).

For most children above age 5, a diet consisting of 30 percent fat calories should be appropriate, with one-third of those fats consisting of monounsaturated fats (e.g., olives and olive oil, peanuts and peanut butter, and products with canola oil), one-third polyunsaturated fats (e.g., sunflower and most vegetable oils), and no more than one-third saturated fats (e.g., meat, butter, dairy products, and foods with tropical oils).

An easy test for identifying saturated fats: they tend to remain solid at room temperature, while monounsaturated and polyunsaturated fats stay liquid.

The rest of the young child's diet should include 15 to 20 percent of calories from protein-based products. And about 50 percent of the daily calories should come from complex carbohydrates.

After a child has reached age 11 or 12, daily fat intake should usually decrease over the next few years to the generally recommended adult level of 20 to 30 percent of total daily calories. At the same time, consumption of complex carbohydrates should increase to about 50 to 60 percent of calories. The crucial point is to eat ample calories with a greater emphasis on carbohydrates and to deemphasize the intake of fats.

Of course, the precise balance of nutrients in your child's diet will depend on his activity and developmental level. For example, if you have a young athlete in the house, you'll want to increase his consumption of complex carbohydrates and overall calorie intake to meet his growth needs and energy requirements. Specific strategies for feeding the young athlete are included in a special section in chapter 10. On the other hand, if you discover that your child is steadily putting on excess weight and increasing body fat, complex carbohydrates and simple sugars may have to be cut as well as fats.

HOW CAN YOU MOTIVATE YOUR CHILD TO EAT SMART?

No matter how much reasonable information about nutrition that a parent reads or hears, the bottom-line question that often comes back to doctors and nutritionists is "Fine, but how do I get my child to *do* it?"

A number of parents have succeeded in motivating their children to eat properly by employing one or more of the following eat smart strategies:

> *#1: Encourage Physical Activity.* The active child is also the hungry
> child. If nutritious snacks of the type we've included in our menu

and recipe sections are made available when hunger strikes, child-hood eating problems often solve themselves.

Furthermore, by *physical activity,* I'm not just referring to formal exercise or even informal sports. The youngster who does regular household chores, such as cleaning her room and washing the car or who walks or bikes to school, rather than being driven, will maintain a better appetite than the one who is more sedentary.

Another facet to this activity strategy is to limit pastimes that allow the child just to sit around. TV watching is the main culprit here. The kid who spends several hours a day in front of the set not only will be less hungry at mealtimes but he'll also be tempted to snack on anything available.

> *#2: Develop Positive Nutritional Thinking and Behavior in Your Boy or Girl.* When discussing nutritional matters, parents should empha-size the best food choices, rather than the negatives of the eating experience.

For example, I believe that parents and eventually children should un-derstand something about the caloric values of food and how certain types of food in certain amounts are likely to put on weight, increase energy, or otherwise affect the body. On the other hand, I agree with the large number of nutritionists who advise against teaching kids to eat primarily by counting calories or avoiding certain "forbidden" or less-healthy foods. That's an inherently negative, uninteresting, and overly complicated way of getting across the message about good nutrition. Not only that, this approach may encourage children to feel excessively guilty about their eating habits and can aggravate eating disorders such as anorexia, bulimia, or obesity.

Also, with most kids, the surest way to get them to eat a less-healthy food is to say, "That's forbidden" or "You must avoid that." Adam and Eve may be our best case studies in this approach to food.

So try training your child to choose low-fat foods, rather than avoid high-fat dishes. Or emphasize how healthy and nutritious natural fruits are—without necessarily belaboring the fact of how unhealthy high-fat, high-sugar desserts may be. The main idea here is to establish lifetime eating habits that are rooted in positive choices, rather than promote a restrictive dieting mentality. If a person thinks, "I can't eat such and such because it's not good for me," he's likely eventually to give in and indulge in that food in times of stress. That's one major reason that the success rate for restrictive dieting is so low and that obesity is a very common manifestation of stress.

There is an exception to this approach. I find nothing wrong with *aversive conditioning* to less-healthy food choices as long as the instruction emphasizes the *specific* drawbacks of certain dishes, rather than presenting them as forbidden fruit. For example, I recall how one mother and father convinced their 11-year-old son about the virtues of low-fat, low-cholesterol foods by pointing out certain newspaper articles that described how the unhealthy eating habits of many children were setting them up for greater risk of heart attacks later in life. After an extensive family discussion on this subject, the parents offered no particular advice about how their son should change his nutrition. They just asked, "What do you think?"

His reply: "I think I should quit having so many hot dogs."

In another family, the mother showed her 9-year-old daughter some pictures of bones damaged by osteoporosis later in life and said, "I expect this woman ate poorly and drank too little milk, even when she was a girl." That was all it took to get the daughter thinking more seriously about finishing her glass of milk at each meal.

In both of these cases, the parents combined the negative message with some solid facts and allowed the children to make up their own minds.

Some other effective visual techniques to teach kids in positive ways about bad foods:

• To show how much sugar one 12-ounce cola contains, scoop out 9 teaspoons of sugar and pile them up in the bottom of a drinking glass.

• To demonstrate how much fat is contained in a typical fast-food hamburger with cheese, deposit 9 teaspoons of some type of solid fat, such as lard into another glass. Just looking at such sights or offering them to children for a "little taste" is often enough to make kids think twice about indulging in such junk foods the next time.

> #3: *Take Regular Physical Measurements.* Children of practically every age are interested in how they are growing. Some simply become fascinated with the mechanical process of checking weight, height, and other measurements. Others, particularly boys and girls who are competing in sports beginning at about age 8, like to see that they're getting bigger and, by implication, stronger and faster.

When the teenage years arrive, another factor emerges: how attractive the child appears to the opposite sex in comparison with peers. This interest in physical measurements automatically makes the child more conscious of his body image and can be a major motivator in firming up flabby muscles or taking off unwanted pounds.

I'm reminded of the response of one athletic 10-year-old boy who experienced the normal increase in body fat that usually occurs a year or so before the onset of adolescence. He saw that there was an extra roll of fat around his stomach, and he asked his parents, "Is this going to make me a slower runner?"

His parents assured him that he was developing quite normally. To prove it, the father measured his body fat, using the calipers and standards described in chapter 7.

But then, just after the season for one of his sports ended and just before the next sport began, the youngster became less active physically. During those two or three weeks, the boy did not change his eating habits, and he gained about 5 pounds. The increase in weight was not hormonal, it was eating too much for his reduced physical activity.

Once again, the 10-year-old asked, "Am I too fat?" And this time, after another body fat measurement, the parents replied quite truthfully, "You're putting on a little too much weight. So you should just exercise more and watch TV less. Then you won't have to worry about your weight."

As a result of this experience, the boy began to measure the circumference of his waist and at the same time monitor the fluctuations of his weight on the bathroom scale. Whenever he felt he was getting too heavy, he would ask his father to measure his percent of body fat to reassure him.

> #4: *Be Aware of Your Influence as a Role Model.* I've already gone into some detail in chapter 5 about how important it is for parents to be involved in all fitness activities, including good nutrition. Parents who eat properly convey principles of healthy nutrition to their children, and without a doubt, this is the best eat smart strategy of all!
>
> #5: *Allow a Regular Splurge.* It's virtually impossible to eliminate less-nutritious foods entirely from the average child's daily menus. Consequently, I advocate a semimonthly splurge—which involves letting your child have a high-fat or high-sugar food about once every two weeks or, in some cases, once a week. This approach works best with younger children, who are still somewhat under the control of adults when they go out for food. With adolescents, the splurge strategy must operate more on the honor system, or as an advised rather than required kind of behavior.

In general, I'd recommend that you try to limit the consumption of a *very* high-calorie, high-fat food, such as a large fast-food hamburger, to once every one to two weeks. These may add up to 1,000 calories or more per serving, most of which comes from fat. Lower-calorie, high-fat foods—say, a high-fat ice cream cone—may be acceptable once a week. Or you may even be able to get your child interested in a real bonus: lower-calorie, low-fat fruit popsicles, frozen yogurt, or popcorn may be consumed *daily*! So may some of the snacks that are included in our kid fitness recipe section.

Here's how the splurge strategy works. Your child may crave fast-food hamburgers. So once every couple of weeks, you might take him out to the local fast-food place for a father-son splurge. Similarly, a mother-daughter outing might involve an ice cream or commercial candy bar once a week. It's up to parents to keep track of how much fat and sugar the child is consuming on these splurges and to be sure that the youngster is maintaining a healthy balance in overall nutrition.

> *#6: Permit nutritious nibbling.* The growth rate slows after age 1, and so does the appetite. Furthermore, throughout childhood, the stomach of a boy or girl is significantly smaller than that of an adult. For example, the average weight of the stomach of an adult is more than 2.5 times that of a 6-year-old and more than 1.5 times that of a 14-year-old.

One implication of these facts is that putting a child on the same eating schedule as an adult may not be a wise move. Many pediatricians, for instance, recommend feeding a child more than three meals a day so as to keep those smaller stomachs filled up and satisfied. In effect, the suggestion is that we legalize "grazing" or nibbling, that great bane of many parents of the past!

I'm all for giving children nutritious snacks at those times of the day when they become especially hungry and then allowing them to cut down on food portions at regular family mealtimes. This strategy fits nicely into the meal plans we've recommended in this book and also conforms to some interesting findings about how nibbling can promote a healthier balance of fats in the blood.

In the October 5, 1989, issue of the *New England Journal of Medicine*, a number of researchers from St. Michael's Hospital, University of Toronto in Canada reported on their investigation of the differences between nibbling and eating three meals a day. They determined that men who nibbled on 17 snacks per day, in contrast to others who ate three square meals daily, enjoyed lower total cholesterol, lower "bad" cholesterol (low-density lipoproteins, or LDL cholesterol), and other benefits.

My conclusion: intelligent nibbling is okay—so long as it's not used as an excuse for constantly raiding the cupboard or refrigerator for high-fat snacks.

> *#7: Let Your Child Participate in Food Preparation.* The more a child helps prepare food, the more inclined he will be to eat it. Part of the fascination of eating what you've made is curiosity: "Did I do a good enough job to satisfy myself and the rest of the family?" And part of the appeal is pride: "I'm not about to let anybody know I don't like what I made!"

Many of the "kid recipes" in this book have been designed simply, so that parents can make them quickly *and* so that children, in some cases rather young children, can at least help in the preparation. Older children and adolescents will find that they can prepare many of these dishes in no time with a little practice.

These seven strategies, when combined with other motivational suggestions in this book, should at least get you off to a good start in inspiring your child to eat smart. Now, let's move directly into the actual Kid Fitness Menus and Recipes. Then in the next chapter, I'll devote some additional time to four special nutritional concerns: obesity, eating disorders, vegetarianism, and nutrition for young athletes.

AN INTRODUCTION TO THE KID FITNESS MENUS AND RECIPES

In the following section you'll find four categories of menus—all of which can be prepared so as to fit into the regular family meal plan.

One Week of 1,000-Calorie Early Childhood Menus. These have been designed for children in the general age range of 3 to 6 years. I regard the feeding of infants and toddlers under 3 as beyond the scope of this book because each pediatrician tends to have his own special set of strategies and advice for such issues as breast-feeding, weaning, and introducing various solid foods to the diet. Consequently, this first set of menus focuses on the somewhat older child. You should consult your pediatrician if your child is 3 or younger.

The average children in the 3- to 6-year range need to eat somewhere between 900 and 1,800 calories per day—obviously quite a wide variation!

So the 1,000-calorie menus should only be regarded as a rough guideline. I've chosen the 1,000-calorie level, by the way, because it's at the low end of this calorie range, and we generally find it's more convenient to *add to,* rather than subtract from, a model menu. With the help of a physician or a qualified nutritionist, portion sizes should be adjusted to fit the precise needs of each child, according to the youngster's level of activity, physical size, and age.

Two Weeks of 2,000-Calorie Menus. These should be used primarily by preteens, aged 7 to 11 years and by female adolescents, aged 12 to 19 years. Children in these categories who engage in average levels of physical activity will most likely find that they can maintain an acceptable weight with this approach. Also, these menus can be effective for weight control for every active male and female adolescent. As with the other menus, calorie levels may be adjusted up or down to suit the needs of the individual child—just add or delete snacks or change portion sizes.

One Week of 3,000-Calorie Menus. This program should be useful mainly for very active teenage boys and some quite active girls, aged 12 to 19. These children need approximately 2,500 to 3,500 calories per day. In some cases, very athletic teenagers may have to take in even more food to maintain a steady weight and high energy.

The best way to tell whether your teenager is eating the right amount of food is his or her ability to maintain a steady weight level. Those who tend to lose weight or who feel listless or fatigued probably aren't consuming enough calories. On the other hand, children who gradually put on body fat are probably getting too much food, too much fat, or too little exercise.

Two Weeks of 1,500-Calorie Weight-Control Menus. These menus have been designed primarily for obese teenagers 12 to 19 years of age, who engage in average or low levels of physical activity. Also, they may be used by *non*obese younger children who require this level of calorie intake for weight maintenance. (For very active teenagers who need to lose weight, refer back to the 2,000-calorie menus.)

In my opinion, growing teenagers should not consume less than 1,500 calories per day because smaller amounts of food are likely to cut into those nutrients necessary for adequate physical and mental development. Furthermore, I discourage weight-loss programs for younger children unless they are conducted under the strict supervision of a physician.

NOTE: For fast-growing teenagers, actual reduction of weight may be inappropriate. Rather, some experts recommend just keeping the same weight or gradually increasing weight as growth occurs. With increases in height, the old weight level will usually be more appropriate than it was when the child was shorter.

On the other hand, if your doctor does determine that some pounds should be taken off, the goal for weight loss should be no more than 1 to 2 pounds per week.

I'll go into other special concerns about obesity and weight loss in the next chapter. If this is one of your main concerns, you should read that part of the book before anyone in your family embarks on a weight-loss program.

The Recipe Section. An extensive set of Kid Fitness Recipes follows the Kid Fitness Menus. Many of the menus include recipes that may be found under the appropriate headings in the recipe section of this chapter. Other recipes in that section, which includes calorie and nutrition content, may be substituted for similar dishes in the menus or may be added as snacks when the child requires additional calories.

Now, let me offer these additional, specific comments about understanding and using the menus and recipes that follow:

• *The nutritional balance.* All menus contain approximately 50 percent complex carbohydrates, 30 percent fats, and 20 percent proteins. As I've already indicated saturated fats and cholesterol have been kept to a minimum.

• *More on fats.* With children, the principles of fat consumption are somewhat different from the guidelines for adults. In general, adults should limit as much as possible their consumption of fats—and especially saturated fats, which contribute to rises in blood cholesterol.

Children, on the other hand, may need more fat in their diets, primarily to keep their calorie levels high enough to sustain proper growth. Our Kid Fitness Menus do average 30 percent fat calories per day. But I don't worry if a child's daily fat consumption goes up a little, say to 35 percent of total calories, *if* these two conditions are met:

1. The child has no cholesterol or other blood lipid problem.
2. The extra calories are necessary to support increasing height, weight, and other requirements of normal development.

To provide the extra calories some children need for growth, a few of the recipes contain more than 10 grams of fat and more than 30 percent of fat calories. Very active children may need this extra energy, and parents can expect any weight gains to be in height and muscle, not in obesity. Of course, if caliper measurements show an increase in body fat, the calories should be cut back or the exercise level increased. Furthermore, an unacceptable rise in blood cholesterol or other blood fats may also dictate a decrease in the child's dietary fat consumption.

• *The milk issue.* The menus and recipes assume the use of 1 or 2 percent fat milk. Parents should lean toward the 2 percent milk for younger children and also for those who need extra calories because of high activity or growth levels.

• *Eggs.* In any recipe, cholesterol-free egg substitutes or egg white may be substituted for eggs. Such substitution may be advisable if blood tests have revealed that the child's cholesterol level is too high. In making such exchanges, use this formula as your guide: 1 whole egg = 2 egg whites = ¼ cup egg substitute.

• *Cereals for kids.* We suggest that you rely on the following approved list of cereals which emphasize solid nutritional content, low sugar, and moderate amounts of fiber.

Recommended List of Cereals

40% Bran Flakes (all brands)
Oat Bran (⅓ cup dry)
Fruit & Fibre (Post)
Fruitful Bran (Kellogg)
Shredded Wheat 'N Bran (Nabisco)
Oatmeal
Shredded Wheat (Nabisco)
Frosted Mini-Wheats (Kellogg)
Raisin Bran (Kellogg, Post)
Total (General Mills)
Wheat Chex (Ralston)
Grape-Nuts (Post)
Nutri-Grain (Kellogg)
Cheerios

• *Calcium and iron.* All menus meet the current Recommended Daily Allowance (RDA) for these very important growth-related nutrients. Specifically, the current RDAs are
For calcium:
Ages 1 to 10: 800 milligrams per day
Ages 11 to 24: 1,200 milligrams per day

For iron:
>Ages 1 to 10: 10 milligrams per day
>Boys ages 11 to 18: 12 milligrams per day
>Girls ages 11 to 18: 15 milligrams per day

• *Margarine.* You may use liquid margarine or soft tub margarine interchangeably.

• *Sugar.* The menus and recipes have been designed to limit a child's consumption of refined sugar to no more than 10 percent of calories each day. Also, we've purposely included real sugar in the recipes rather than artificial sweeteners because current research hasn't established the long-term effects of the artificial substances.

My philosophy is that it's best to build good habits in consuming moderate amounts of natural foods. Such an approach to calorie control is usually preferable to an emphasis on completely abstaining from "bad" foods or relying too heavily on commercially produced substitutes.

BUT NOTE: Some children may be especially sensitive to sugar, and their behavior may be affected by excessive consumption. Yale University medical researchers reported at the 1990 annual meeting of the Society for Pediatric Research that children who were given a sugar dose for breakfast experienced significant increases in the adrenaline in their blood. Adrenaline is the gland secretion that prepares the body for a flight-or-fight response by increasing the heart rate and constricting the blood vessels. Excessive amounts can cause shakiness and nervousness.

Most of the 14 children tested complained of feeling shaky and weak. Similarly, in nonclinical settings, many parents have reported that after eating sugary foods, their children became irritable, aggressive, or hyperactive.

Consequently, parents must monitor each child's response and adjust sugar in the diet accordingly. For most children, however, the modest amounts of sugar contained in the menus and recipes in this book should pose no problem.

• *Peanut butter.* All recipes and menus assume the use of natural non-hydrogenated peanut butter such as Smucker's Natural Peanut Butter. You can purchase it in many supermarkets, or you can make your own from crushed peanuts. But be sure you stay away from commercially produced peanut butter with hydrogenated or partially hydrogenated ingredients. As you already know, hydrogenation produces saturated fats, which may increase the body's level of cholesterol.

Finally, in using these menus and recipes with your child, you should feel free to make necessary adjustments to merge them into regular family meals. In fact, *all* family members should be eating according to the healthy meal principles outlined in this book. Among other things, the menus adhere to principles approved by the American Heart Association and the American Cancer Society. Consequently—although many adults will want to skip some of the high-calorie snacks or other kid-oriented recipes—these menus have been designed to provide a model for what children *and* adults with various calorie needs should be eating.

The Kid Fitness
MENUS

1,000-CALORIE EARLY CHILDHOOD WEEKLY MENU
(FOR CHILDREN 3 TO 6 YEARS OLD)

DAY 1

BREAKFAST
- ½ cup dry cereal, see recommended cereals list, p. 182
- ¼ cup skim or low-fat milk
- ½ small banana
- 4 ounces orange juice

Suggestion: Slice banana to form shape of a happy face on dry cereal.

SNACK
- 1 fig newton
- ½ cup skim or low-fat milk

LUNCH
- ½ ham and cheese sandwich:
    - 1 slice whole wheat bread
    - ½ ounce sliced ham
    - ½ ounce American cheese
    - 1 slice tomato
    - 1 lettuce leaf
    - ½ tablespoon mayonnaise
- 1 raw carrot stick
- ¼ cup grapes
- 4 ounces unsweetened pineapple juice

Suggestion: Cut sandwich into three triangles.

AFTER-SCHOOL SNACK
- 1 whole wheat cracker with
    - 1 teaspoon natural peanut butter
- ½ cup skim or low-fat milk

DINNER
2 ounces roast turkey
4 medium Oven French Fries, see p. 247
¼ cup steamed green peas
One 1-inch square piece Corny Cornbread, see p. 236 with
    1 teaspoon margarine
¼ cup vanilla yogurt with
    2 sliced fresh strawberries
½ cup skim or low-fat milk

DAY 2

BREAKFAST
½ slice whole wheat toast with
    ½ tablespoon natural peanut butter
fruit cup:
    ⅛ cup fresh or unsweetened, canned pineapple chunks
    ⅛ cup fresh orange sections
    4 ounces hot cocoa

Suggestion: Serve fruit cup in a hollowed-out orange half.

SNACK
¼ cup fresh or unsweetened, canned fruit cocktail (grapes, peaches, pears, pineapple, etc.)
½ cup skim or low-fat milk

LUNCH
½ turkey sandwich:
    1 slice whole wheat bread
    1 ounce sliced turkey
    1 slice tomato
    1 lettuce leaf
    ½ tablespoon mayonnaise
1 pretzel log
2 slices cucumber
1 fresh small plum
½ cup skim or low-fat milk

Suggestions: Cut sandwich into thirds for small finger sandwiches. "Score" edges of sliced cucumbers with fork tines.

AFTER-SCHOOL SNACK
One 1-ounce part-skim mozzarella cheese
2 whole wheat crackers
4 ounces orange juice

Suggestion: Cut cheese in skinny sticks; may put on plate to create "stick-man" figure.

DINNER
2 ounces Fine Turkey Meat Loaf, see p. 243
¼ cup steamed green beans
¼ cup cooked brown rice
¼ cup Carrot-Raisin Salad, see p. 238, placed on
    1 lettuce leaf
1 Country Garden Muffin, see p. 234, with
    1 teaspoon margarine
½ cup skim or low-fat milk

DAY 3

BREAKFAST
½ slice whole wheat toast with
    ½ ounce American cheese
3 sliced fresh strawberries
4 ounces orange juice

Suggestion: Melt cheese if desired.

SNACK
¼ cup low-fat, flavored yogurt
4 ounces apple juice

Suggestion: Top yogurt with ½ strawberry or 1 grape for color.

LUNCH
½ tuna salad sandwich:
1 slice whole wheat bread
⅛ cup "Charlie Tuna" Salad, see p. 237
½ cup Colorful Veggie Soup, see p. 240
¼ cup fresh or unsweetened, canned peach slices
¼ cup oyster crackers
½ cup skim or low-fat milk

Suggestion: Arrange peach slices to create a pinwheel pattern on plate.

AFTER-SCHOOL SNACK
¼ cup trail mix
3 ounces grape juice

DINNER
½ cup cooked spaghetti with tomato sauce and
1-ounce meatball
1 tossed salad:
½ cup lettuce
1 tablespoon grated carrots
⅛ chopped tomato
1 teaspoon Italian dressing
½ slice whole wheat bread with
½ teaspoon margarine
¼ cup vanilla pudding
½ cup skim or low-fat milk

DAY 4

BREAKFAST
½ slice French Toast Delight, see p. 231 with
½ teaspoon powdered sugar
2 fresh orange sections
4 ounces hot cocoa

Suggestion: Cut French toast in three triangles and alternate toast and orange sections on plate.

SNACK
¼ cup low-fat cottage cheese with
    2 tablespoons fresh or unsweetened, canned peach slices
8 ounces water

Suggestion: Place cottage cheese on plate and surround with fruit.

LUNCH
1 ounce cheddar cheese, in cubes
1 ounce part-skim mozzarella cheese, in cubes
3 whole wheat crackers
¼ cup grapes
1 Lunch Box Favorite Oatmeal Cookie, see p. 250
4 ounces pineapple-orange juice

Suggestion: Arrange three crackers on plate as three corners of a triangle; add grapes clustered in the center; arrange cheese cubes as arms, hat, etc., of a clown.

AFTER-SCHOOL SNACK
4 ounces Strawberry Smoothie, see p. 265

Suggestion: Serve in a favorite glass or cup with a straw.

DINNER
2 ounces Special Fried Chicken, see p. 243
¼ cup Country Red Potato Salad, see p. 238
2 fresh, steamed asparagus spears
½ cup sliced cantaloupe
½ cup skim or low-fat milk

DAY 5

BREAKFAST
½ slice raisin toast with
   ½ tablespoon part-skim ricotta cheese
fruit cup:
   ⅛ cup sliced fresh strawberries
   ⅛ cup sliced bananas
   ½ cup skim or low-fat milk

Suggestions: Top ricotta cheese with extra raisins in shape of design or alphabet letter or face, etc. Arrange berries and bananas as design or circle, alternating fruit.

SNACK
¼ cup low-fat, flavored yogurt
6 ounces water

Suggestion: Top with grape or strawberry or three raisins.

LUNCH
½ chicken sandwich:
   1 slice whole wheat bread
   1 ounce sliced chicken
   1 slice tomato
   1 lettuce leaf
   ½ tablespoon mayonnaise
¼ cup corn chips
¼ fresh small pear
2 vanilla wafers
4 ounces orange juice

Suggestions: Cut as finger sandwiches. Put two wafers stacked in center of plate with pear slices as "sunbeams."

AFTER-SCHOOL SNACK
2 fresh or dried apricots
½ cup skim or low-fat milk

DINNER

1 slice medium cheese and green pepper pizza

1 spinach salad:

½ cup raw spinach

4 mandarin orange sections

1 teaspoon Italian dressing

4 ounces Lemonade Refresher, see p. 260

DAY 6

BREAKFAST

1 Feeling Your Oats Bran Muffin, see p. 234, with

1 teaspoon margarine

1 fresh or canned peach half topped with

¼ cup low-fat cottage cheese

4 ounces unsweetened pineapple juice

SNACK

2 graham cracker squares

4 ounces apple juice

Suggestion: Freeze apple juice in popsicle mold.

LUNCH

½ peanut butter and jelly sandwich:

1 slice whole wheat bread

1 tablespoon natural peanut butter

1 teaspoon all-fruit jelly

2 raw carrot sticks

½ tangerine

1 Lunch Box Favorite Oatmeal Cookie, see p. 250

½ cup skim or low-fat milk

Suggestion: Cut sandwich with a favorite small cookie cutter.

AFTER-SCHOOL SNACK
1 slice Banana Bread, see p. 235
½ cup skim or low-fat milk

DINNER
1 beef and cheese taco:
    1 taco shell
    1 ounce cooked ground beef
    ½ ounce (1½ tablespoons) grated cheddar cheese
    2 tablespoons shredded lettuce
    1 tablespoon chopped tomato
    1 tablespoon grated zucchini
¼ cup watermelon balls
½ cup skim or low-fat milk

DAY 7

BREAKFAST
1 whole wheat English muffin half with
    1 teaspoon margarine
½ ounce cooked ham slice
¼ cup unsweetened applesauce
½ cup skim or low-fat milk

Suggestion: Roll ham slice and use a toothpick to hold.

SNACK
½ cup dry cereal (see recommended cereals list, p. 182)
4 ounces apple juice

Suggestion: Serve cereal as finger food.

LUNCH
½ pimiento cheese sandwich:
    1 slice whole wheat bread
    ⅛ cup pimiento cheese
2 raw celery sticks
½ nectarine
1 small slice (¹/₂₄ cake) angel food cake
4 ounces orange juice

Suggestions: Cut sandwich half into three finger sandwiches. Place small orange wedge on side of juice glass.

AFTER-SCHOOL SNACK
½ granola bar
½ cup skim or low-fat milk

DINNER
2 ounces broiled tuna steak
¼ cup macaroni and cheese
¼ cup steamed peas and carrots
1 whole wheat dinner roll with
    ½ teaspoon margarine
¼ cup nonfat frozen yogurt
6 ounces water

Suggestion: Top yogurt with 1 tablespoon Cheerios or nuts or 1 fruit slice.

2,000-CALORIE PRE-TEEN AND TEENAGE FEMALE TWO-WEEK MENU

(FOR BOYS AND GIRLS 7 TO 11 YEARS OLD AND AVERAGE TEENAGE FEMALES 12 TO 19 YEARS OLD)

PREADOLESCENT AND FEMALE TEEN MENU
WEEK 1, DAY 1

BREAKFAST
¾ cup dry cereal, see recommended cereals list, p. 182
½ cup skim milk
½ banana
4 ounces orange juice

LUNCH
1 ham and cheese sandwich:
   2 slices whole wheat bread
   1 ounce sliced ham
   1 ounce part-skim mozzarella cheese
   2 slices tomato
   2 lettuce leaves
   1 tablespoon mayonnaise
2 raw carrot sticks
½ cup grapes
4 ounces unsweetened pineapple juice

AFTER-SCHOOL SNACK
3 whole wheat crackers with
   3 teaspoons natural peanut butter
½ cup skim milk

DINNER
3 ounces roast turkey
8 medium Oven French Fries, see p. 247
¼ cup steamed green peas
One 1-inch by 4-inch piece Corny Cornbread, see p. 236 with
   1 teaspoon margarine
½ cup vanilla yogurt with
   2 sliced fresh strawberries
1 cup skim milk

DAY 2

BREAKFAST
1 slice whole wheat toast with
    1 tablespoon natural peanut butter
fruit cup:
    ¼ cup fresh or unsweetened, canned pineapple chunks
    ¼ cup fresh orange sections
8 ounces hot cocoa

LUNCH
1 turkey sandwich:
    2 slices whole wheat bread
    2 ounces sliced turkey
    2 slices tomato
    2 lettuce leaves
    1 tablespoon mayonnaise
3 pretzel logs
4 slices cucumber
2 fresh plums
1 cup skim milk

AFTER-SCHOOL SNACK
Two 1-ounce part-skim mozzarella cheese sticks
4 whole wheat crackers
4 ounces orange juice

DINNER
3 ounces Fine Turkey Meat Loaf, see p. 243
½ cup steamed green beans
½ cup cooked brown rice
½ cup Carrot-Raisin Salad, see p. 238
1 Country Garden Muffin, see p. 234, with
    1 teaspoon margarine
1 cup skim milk

DAY 3

BREAKFAST

1½ slices whole wheat toast with
    1½ ounces low-fat cheddar cheese
  6 sliced fresh strawberries
  4 ounces orange juice

LUNCH

  1 tuna salad sandwich:
    2 slices whole wheat bread
    ¼ cup "Charlie Tuna" Salad, see p. 237
  ¾ cup Colorful Veggie Soup, see p. 240
  ½ cup fresh or unsweetened, canned peach slices
  ¼ cup oyster crackers
  1 cup skim milk

AFTER-SCHOOL SNACK

  ½ cup trail mix
  4 ounces grape juice

DINNER

  1 cup cooked spaghetti with tomato sauce and
    Three 1-ounce meatballs
  1 tossed salad:
    1 cup lettuce
    1 tablespoon grated carrots
    ¼ chopped tomato
    2 teaspoons Italian dressing
  1 slice whole wheat bread with
    1 teaspoon margarine
  ½ cup vanilla pudding
  1 cup skim milk

DAY 4

BREAKFAST
2 slices French Toast Delight, see p. 231, with
2 teaspoons powdered sugar
4 fresh orange sections
4 ounces hot cocoa

LUNCH
One 1-ounce cube low-fat cheddar cheese
Two 1-ounce cubes part-skim mozzarella cheese
10 whole wheat crackers
½ cup grapes
2 Lunch Box Favorite Oatmeal Cookies, see p. 250
4 ounces pineapple-orange juice

AFTER-SCHOOL SNACK
8 ounces Strawberry Smoothie, see p. 265

DINNER
3 ounces Special Fried Chicken, see p. 243
½ cup Country Red Potato Salad, see p. 238
3 fresh, steamed asparagus spears
1 cup sliced cantaloupe
1 cup skim milk

DAY 5

BREAKFAST
1 slice raisin toast with
1 tablespoon part-skim ricotta cheese
fruit cup:
¼ cup sliced fresh strawberries
¼ cup sliced bananas
1 cup skim milk

LUNCH
1 chicken sandwich:
    2 slices whole wheat bread
    2 ounces sliced chicken
    2 slices tomato
    2 lettuce leaves
    1 tablespoon mayonnaise
½ cup corn chips
1 fresh pear
8 vanilla wafers
8 ounces orange juice

AFTER-SCHOOL SNACK
4 dried apricots
⅓ cup dry roasted peanuts
½ cup skim milk

DINNER
3 slices medium cheese and green pepper pizza
1 spinach salad:
    1 cup raw spinach
    8 mandarin orange sections
    2 teaspoons Italian dressing
8 ounces Lemonade Refresher, see p. 260

DAY 6

BREAKFAST
2 Feeling Your Oats Bran Muffins, see p. 234, with
    2 teaspoons margarine
½ sliced cantaloupe with
    ¼ cup low-fat cottage cheese
4 ounces unsweetened pineapple juice

LUNCH
1 peanut butter and jelly sandwich:
    2 slices whole wheat bread
    2 tablespoons natural peanut butter
    2 teaspoons all-fruit jelly
2 raw carrot sticks
1 tangerine
2 Lunch Box Favorite Oatmeal Cookies, see p. 250
1 cup skim milk

AFTER-SCHOOL SNACK
2 slices Banana Bread, see p. 235
1 cup skim milk

DINNER
2 beef and cheese tacos:
    2 taco shells
    2 ounces cooked ground beef
    1 ounce (3 tablespoons) grated low-fat cheddar cheese
    4 tablespoons shredded lettuce
    2 tablespoons chopped tomato
    2 tablespoons grated zucchini
½ cup watermelon balls
1 cup skim milk

DAY 7

BREAKFAST
2 whole wheat English muffin halves with
    2 teaspoons margarine
1 ounce cooked ham slice
½ cup unsweetened applesauce
1 cup skim milk

LUNCH
  1 pimiento cheese sandwich:
      2 slices whole wheat bread
      ¼ cup pimiento cheese
  2 raw celery sticks
  1 nectarine
  1 slice (1/16 cake) angel food cake
  8 ounces orange juice

AFTER-SCHOOL SNACK
  1 granola bar
  1 fresh peach
  1 cup skim milk

DINNER
  3 ounces broiled tuna steak
  ½ cup macaroni and cheese
  ½ cup steamed peas and carrots
  1 whole wheat dinner roll with
      1 teaspoon margarine
  ½ cup nonfat frozen yogurt
  8 ounces water

WEEK 2, DAY 1

BREAKFAST
  3 pieces French Toast Delight, see p. 231, with
      2 tablespoons molasses and
      1 tablespoon margarine
  8 ounces orange juice
  1 cup skim milk

LUNCH
  1 Bagel Bonanza, see p. 242
  1 apple
  1 cup skim milk

AFTER-SCHOOL SNACK

2 Lunch Box Favorite Oatmeal Cookies, see p. 250
12 ounces Frothy Fruit Frostie, see p. 259

DINNER

2 slices cheese pizza
1 tossed salad:
    1½ cups lettuce
    1 tablespoon grated carrots
    ¼ chopped tomato
    1 tablespoon Italian dressing
1 Brownie Delight, see p. 251
1 cup skim milk

DAY 2

BREAKFAST

½ cup dry cereal, see recommended cereals list, p. 182
2 slices Sweet Cinnamon Toast, see p. 232
8 ounces unsweetened apple juice
1 cup skim milk

LUNCH

1 tuna salad sandwich:
    2 slices whole wheat bread
    ½ cup "Charlie Tuna" Salad, see p. 237
1 fresh nectarine
1 Brownie Delight, see p. 251
1 cup skim milk

AFTER-SCHOOL SNACK

4 cups Calico Corn, see p. 249
3 pieces Fruit Cube Fizz, see p. 259

DINNER
   1 cup Magic Bean Soup, see p. 240
3½ ounces roasted turkey
  ½ cup steamed broccoli
  ½ cup steamed carrots
  ¼ cup cranberry sauce
  1 cup skim milk

DAY 3

BREAKFAST
  1 Egg on a Nest, see p. 231
  1 ounce grilled Canadian bacon
  8 ounces grape juice
  1 cup skim milk

LUNCH
  1 peanut butter sandwich:
     2 slices whole wheat bread
     2 tablespoons natural peanut butter
  ½ cup sliced cantaloupe
  1 cup sliced honeydew melon
  1 banana
  1 cup skim milk

AFTER-SCHOOL SNACK
  1 Frozen Fruit Spear, see p. 251
  8 ounces water

DINNER
- 1 cup cooked spaghetti with tomato sauce and
    - 2 tablespoons Parmesan cheese
- 1 spinach salad:
    - ½ cup raw spinach
    - 1 tablespoon chopped onion
    - 1 tablespoon Italian dressing
- 2 slices Italian bread
- 1 piece Terrific Tapioca Dessert, see p. 270
- 1 cup skim milk

DAY 4

BREAKFAST
- 1 packet instant cinnamon and spice oatmeal
- 2 English muffin halves
- 1 fresh peach
- 1 cup skim milk

LUNCH
- 1 turkey salad sandwich:
    - 2 slices whole wheat bread
    - ½ cup Gobblin' Turkey Salad, see p. 237
- 1 fresh pear
- 3 gingersnaps
- 1 cup skim milk

AFTER-SCHOOL SNACK
- ½ cup Fit Fries, see p. 250
- 2 tablespoons chili sauce
- 8 ounces water

DINNER
- 2 cups Magic Bean Soup, see p. 240
- Two 1-inch by 4-inch pieces Corny Cornbread, see p. 236, with
    - 2 teaspoons margarine
- 1 piece Festive Fruit-Filled Yogurt, see p. 270
- 1 cup skim milk

DAY 5

BREAKFAST
2 Blueberry Blintzes, see p. 233, with
1 tablespoon honey
1 cup skim milk

LUNCH
1 French Dip Sandwich, see p. 242
8 raw celery sticks
8 raw carrot sticks
8 ounces plain nonfat yogurt mixed with
1 cup sliced fresh strawberries
2 teaspoons brown sugar
5 vanilla wafers
1 cup skim milk

AFTER-SCHOOL SNACK
12 Seasoned Fiesta Chips, see p. 249
6 tablespoons jalapeño bean dip
8 ounces water

DINNER
3 ounces Fish with Garden Gems, see p. 244
½ cup steamed summer squash
½ cup steamed brussels sprouts
1 whole wheat dinner roll with
1 teaspoon margarine
1 slice Pumpkin Pie, see p. 271
1 cup skim milk

DAY 6

BREAKFAST
½ cup dry cereal, see recommended cereals list, p. 182
1 slice Banana Bread, see p. 235
½ fresh grapefruit
1 cup skim milk

LUNCH

1 hamburger:

    One 3-ounce cooked, lean hamburger patty

    1 bun

    1 lettuce leaf

    1 slice tomato

    2 teaspoons mustard

8 ounces Chilled Chocolate Cow, see p. 261

AFTER-SCHOOL SNACK

1 Frozen Fruit Spear, see p. 251

1 slice whole wheat bread

1 ounce part-skim mozzarella cheese

8 ounces water

DINNER

3 ounces braised or baked pork tenderloin with

    1 tablespoon horseradish

1 cup cooked egg noodles

½ cup steamed cabbage

½ cup unsweetened applesauce

1 cup skim milk

DAY 7

BREAKFAST

2 Johnny Appleseed Walnut Muffins, see p. 232, with

    2 teaspoons margarine

8 ounces pear nectar

1 cup skim milk

LUNCH

2 ounces Fine Turkey Meat Loaf, see p. 243

1 cup boiled potatoes with skin with

1 teaspoon margarine

½ cup steamed turnip greens

2 slices whole wheat bread

1 cup cantaloupe balls

1 cup skim milk

AFTER-SCHOOL SNACK

1 cup Colorful Veggie Soup, see p. 240

¾ cup sliced jicama

8 ounces water

DINNER

1 bean burrito

½ cup unsweetened fruit cocktail

1 slice (1/16 cake) angel food cake

1 cup skim milk

3,000-CALORIE TEENAGE MALE WEEKLY MENU

(FOR ACTIVE TEENAGE MALES 12 TO 19 YEARS OLD)

MALE TEEN MENU
WEEK 1, DAY 1

BREAKFAST
1½ cups dry cereal, see recommended cereals list, p. 182
1 cup 2% milk
1 banana
8 ounces orange juice

LUNCH
1 ham and cheese sandwich:
    2 slices whole wheat bread
    1 ounce sliced ham
    1 ounce part-skim mozzarella cheese
    2 slices tomato
    2 lettuce leaves
    1 tablespoon mayonnaise
3 raw carrot sticks
1 cup grapes
8 ounces unsweetened pineapple juice

AFTER-SCHOOL SNACK
6 whole wheat crackers with
    6 teaspoons natural peanut butter
1 cup 2% milk

DINNER
4 ounces roast turkey
16 medium Oven French Fries, see p. 247
½ cup steamed green peas
Two 1-inch by 4-inch pieces Corny Cornbread, see p. 236, with
    2 teaspoons margarine
1 cup vanilla yogurt with
    2 sliced fresh strawberries
1 cup 2% milk

DAY 2

BREAKFAST
2 slices whole wheat toast with
    2 tablespoons natural peanut butter
fruit cup:
    ½ cup fresh or unsweetened, canned pineapple chunks
    ½ cup fresh orange sections
8 ounces hot cocoa

LUNCH
1 turkey sandwich:
    2 slices whole wheat bread
    2 ounces sliced turkey
    2 slices tomato
    2 lettuce leaves
    1 tablespoon mayonnaise
6 pretzel logs
4 slices cucumber
2 fresh plums
1 cup 2 % milk

AFTER-SCHOOL SNACK
Two 1-ounce part-skim mozzarella cheese sticks
8 whole wheat crackers
8 ounces orange juice

DINNER
4 ounces Fine Turkey Meat Loaf, see p. 243
1 cup steamed green beans
1 cup cooked brown rice
1 cup Carrot-Raisin Salad, see p. 238
2 Country Garden Muffins, see p. 234, with
    2 teaspoons margarine
1 cup 2% milk

DAY 3

BREAKFAST
3 slices whole wheat toast with
   3 ounces low-fat cheddar cheese
9 sliced fresh strawberries
8 ounces orange juice

LUNCH
1 tuna salad sandwich:
   2 slices whole wheat bread
   ¼ cup "Charlie Tuna" Salad, see p. 237
1½ cups Colorful Veggie Soup, see p. 240
1 cup fresh or unsweetened, canned peach slices
1 cup oyster crackers
1 cup 2% milk

AFTER-SCHOOL SNACK
1 cup trail mix
6 ounces grape juice

DINNER
2 cups cooked spaghetti with tomato sauce and
   Four 1-ounce meatballs
1 tossed salad:
   1½ cups lettuce
   1 tablespoon grated carrots
   ¼ chopped tomato
   1 tablespoon Italian dressing
1 slice whole wheat bread with
   1 teaspoon margarine
1 cup vanilla pudding
1 cup 2% milk

DAY 4

BREAKFAST
　　2 slices French Toast Delight, see p. 231, with
　　　　2 teaspoons powdered sugar
　　6 fresh orange sections
　　8 ounces hot cocoa

LUNCH
　Two 1-ounce cubes low-fat cheddar cheese
　Two 1-ounce cubes part-skim mozzarella cheese
　12 whole wheat crackers
　　1 cup grapes
　　4 Lunch Box Favorite Oatmeal Cookies, see p. 250
　　8 ounces pineapple-orange juice

AFTER-SCHOOL SNACK
　12 ounces Strawberry Smoothie, see p. 265

DINNER
　　4 ounces Special Fried Chicken, see p. 243
　　1 cup Country Red Potato Salad, see p. 238
　　4 fresh, steamed asparagus spears
　　1 cup sliced cantaloupe
　　1 cup 2% milk

DAY 5

BREAKFAST
　　2 slices raisin toast with
　　　　2 tablespoons part-skim ricotta cheese
　fruit cup:
　　　　½ cup sliced fresh strawberries
　　　　½ cup sliced bananas
　　　　1 cup 2% milk

LUNCH

1 chicken sandwich:
  2 slices whole wheat bread
  2 ounces sliced chicken
  2 slices tomato
  2 lettuce leaves
  1 tablespoon mayonnaise
1 cup corn chips
1 fresh pear
8 vanilla wafers
8 ounces orange juice

AFTER-SCHOOL SNACK

6 dried apricots
⅔ cup dry roasted peanuts
1 cup 2% milk

DINNER

6 slices medium cheese and green pepper pizza
1 spinach salad:
  1 cup raw spinach
  8 mandarin orange sections
  2 teaspoons Italian dressing
8 ounces Lemonade Refresher, see p. 260

DAY 6

BREAKFAST

2 Feeling Your Oats Bran Muffins, see p. 234, with
  2 teaspoons margarine
½ sliced cantaloupe with
  ½ cup low-fat cottage cheese
8 ounces unsweetened pineapple juice

LUNCH
    2 peanut butter and jelly sandwiches:
        4 slices whole wheat bread
        4 tablespoons natural peanut butter
        4 teaspoons all-fruit jelly
    4 raw carrot sticks
    1 tangerine
    3 Lunch Box Favorite Oatmeal Cookies, see p. 250
    1 cup 2% milk

AFTER-SCHOOL SNACK
    2 slices Banana Bread, see p. 235
    1 cup 2% milk

DINNER
    4 beef and cheese tacos:
        4 taco shells
        4 ounces cooked ground beef
        2 ounces (6 tablespoons) grated low-fat cheddar cheese
        8 tablespoons chopped lettuce
        4 tablespoons chopped tomato
        4 tablespoons grated zucchini
    1 cup watermelon balls
    1 cup 2% milk

DAY 7

BREAKFAST
    4 whole wheat English muffin halves with
        2 teaspoons margarine
    2 ounces cooked ham slices
    ½ cup unsweetened applesauce
    1 cup 2% milk

LUNCH
- 2 pimiento cheese sandwiches:
    - 4 slices whole wheat bread
    - ½ cup pimiento cheese
- 3 raw celery sticks
- 1 nectarine
- 1 large slice (1/12 cake) angel food cake
- 8 ounces orange juice

AFTER-SCHOOL SNACK
- 2 granola bars
- 1 cup 2% milk

DINNER
- 4 ounces broiled tuna steak
- 1 cup macaroni and cheese
- ½ cup steamed peas and carrots
- 2 whole wheat dinner rolls with
    - 2 teaspoons margarine
- 1 cup nonfat frozen yogurt
- 12 ounces water

1,500-CALORIE TEENAGE WEIGHT-LOSS TWO-WEEK MENU
(FOR TEENAGERS 12 TO 19 YEARS OLD)

1,500-CALORIE WEIGHT-LOSS MENU
WEEK 1, DAY 1

BREAKFAST
¾ cup dry cereal, see recommended cereals list, p. 182
½ cup skim milk
½ banana
4 ounces orange juice

LUNCH
1 ham and cheese sandwich:
  2 slices reduced-calorie whole wheat bread
  1 ounce sliced ham
  1 slice low-calorie, low-fat cheese (35 calories/slice)
  2 slices tomato
  2 lettuce leaves
  2 teaspoons mustard
½ cup grapes
4 ounces unsweetened pineapple juice

AFTER-SCHOOL SNACK
3 whole wheat crackers with
  3 teaspoons natural peanut butter
½ cup skim milk

DINNER
2 ounces roast turkey
8 medium Oven French Fries, see p. 247
¼ cup steamed green peas
One 1-inch by 4-inch piece Corny Cornbread, see p. 236
½ cup vanilla yogurt with
  1 cup sliced fresh strawberries
1 cup skim milk

DAY 2

BREAKFAST
1 slice reduced-calorie whole wheat bread with
    1 tablespoon natural peanut butter
fruit cup:
    ¼ cup fresh or unsweetened, canned pineapple chunks
    ¼ cup fresh orange sections
1 cup skim milk

LUNCH
1 turkey sandwich:
    2 slices reduced-calorie whole wheat bread
    2 ounces sliced turkey
    2 slices tomato
    2 lettuce leaves
    2 teaspoons low-calorie mayonnaise
4 slices cucumber
2 small fresh plums
1 cup skim milk

AFTER-SCHOOL SNACK
Two 1-ounce part-skim mozzarella cheese sticks
4 whole wheat crackers
4 ounces orange juice

DINNER
2 ounces Fine Turkey Meat Loaf, see p. 243
1 cup steamed green beans
½ cup cooked brown rice
½ cup Carrot-Raisin Salad, see p. 238
1 Country Garden Muffin, see p. 234
1 cup skim milk

DAY 3

BREAKFAST
1 slice reduced-calorie whole wheat toast with
  2 slices low-calorie, low-fat cheese (35 calories/slice)
6 sliced fresh strawberries
4 ounces orange juice

LUNCH
1 tuna salad sandwich:
  2 slices reduced-calorie whole wheat bread
  ¼ cup "Charlie Tuna" Salad, see p. 237
1 cup Colorful Veggie Soup, see p. 240
½ cup fresh or unsweetened, canned peach slices
¼ cup oyster crackers
1 cup skim milk

AFTER-SCHOOL SNACK
¼ cup trail mix
1 small apple
8 ounces water

DINNER
1 cup cooked spaghetti with tomato sauce and
  Two 1-ounce meatballs
1 tossed salad:
  1 cup lettuce
  1 tablespoon grated carrots
  ¼ chopped tomato
  2 teaspoons Italian dressing
1 slice reduced-calorie whole wheat bread
½ cup flavored gelatin
1 cup skim milk

DAY 4

BREAKFAST
1 slice French Toast Delight, see p. 231, with
    1 teaspoon powdered sugar
4 fresh orange sections
1 cup skim milk

LUNCH
One 1-ounce cube low-fat cheddar cheese
One 1-ounce cube part-skim mozzarella cheese
10 whole wheat crackers
½ cup grapes
2 Lunch Box Favorite Oatmeal Cookies, see p. 250
4 ounces pineapple-orange juice

AFTER-SCHOOL SNACK
8 ounces Strawberry Smoothie, see p. 265

DINNER
3 ounces Special Fried Chicken, see p. 243
½ cup Country Red Potato Salad, see p. 238
3 fresh steamed asparagus spears
½ cup sliced cantaloupe
1 cup skim milk

DAY 5

BREAKFAST
1 slice raisin toast with
    1 tablespoon part-skim ricotta cheese
fruit cup:
    ¼ cup fresh sliced strawberries
    ¼ cup sliced bananas
1 cup skim milk

LUNCH

1 chicken sandwich:
    2 slices reduced-calorie whole wheat bread
    2 ounces sliced chicken
    2 slices tomato
    2 lettuce leaves
    2 teaspoons low-calorie mayonnaise
1 fresh pear
8 vanilla wafers
4 ounces orange juice

DINNER

2 slices medium cheese and green pepper pizza
1 spinach salad:
    1 cup raw spinach
    8 mandarin orange sections
    2 teaspoons Italian dressing
12 ounces water

DAY 6

BREAKFAST

1 Feeling Your Oats Bran Muffin, see p. 234, with
    1 teaspoon margarine
½ sliced cantaloupe with
    ¼ cup low-fat cottage cheese
4 ounces unsweetened pineapple juice

LUNCH

1 peanut butter and jelly sandwich:
    2 slices reduced-calorie whole wheat bread
    1 tablespoon natural peanut butter
    2 teaspoons all-fruit jelly
4 raw carrot sticks
1 tangerine
2 Lunch Box Favorite Oatmeal Cookies, see p. 250
1 cup skim milk

AFTER-SCHOOL SNACK
    1 slice Banana Bread, see p. 235
    1 cup skim milk

DINNER
    2 beef and cheese tacos:
        2 taco shells
        2 ounces cooked ground beef
        1 ounce (3 tablespoons) grated low-fat cheddar cheese
        4 tablespoons shredded lettuce
        2 tablespoons chopped tomato
        2 tablespoons grated zucchini
    ½ cup watermelon balls
    1 cup skim milk

DAY 7

BREAKFAST
    2 whole wheat English muffin halves with
        1 tablespoon low-calorie margarine
    1 ounce cooked ham slice
    ½ cup unsweetened applesauce
    1 cup skim milk

LUNCH
    1 pimiento cheese sandwich:
        2 slices reduced-calorie whole wheat bread
        ¼ cup pimiento cheese
    4 raw celery sticks
    1 nectarine
    1 small slice ($1/_{24}$ cake) angel food cake
    4 ounces orange juice

AFTER-SCHOOL SNACK

  1 granola bar
  1 cup skim milk

DINNER

  3 ounces broiled tuna steak
  ¼ cup macaroni and cheese
  ½ cup steamed peas and carrots
  1 whole wheat dinner roll
  ½ cup nonfat frozen yogurt
  12 ounces water

DAY 1

BREAKFAST

  2 pieces French Toast Delight, see p. 231, with
     2 tablespoons low-calorie syrup and
     2 teaspoons margarine
  4 ounces orange juice
  1 cup skim milk

LUNCH

  1 Bagel Bonanza, see p. 242
  1 apple
  1 cup skim milk

AFTER-SCHOOL SNACK

  2 fig newtons
  4 cups Calico Corn, see p. 249
  8 ounces water

DINNER

  1 slice cheese pizza
  1 tossed salad:
     1½ cups lettuce
     1 tablespoon grated carrots
     ¼ chopped tomato
     2 tablespoons low-calorie Italian dressing
  4 pieces Fruit Cube Fizz, see p. 259
  1 cup skim milk

DAY 2

BREAKFAST
½ cup dry cereal, see recommended cereals list, p. 182
1 slice Sweet Cinnamon Toast, see p. 232
8 ounces unsweetened apple juice
½ cup skim milk

LUNCH
1 tuna salad sandwich:
    2 slices reduced-calorie whole wheat bread
    ¼ cup "Charlie Tuna" Salad, see p. 237
1 fresh nectarine
½ Brownie Delight, see p. 251
1 cup skim milk

AFTER-SCHOOL SNACK
4 cups Calico Corn, see p. 249
8 ounces water

DINNER
1 cup Magic Bean Soup, see p. 240
1 ounce roast turkey
½ cup steamed broccoli
½ cup steamed carrots
¼ cup cranberry sauce
1 cup skim milk

DAY 3

BREAKFAST
   1 Egg on a Nest, see p. 231
   1 ounce grilled Canadian bacon
   4 ounces grape juice
   1 cup skim milk

LUNCH
   1 peanut butter sandwich:
      2 slices reduced-calorie whole wheat bread
      2 tablespoons natural peanut butter
   ½ cup sliced cantaloupe
   ½ cup sliced honeydew melon
   ½ banana
   1 cup skim milk

AFTER-SCHOOL SNACK
   3 Frozen Fruit Spears, see p. 251
   8 ounces water

DINNER
   ½ cup cooked spaghetti with tomato sauce and
      1 tablespoon grated Parmesan cheese
   1 spinach salad:
      ½ cup raw spinach
      1 tablespoon chopped onion
      1 tablespoon low-calorie Italian dressing
   1 slice Italian bread
   ½ piece Terrific Tapioca Dessert, see p. 270
   1 cup skim milk

DAY 4

BREAKFAST
  1 packet instant cinnamon and spice oatmeal
  1 English muffin half
  1 fresh peach
  1 cup skim milk

LUNCH
  1 turkey salad sandwich:
      2 slices reduced-calorie whole wheat bread
      ¼ cup Gobblin' Turkey Salad, see p. 237
  1 fresh pear
  2 gingersnaps
  1 cup skim milk

AFTER-SCHOOL SNACK
  ½ cup Fit Fries, see p. 250
  1 tablespoon chili sauce
  8 ounces water

DINNER
  1 cup Magic Bean Soup, see p. 240
  One 1-inch by 4-inch piece Corny Cornbread, see p. 236, with
      1 teaspoon margarine
  1 piece Festive Fruit-Filled Yogurt, see p. 270
  1 cup skim milk

DAY 5

BREAKFAST
  2 Blueberry Blintzes, see p. 233, with
      1 tablespoon honey
  1 cup skim milk

LUNCH

½ French Dip Sandwich, see p. 242
8 raw celery sticks
8 raw carrot sticks
4 ounces plain nonfat yogurt mixed with
  ½ cup sliced fresh strawberries
  2 teaspoons brown sugar
2 vanilla wafers
1 cup skim milk

AFTER-SCHOOL SNACK

4 Seasoned Fiesta Chips, see p. 249
3 tablespoons jalapeño bean dip
8 ounces water

DINNER

3 ounces Fish with Garden Gems, see p. 244
½ cup steamed summer squash
½ cup steamed brussels sprouts
1 whole wheat dinner roll with
  1 teaspoon margarine
½ cup fruit gelatin made with
  2 tablespoons fresh fruit of choice
1 cup skim milk

DAY 6

BREAKFAST

½ cup dry cereal, see recommended cereals list, p. 182
1 slice Banana Bread, see p. 235
½ fresh grapefruit
1 cup skim milk

LUNCH

1 hamburger:
  One 3-ounce cooked, lean hamburger patty
  1 bun
  1 lettuce leaf
  1 slice tomato
  2 teaspoons mustard
6 ounces Chilled Chocolate Cow, see p. 261

AFTER-SCHOOL SNACK

    1 Frozen Fruit Spear, see p. 251

    8 ounces water

DINNER

    3 ounces braised or baked pork tenderloin with

        1 tablespoon horseradish

    1 cup cooked egg noodles

    ½ cup steamed cabbage

    ½ cup unsweetened applesauce

    1 cup skim milk

DAY 7

BREAKFAST

    1 Johnny Appleseed Walnut Muffin, see p. 232, with

        1 teaspoon margarine

    4 ounces orange juice

    ½ cup skim milk

LUNCH

    2 ounces Fine Turkey Meat Loaf, see p. 243

    ½ cup boiled potatoes with skin with

        1 teaspoon margarine

    ½ cup steamed turnip greens

    1 slice reduced-calorie whole wheat bread

    1 cup cantaloupe balls

    1 cup skim milk

AFTER-SCHOOL SNACK

1 cup Colorful Veggie Soup, see p. 240

¾ cup sliced jicama

8 ounces water

DINNER

1 bean burrito

½ cup unsweetened fruit cocktail

1 slice (1⁄16 cake) angel food cake

1 cup skim milk

The Kid Fitness
RECIPES

NOTE: g = gm = gram
mg = milligram

Egg on a Nest

1 slice whole wheat bread
 nonstick cooking spray
⅛ teaspoon pepper
¼ cup egg substitute*
1 slice part-skim mozzarella cheese

Cut a hole out of the center of the bread. Toast bread lightly. Spray a skillet with nonstick cooking spray. Sprinkle pepper into egg substitute. Beat egg mixture vigorously. Pour into hot skillet and scramble until egg no longer runs but is not dry. Remove from skillet and place in hole in toast. Place cheese slice over toast. Place back in skillet, cover, and cook 1 minute more.

*May substitute 1 egg.

Yields: 1 serving
Per serving
(1 egg/toast):

Calories = 155
Cholesterol = 15 mg
Fat = 6 g

French Toast Delight

½ cup egg substitute*
¾ cup skim milk
1 teaspoon vanilla
1 teaspoon ground cinnamon
⅛ teaspoon ground nutmeg
8 slices whole wheat bread
 nonstick cooking spray
 syrup or puréed fruit, to top

Mix all ingredients together except bread, nonstick cooking spray, and syrup. Dip each slice of bread in the mixture. Brown bread on each side in large skillet sprayed with nonstick cooking spray. Serve with a light drizzle of syrup (2 teaspoons) or top with fresh puréed fruit of your choice.

*May substitute 2 eggs.

Yields: 8 slices
Per serving (1 slice):

Calories = 85
Cholesterol = 0 mg
Fat = 1 g

Sweet Cinnamon Toast

Yields: 1 serving
Per serving (1 slice):

Calories = 110
Cholesterol = 0 mg
Fat = 5 g

1 teaspoon liquid or soft tub margarine
1 slice whole wheat bread
1 teaspoon ground cinnamon
1 teaspoon sugar

Preheat oven broiler. Squeeze margarine on bread. Mix cinnamon and sugar in an empty salt shaker. Shake mixture evenly over the bread. Or let your child create his own happy face with the cinnamon sugar mixture on buttered toast. Toast under the broiler until lightly browned.

Johnny Appleseed Walnut Muffins

Yields: 12 servings
Per serving
(1 muffin):

Calories = 130
Cholesterol = 0 mg
Fat = 3 g

1 large apple
1½ cups flour
½ cup bran
2½ teaspoons baking powder
1 teaspoon ground cinnamon
¼ teaspoon ground nutmeg
2 egg whites*
⅔ cup concentrated apple juice
½ cup chopped walnuts

Preheat oven to 400°. Peel, core, and chop apple. Mix all dry ingredients until well blended. Mix egg whites, apple juice, and walnuts together. Pour the liquid ingredients into the dry ingredients and mix well. Pour mixture evenly in a 12-cup muffin tin. Cook 15 to 20 minutes, or until brown.

*May substitute 1 egg.

Blueberry Blintzes

CREPE BATTER

2 eggs
6 egg whites
4 tablespoons flour
2 tablespoons cold water
⅛ teaspoon salt

FILLING

2 cups fresh blueberries
1 tablespoon sugar
1 teaspoon lemon juice
½ teaspoon margarine per crepe for cooking

Yields: 16 blintzes
Per serving
(1 blintz):

Calories = 54
Cholesterol = 27 mg
Fat = 3 g

To make the crepe batter, put eggs, egg whites, flour (sifted twice), cold water, and salt in a mixing bowl. Beat the mixture vigorously until it has the consistency of thin cream; set aside.

To make the filling, stew blueberries with sugar and lemon juice. Pour off the juice, leaving the berries fairly moist; set aside.

In a small nonstick frying or crepe pan, heat ½ teaspoon margarine until it bubbles. Pour in 1 generous tablespoon of batter to cover the bottom of the pan with a thin layer. Rotate the pan quickly to spread the batter as thinly and evenly as possible. Cook the crepe for about 1 minute on one side. Remove from pan; set and stack all the crepes, brown side up, on a heated plate or on a towel. Spoon 2 tablespoons of the blueberry filling in the center of each crepe. Fold both sides of the crepe over the filling in the center and put as many as will fit back in the frying pan and cook until golden brown. Then finish cooking the others. Place on a serving plate and sprinkle lightly with sifted powdered sugar.

Feeling Your Oats Bran Muffins

Yields: 12 servings
Per serving
(1 muffin):

Calories = 130
Cholesterol = 2 mg
Fat = 4 g

2 cups oat bran cereal
¼ cup brown sugar
2 teaspoons baking powder
1 cup low-fat milk
2 egg whites*
¼ cup honey
2 tablespoons vegetable oil

Preheat oven to 425°. Mix together dry ingredients. Add milk, egg whites, honey, and oil. Mix just enough so dry ingredients are moistened. Divide mixture evenly in a 12-cup muffin tin. Bake for 18 to 20 minutes or until lightly browned.

*May substitute 1 egg.

Country Garden Muffins

Yields: 24 servings
Per serving
(1 muffin):

Calories = 125
Cholesterol = 0 mg
Fat = 5 g

3 egg whites
½ cup oil
1 tablespoon vanilla
2 cups shredded zucchini, unpeeled, or carrot, peeled
1½ cups sugar
1½ cups flour
½ cup whole wheat flour
1 tablespoon ground cinnamon
1½ teaspoons baking soda
¼ teaspoon baking powder

Preheat oven to 400°. Combine egg whites, oil, vanilla, and zucchini. Add remaining ingredients; stir by hand until moistened. Fill paper-lined muffin cups two-thirds full. Bake for 18 minutes or until lightly browned.

Banana Bread

1¾ cups sifted flour
2¼ teaspoons baking powder
½ teaspoon salt
⅓ cup shortening
⅔ cup sugar
¾ teaspoon grated lemon rind
2 eggs, beaten
1¼ cups ripe, mashed bananas

Yields: 1 loaf/
16 servings
Per serving (1 slice):

Calories = 140
Cholesterol = 27 mg
Fat = 5 g

Preheat oven to 350°. Sift together flour, baking powder, and salt; set aside. Blend together shortening, sugar, and lemon rind until creamy. Beat in eggs and bananas. Add sifted ingredients one-third at a time to the batter. Beat the batter after each addition until smooth. Place the batter in a greased 9- × 5-inch loaf pan. Bake the bread for about 1 hour or until done. Cool before slicing.

Yields: 16 servings
Per serving (1-inch
× 4-inch piece):

Calories = 83
Cholesterol = 0 mg
Fat = 2 g

Corny Cornbread

1¼ cups yellow or white cornmeal
¾ cup flour
1 tablespoon sugar
2½ teaspoons baking powder
½ teaspoon salt
2 egg whites, beaten (or ¼ cup egg substitute)*
2 tablespoons melted margarine
1 cup skim milk

Preheat oven to 425°. Mix dry ingredients; set aside. Mix egg whites (or egg substitute) and liquid ingredients. Pour the liquid mixture into the dry mixture. Blend with a few rapid strokes. Grease a heavy 8- × 8-inch baking pan with margarine or oil. Place the pan by itself in the oven until sizzling hot. Pour the batter into the hot pan. Bake 20 to 25 minutes until golden brown.

*May substitute 1 egg.

"Charlie Tuna" Salad

Yields: 3 servings
Per serving (½ cup):

Calories = 144
Cholesterol = 12 mg
Fat = 7 g

1 chopped green onion (or ¼ chopped apple)
1 stalk chopped celery
1 (6½-ounce) can water-packed tuna
⅛ teaspoon pepper
¼ cup low-calorie mayonnaise

Chop green onion (or apple) and celery. Flake the tuna. Combine with remaining ingredients and refrigerate. Cut bread with favorite cookie cutter and spread tuna salad on top.

Gobblin' Turkey Salad

Yields: 4 servings
Per serving (½ cup):

Calories = 200
Cholesterol = 73 mg
Fat = 4 g

12 ounces cooked, skinless turkey
3 stalks celery
1 large apple
¼ cup raisins
1 tablespoon light sour cream
1 tablespoon low-calorie mayonnaise
2 teaspoons sesame seeds

Dice the turkey, celery, and apple. Combine all ingredients and refrigerate. Try this turkey pleaser stuffed in a garden-ripe tomato or stuffed into a pita pocket.

Country Red Potato Salad

Yields: 4 servings
Per serving (½ cup):

Calories = 115
Cholesterol = 0 mg
Fat = 5 g

2 medium red potatoes (or 8 small new potatoes)
5 green onions, chopped
2 celery stalks, finely chopped
1 tablespoon chopped parsley
⅛ teaspoon salt
⅛ teaspoon pepper
4 tablespoons mayonnaise
  paprika, for garnish

Wash and scrub potatoes, leaving skins on. Cut into small pieces. Steam 20 to 30 minutes or microwave 5 to 10 minutes, until firm, but cooked. Chill 1 hour. Combine potatoes, green onions, celery, parsley, salt, pepper, and mayonnaise. Sprinkle with paprika. Keep chilled until served.

Carrot-Raisin Salad

Yields: 2 servings
Per serving (½ cup):

Calories = 130
Cholesterol = 1 mg
Fat = 5 g

2 carrots, grated
4 tablespoons raisins
2 tablespoons mayonnaise
2 teaspoons sugar
⅛ teaspoon salt

Mix all ingredients. Chill for 1 hour before serving.

Holiday Cranberry Mold

Yields: 6 servings
Per serving (½ cup):

Calories = 60
Cholesterol = 0 mg
Fat = 0 g

1 cup boiling water
1 envelope strawberry gelatin
½ cup cold water
1 tablespoon lemon juice
1 cup coarsely ground cranberries
1 cup chopped celery

Add boiling water to gelatin. Stir until dissolved. Add cold water. Chill until partly set. Add lemon juice, cranberries, and celery. Chill until set. Unmold salad on serving plate lined with bright green leaf lettuce.

Colorful Veggie Soup

Yields: 8 servings
Per serving (1 cup):

Calories = 70
Cholesterol = 0 mg
Fat = 1 g

3 carrots, chopped
1 head of cabbage, shredded
2 celery stalks, chopped
1 onion, chopped
1 cup frozen yellow corn
½ cup frozen green beans
2 teaspoons basil
1 teaspoon parsley
½ teaspoon salt
¼ teaspoon pepper
1 (28-ounce) can tomatoes
6 beef bouillon cubes, dissolved in 6 cups boiling water

Place vegetables and spices in a large pot with sliced chunks of tomatoes and bouillon. Bring to a boil and simmer, covered, until thick, about 45 minutes. Season to taste with salt and pepper.

Magic Bean Soup

Yields: 10 servings
Per serving (1 cup):

Calories = 120
Cholesterol = 0 mg
Fat = 1 g

1 (16-ounce) bag mixed dried beans and lentils
5 cups water
1 (28-ounce) can stewed tomatoes
1 (9-ounce) package frozen green beans
1 large onion, chopped
2 carrots, sliced
½ cup chopped green pepper
1 tablespoon worcestershire sauce
¼ teaspoon oregano
2 cloves garlic, minced

Follow package directions for washing and soaking beans and lentils. Pour off water from soaked beans, add 5 cups water and remaining ingredients. Bring to a boil. Cover, reduce heat, and simmer 1 hour until beans are tender.

French Dip Sandwich

Yields: 4 servings
Per serving
(1 sandwich):

Calories = 565
Cholesterol = 60 mg
Fat = 16 g

½ cup water
½ cup beef broth
1 cup unsweetened pineapple juice
1 pound flank steak
1 tablespoon worcestershire sauce
1 tablespoon minced onion
1 clove garlic, pressed
⅛ teaspoon pepper
4 French rolls

Heat water, broth, and pineapple juice for dipping broth. Season the steak with worcestershire sauce, onion, garlic, and pepper. Broil approximately 10 minutes on each side or until medium-well done. Toast the rolls. Thinly slice the steak and place on the rolls. Pour a small amount of broth over the meat. Serve the remaining broth in a bowl to use as a dip for the sandwiches. Add fresh crisp vegetable sticks to the side of the plate or 1 to 2 cherry tomatoes.

Bagel Bonanza

Yields: 1 serving
Per serving
(1 bagel):

Calories = 340
Cholesterol = 55 mg
Fat = 9 g

1 (2-ounce) onion bagel
1 tablespoon whipped cream cheese
1 teaspoon finely chopped black olives
4 lettuce leaves
2 ounces turkey, thinly sliced
½ sliced medium tomato
¼ lemon

Split bagel and toast. Fold olives into cream cheese. Spread open face of bagel with mixture. Place lettuce on half of bagel. Top with sliced turkey and tomato. Squeeze lemon over all and top with other half of bagel.

Fine Turkey Meat Loaf

Yields: 6 servings
Per serving (1½-inch slice):

Calories = 156
Cholesterol = 43 mg
Fat = 4 g

   1 pound ground turkey breast
  ¾ cup tomato sauce
  ¾ cup uncooked oatmeal
  2 egg whites*
  ½ diced onion
  1 clove garlic, minced
  1 teaspoon salt
  ¼ teaspoon oregano

Preheat oven to 350°. Combine all ingredients and mix well. Pat mixture into a 9- × 5-inch loaf pan. Bake for 1 hour.

*May substitute 1 egg.

Special Fried Chicken

Yields: 4 servings
Per serving
(3 ounces cooked):

Calories = 260
Cholesterol = 72 mg
Fat = 11 g

  ½ cup flour
  ¼ teaspoon pepper
  1 teaspoon salt
  4 (4-ounce) skinless chicken breast halves
  8 teaspoons margarine

Preheat oven to 425°. Mix together flour, pepper, and salt. Coat chicken thoroughly with flour mixture. Place chicken in baking pan and top each piece of chicken with 2 teaspoons margarine. Bake uncovered for 30 minutes in 13- × 9-inch baking pan. Turn chicken pieces over and bake for another 30 minutes or until fork tender and golden brown.

Fish with Garden Gems

Yields: 8 servings
Per serving (3-ounce
cooked fillet):

Calories = 118
Cholesterol = 58 mg
Fat = 2 g

½ cup chopped green pepper
½ cup chopped onion
½ cup water
1 teaspoon chicken-flavored bouillon granules
½ cup chopped fresh parsley
½ teaspoon oregano
1 (16-ounce) can whole tomatoes, undrained and chopped
8 (4-ounce) white fish fillets of your choice (each 4-ounce raw
fish fillet equals one 3-ounce serving cooked)

Preheat oven to 350°. Place green pepper, onion, water, and bouillon granules in a saucepan; bring to a boil. Cover, reduce heat, and simmer 5 minutes or until vegetables are tender. Remove from heat; stir in parsley, oregano, and tomatoes. Place fish fillets in a single layer in a 13- × 9- × 2-inch baking dish. Spoon the vegetable mixture on top. Bake, uncovered, for 30 minutes or until fish fillets flake easily when tested with a fork.

Sweet Potato Pleaser

Yields: 8 servings
Per serving (¼ cup):

2 whole sweet potatoes or yams, sliced
1 (4-ounce) can unsweetened crushed pineapple
1 teaspoon cornstarch
   ground cinnamon to taste

Calories = 90
Cholesterol = 0 mg
Fat = 0 g

In a 2-quart casserole dish, cook 2 sliced sweet potatoes or yams in microwave for 10 minutes, or steam for 15 minutes. Set aside. Preheat oven to 325°. Drain juice from pineapple and reserve. Mix pineapple juice with cornstarch in small saucepan. Add cinnamon. Heat over medium heat, stirring until thickened. Mix sauce with pineapple. Pour over sweet potatoes. Bake for 20 minutes until hot and bubbly.

Peter Piper Pizza

Yields: 1 serving
Per serving (1 pizza):

1 flour tortilla
1 tablespoon canned pizza or spaghetti sauce
1 ounce sliced or grated part-skim mozzarella cheese

Calories = 170
Cholesterol = 15 mg
Fat = 7 g

Preheat oven broiler. Place flour tortilla under broiler for 2 minutes. Remove and flip tortilla. Place pizza or spaghetti sauce and cheese on the unbroiled side of the tortilla. Broil pizza about 5 minutes until cheese melts. Can be prepared with bagels or English muffins. For variety have available additional toppings such as chopped onions, green peppers, fresh sliced mushrooms, Canadian bacon, or lean ham. Let everyone build his own pizza.

Yields: 4 servings
Per serving (1 cup):

Calories = 20
Cholesterol = 0 mg
Fat = 0 g

Veggie Skinny Dippers

  1 stalk celery
  1 stalk uncooked broccoli
  1 carrot, peeled
  1 uncooked yellow squash
  1 green pepper
  1 cucumber, peeled
 10 cherry tomatoes

Wash and prepare all vegetables, as needed. Cut celery into 9 strips. At the top of each strip, make 2 cuts with a knife to resemble "celery fans." Slice broccoli into flowerets. Slice carrot into sticks. Slice squash into short sticks. Slice green pepper into rings. Run fork tines down the sides of the cucumber to make ridges. Slice the cucumber into rounds, which will have frilled edges. Serve the tomatoes whole. Try dipping vegetables in zippy dips of your choice (see pages 252 to 254).

Yields: 2 servings
Per serving
(8 chips):

Calories = 135
Cholesterol = 2 mg
Fat = 2 g

Fiesta Tortilla Chips

  4 medium corn or whole wheat tortillas

Preheat oven broiler. Cut each tortilla into 4 wedges. Place on baking sheet. Place under broiler for 5 to 7 minutes until slightly brown. Serve with healthy dips (see pages 252 to 254).

Note: If chips stick to the baking sheet, spray the baking sheet with nonstick cooking spray before placing the chips on the sheet.

Variation: Bake chips at 400° for 8 minutes. Remove from oven. Use tongs to turn each chip over. Bake another 3 minutes.

Oven French Fries

Yields: 1 serving
Per serving (10 to 12 pieces):

Calories = 220
Cholesterol = 0 mg
Fat = 0 g

1 medium potato with skin
  nonstick cooking spray

Preheat oven to 425°. Cut the potato into strips. Arrange on a cookie sheet that has been sprayed with nonstick cooking spray. Bake 15 to 20 minutes or until brown. Turn the potatoes over with a spatula and bake another 15 minutes or until tender.

Variation: Broil potatoes 10 minutes on each side until tender and crisp.

Peanut Butter Banana Crunch

Yields: 4 servings
Per serving
(½ banana):

Calories = 160
Cholesterol = 1 mg
Fat = 7 g

2 tablespoons natural peanut butter
½ cup evaporated skim milk
2 bananas cut in half
¼ cup chopped peanuts (or 1 cup crushed flaked cereal)

Mix peanut butter with evaporated skim milk until creamy. Roll bananas in peanut butter and milk mixture. Then roll in nuts (or cereal). Place in freezer until frozen.

Fruit Yogurt Fun Pops

Yields: 5 servings
Per serving
(4 ounces):

Calories = 95
Cholesterol = 1 mg
Fat = 0 g

6 ounces orange juice concentrate
6 ounces water
1 cup plain nonfat yogurt
1 teaspoon vanilla

Combine all ingredients in a blender container. Cover and blend on high speed for 1 minute, or until smooth. Pour into 5 individual 4-ounce paper cups. Put a plastic spoon or drinking straw into each cup before freezing. Place in freezer and freeze for several hours.

Variation: May replace orange juice with 1 cup puréed fruit of choice.

Yummy Chocolate Yogurt

Yields: 1 serving
Per serving (1 cup):

Calories = 190
Cholesterol = 4 mg
Fat = 1 g

1 cup plain nonfat yogurt
1 tablespoon sugar
2 teaspoons cocoa powder
½ teaspoon vanilla
¼ teaspoon flavoring extract, if desired (e.g., chocolate, strawberry, almond, or banana)

Combine all ingredients. Stir until smooth to resemble pudding. Serve in a favorite dish. Top with 1 tablespoon chopped nuts, grape nuts, or granola.

Variations: Add to the plain nonfat yogurt any one of the following:
6 fresh strawberries and 2 teaspoons sugar
½ banana and 2 teaspoons sugar
¼ cup fresh or water-packed canned cherries and 1 tablespoon sugar
½ cup fresh or frozen blueberries and 1 tablespoon sugar

Calico Corn

Yields: 1 serving
Per serving (5 cups):

Calories = 185
Cholesterol = 0 mg
Fat = 2 g

4 tablespoons popcorn kernels
    seasoning suggestions: fajita seasoning, soy sauce, Parmesan
        cheese, taco seasoning mix, cinnamon, garlic powder or
        garlic salt, cayenne pepper, curry powder, paprika, onion
        powder or onion salt, Italian seasonings, powdered salad
        dressing mixes, butter substitute sprinkles

Pop popcorn in air popper or microwave container in microwave. Sprinkle
with seasoning of your choice.

Note: To get seasonings to adhere without lots of butter or oil, spray popcorn
with nonstick cooking spray, buy seasoned popcorn sprays, or mix salt and
water in a spray bottle and mist the popcorn.

Seasoned Fiesta Chips

Yields: 1 serving
Per serving
(4 pieces):

Calories = 70
Cholesterol = 1 mg
Fat = 1 g

1 (6-inch) corn tortilla
    garlic salt or garlic powder, chili powder, fajita seasoning
        mix, or other seasonings as desired

Preheat oven to 250°. Cut tortilla into 4 wedges. Use the seasonings of your
choice. Toast for 20 minutes or until crisp.

Fit Fries

Yields: 2 servings
Per serving (1 cup):

Calories = 330
Cholesterol = 0 mg
Fat = 6 g

2 large baking potatoes
2 teaspoons canola oil
¼ teaspoon salt
  picante sauce to taste

Preheat oven to 400°. Cut scrubbed potatoes into long, very thin pieces. Put into a large bowl and add oil and salt. Mix until the oil and salt cover potatoes. Lay potatoes on a cookie sheet and put in hot oven. Bake for 15 minutes; remove the pan and turn potatoes. Return the potatoes to oven and bake another 15 minutes. Dip potatoes in picante sauce, if desired, before eating. Serve in a basket lined with a brightly colored napkin.

Lunch Box Favorite Oatmeal Cookies

Yields: 24 servings
Per serving
(1 cookie):

Calories = 65
Cholesterol = 0 mg
Fat = 4 g

½ cup chopped walnuts
½ cup uncooked oatmeal
¾ cup flour
1 tablespoon raisins
¼ cup canola oil
¼ cup maple syrup
2 teaspoons vanilla
1 tablespoon water

Preheat oven to 350°. Mix walnuts, oatmeal, flour, and raisins in a bowl. In another bowl, mix oil, syrup, vanilla, and water. Then add the liquid mixture to the flour mixture. Lightly grease a cookie sheet with a small amount of oil. With wet hands, make 2-inch balls with the cookie dough and then flatten them onto the greased cookie sheet. Bake for 15 minutes, turn cookies with spatula, and bake another 10 minutes until cookies are lightly browned.

Brownie Delight

Yields: 9 servings
Per serving (2½-inch square piece):

Calories = 225
Cholesterol = 0 mg
Fat = 4 g

    1 cup flour
    ¾ cup sugar
    2 tablespoons cocoa powder
    2 teaspoons baking powder
    1 teaspoon salt
    ½ cup skim milk
    2 tablespoons plus 1 teaspoon canola oil
    2 teaspoons vanilla
    ¾ cup brown sugar
    ¼ cup cocoa powder
    1¾ cups hot water

Preheat oven to 350°. Mix flour, sugar, 2 tablespoons cocoa powder, baking powder, and salt. Add milk, oil, and vanilla. Mix well. Pour into a lightly greased 8- × 8-inch baking pan. Mix brown sugar, ¼ cup cocoa powder, and hot water. Pour on top of batter. Bake for 40 minutes. Cut and serve warm or cool. For a special occasion, top with a scoop of vanilla ice milk.

Frozen Fruit Spears

Yields: 18 servings
Per serving (1 kabob):

Calories = 20
Cholesterol = 0 mg
Fat = 0 g

    1 (15¼-ounce) can unsweetened pineapple chunks
    ½ cup unsweetened orange juice
    1 tablespoon lemon juice
    2 small bananas, cut into ½-inch slices
    1 cup seedless red grapes
    18 wooden skewers

Drain pineapple juice and mix it with orange juice and lemon juice in a shallow 8- × 8-inch baking dish. Add bananas. Cover and marinate in refrigerator 8 hours. Store pineapple chunks in covered container in refrigerator until ready to thread on skewers. Thread fruit alternately on wooden skewers. Place on baking sheet and freeze until firm.

Big Dipper Ricotta Cheese Ranch Dip

Yields: 2 servings
Per serving
(¼ cup):

Calories = 95
Cholesterol = 20 mg
Fat = 5 g

½ cup part-skim ricotta cheese
1 heaping tablespoon plain nonfat yogurt
1 teaspoon dry ranch dressing mix
   paprika, for garnish

Combine all ingredients. Mix until well blended. Sprinkle with a dash of paprika.

Note: May be served with Veggie Skinny Dippers (see p. 246) and Fiesta Tortilla Chips (p. 246).

Zippity Dippity Dip

Yields: 5 servings
Per serving
(¼ cup):

Calories = 45
Cholesterol = 5 mg
Fat = 1 g

¼ cup part-skim ricotta cheese
1 cup plain nonfat yogurt
1 tablespoon dry soup mix or salad dressing mix

Combine all ingredients. Mix until well blended. Refrigerate for at least 2 hours. Serve chilled. Garnish with a broccoli floweret or serve in a hollowed-out red cabbage head.

Note: May be served with Veggie Skinny Dippers (p. 246) and Fiesta Tortilla Chips (p. 246).

Funion Dip

Yields: 2 servings
Per serving (¼ cup):

½ cup low-fat cottage cheese
2 tablespoons skim or low-fat milk
¼ package dry onion soup mix
carrot curls, for garnish

Calories = 50
Cholesterol = 7 mg
Fat = 1 g

Combine all ingredients in a blender container. Cover and blend on high until smooth. Refrigerate for 1 hour. Serve chilled. To garnish place carrot curls on top of chilled dip.

Note: May be served with Veggie Skinny Dippers (p. 246) and Fiesta Tortilla Chips (p. 246).

Peppy Parmesan Dip

Yields: 4 servings
Per serving (¼ cup):

½ cup part-skim ricotta cheese
¼ cup Parmesan cheese
¼ cup plain nonfat yogurt
cherry tomato, for garnish

Calories = 75
Cholesterol = 14 mg
Fat = 4 g

Combine all ingredients in blender container. Cover and blend on high until smooth. Refrigerate for 1 hour. Serve chilled. Garnish with a cherry tomato cut in fourths.

Note: May be served with Veggie Skinny Dippers (p. 246) and Fiesta Tortilla Chips (p. 246).

Yields: 6 servings
Per serving (¼ cup):

Calories = 30
Cholesterol = 2 mg
Fat = 0 g

Little Dipper Ranch Dressing

1 cup skim or low-fat milk
½ cup plain nonfat yogurt
1 package dry ranch dressing mix

Combine milk and yogurt in a bowl. Add dressing mix one tablespoon at a time. Mix vigorously with a wire whisk or fork for 60 seconds. Taste-test and add extra ranch mix as desired. Refrigerate for 1 hour in covered container. Stir before serving.

Note: May be served with Veggie Skinny Dippers (p. 246) and Fiesta Tortilla Chips (p. 246).

Chocolate Peanutty Pops

Yields: 6 servings
Per serving (1 frozen pop):

Calories = 350
Cholesterol = 3 mg
Fat = 23 g

   1 envelope unflavored gelatin
  ½ cup sugar
   1 cup boiling water
   1 cup creamy natural peanut butter
   1 cup low-fat chocolate milk

In a medium bowl mix gelatin and sugar; add boiling water and stir until gelatin is completely dissolved. With wire whisk or beater, blend in peanut butter; stir in milk. Pour into 5-ounce paper cups and place in freezer until partially frozen. Insert wooden ice cream sticks or plastic spoons; freeze until firm.

Grandma's Favorite Custard

Yields: 6 servings
Per serving (½ cup):

Calories = 135
Cholesterol = 114 mg
Fat = 5 g

   3 eggs
  ⅛ teaspoon salt
  ⅓ cup sugar
   1 teaspoon vanilla
 2½ cups scalded low-fat milk
  ⅛ teaspoon ground nutmeg

Preheat oven to 350°. Blend eggs, salt, sugar, and vanilla. Gradually stir in milk. Pour into 6 custard cups and sprinkle with nutmeg. Place cups in a 13- × 9- × 2-inch baking pan. Fill pan with 1 inch of hot water. Bake 45 minutes or until tip of knife inserted into center of custard comes out clean.

Yields: 6 servings
Per serving (½ cup):

Calories = 210
Cholesterol = 114 mg
Fat = 5 g

Rice Raisin Pudding

½ cup water
½ cup uncooked instant rice
3 eggs, slightly beaten
½ cup sugar
2 teaspoons vanilla
¼ teaspoon salt
2½ cups scalded low-fat milk
½ cup raisins (if desired)
ground cinnamon to taste

Preheat oven to 350°. Heat water to boiling in a medium saucepan. Remove from heat; stir in rice. Cover and let stand about 5 minutes. Blend eggs, sugar, vanilla, and salt. Gradually stir in milk. Mix in rice and raisins (if desired). Pour into ungreased 1½- quart casserole; sprinkle with cinnamon. Place casserole in 9- × 9- × 2-inch pan and pour 1 inch of very hot water into pan. Bake about 70 minutes or until knife inserted halfway between center and edge comes out clean. Remove casserole from water. Serve pudding warm or cold in child's favorite small dish. Top with cinnamon sprinkled in shape of child's first initial or a heart.

Yields: 8 servings
Per serving (2-inch by 4-inch log):

Calories = 365
Cholesterol = 3 mg
Fat = 17 g

Peanut Butter Logs

1 cup nonfat powdered milk
1 cup creamy natural peanut butter
½ cup honey
1 cup Rice Krispies
1 cup bran flakes
½ cup raisins

Combine all ingredients well. Flatten mixture in an 8- × 8-inch pan. Chill overnight. Cut into eight 2-inch × 4-inch "logs."

Crunchy Energy Squares

Yields: 16 servings
Per serving (2-inch
× 2-inch square):

Calories = 145
Cholesterol = 1 mg
Fat = 7 g

½ cup honey
½ cup creamy natural peanut butter
3 tablespoons margarine
½ cup nonfat powdered milk
2½ cups bran cereal
3 tablespoons toasted sesame seed

Combine first 3 ingredients until well blended. Stir in powdered milk and cereal. Press firmly into a buttered 8- × 8-inch baking pan. Sprinkle with sesame seeds and press them into the surface. Chill for at least 1 hour. Cut into 2-inch squares.

Golden Whole Wheat Pound Cake

Yields: 8 servings
Per serving (1 slice):

Calories = 745
Cholesterol = 160 mg
Fat = 45 g

1½ cups honey
1½ cups vegetable oil
¼ teaspoon salt
6 eggs, separated
2 cups whole wheat flour
¾ cup orange juice
⅓ cup nonfat powdered milk
2 tablespoons grated orange rind
¼ teaspoon ground mace

Preheat oven to 300°. Place honey, oil, and salt in a large mixing bowl. Blend in egg yolks one at a time. Beat until well mixed. Stir in rest of ingredients except for egg whites. Beat egg whites until stiff and fold into mixture. Turn into oiled 9- × 5-inch loaf pan. Bake for about 1 hour or until cake springs back when touched lightly in center. Serve with a glass of milk.

Peanut Butter Crispies

Yields: 24 bars
Per serving (1½-inch
× 2¼-inch bar):

Calories = 110
Cholesterol = 1 mg
Fat = 7 g

¾ cup creamy natural peanut butter
¼ cup vegetable oil
½ cup nonfat powdered milk
4 cups mixed cereal (e.g., Cheerios, Total, and Special K)
1 cup raisins

Melt peanut butter and oil over low heat. Stir in powdered milk, cereal, and raisins until evenly coated. Pat evenly into a 9- × 9-inch pan. Cool thoroughly, and cut into bars.

Frothy Fruit Frostie

½ cup ice cubes
1 cup unsweetened pineapple juice
½ cup low-fat yogurt or 1% milk
½ cup fruit (pineapple, melon, or your choice)

Put all ingredients in blender container, cover, and blend until smooth. Pour into a glass and serve. Alternate cubes of fruit on a wooden skewer and place in drink.

Yields: 1 serving
Per serving
(1 drink):

Calories = 250
Cholesterol = 7 mg
Fat = 2 g

Fruit Cube Fizz

3 empty ice cube trays
2 cups apple juice*
2 cups apple-strawberry juice*
2 cups apple-boysenberry juice*
1 quart carbonated water

Fill each ice cube tray (16 cubes per tray) with a different flavor of juice. Freeze overnight. Place one cube of each flavor in a glass. Fill with carbonated water. Flavor surprises abound as each cube melts.

*Or use a total of 6 cups of any mixture of your favorite fruit juices.

Yields: 16 servings
Per serving
(3 cubes):

Calories = 48
Cholesterol = 0 mg
Fat = 0 g

Lemonade Refresher

Yields: 1 serving
Per serving
(8 ounces):

Calories = 65
Cholesterol = 0 mg
Fat = 0 g

¼ cup freshly squeezed lemon juice
1 tablespoon sugar
¾ cup water
ice cubes
lemon slice (optional)

Combine lemon juice and sugar. Stir in water. Add ice cubes. Pour into a glass and garnish with a lemon slice, if desired.

Orange Sparkler

Yields: 1 serving
Per serving
(8 ounces):

Calories = 55
Cholesterol = 0 mg
Fat = 0 g

4 ounces orange juice
4 ounces club soda
ice cubes

Combine orange juice and club soda in a glass. Add ice cubes.

Winter Warmer Tea

Yields: 1 serving
Per serving
(8 ounces):

Calories = 0
Cholesterol = 0 mg
Fat = 0 g

1 decaffeinated tea bag
1 lemon slice
1 cinnamon stick
1 whole clove
1 cup boiling water

Combine first 4 ingredients in a teapot. Add boiling water. Steep for 3 to 5 minutes and strain. Pour into a teacup and add sugar or honey, if desired.

Chilled Chocolate Cow

Yields: 1 serving
Per serving
(8 ounces):

Calories = 210
Cholesterol = 8 mg
Fat = 0 g

2 teaspoons cocoa powder
1 tablespoon sugar
⅓ cup nonfat powdered milk
2 teaspoons vanilla
½ cup water
5 ice cubes

Combine all ingredients in blender container. Cover and blend on high speed for 1 minute or until smooth. Pour into a glass and serve immediately.

Chocolate-Covered Cherry Milk Shake

Yields: 1 serving
Per serving
(8 ounces):

Calories = 175
Cholesterol = 5 mg
Fat = 0 g

½ cup evaporated skim milk
¼ cup unsweetened canned cherries
1 tablespoon sugar
½ teaspoon almond extract
¼ teaspoon chocolate extract
4 ice cubes
1 reserved cherry, for garnish

Combine all ingredients in blender container. Cover and blend on high speed for 1 minute or until smooth. Pour into a glass and serve immediately. Top with a cherry.

Pink Cow

Yields: 1 serving
Per serving
(8 ounces):

Calories = 235
Cholesterol = 8 mg
Fat = 1 g

    1 cup or 6 large fresh strawberries
    ½ cup water
    ⅓ cup nonfat powdered milk
    1 tablespoon sugar
    5 to 8 ice cubes

Combine all ingredients in blender container. Cover and blend on high speed for 1 minute or until smooth. Pour into a glass and serve immediately.

Variations: Substitute ⅓ cup crushed pineapple, ½ ripe banana, or 1 fresh peach for the strawberries.

Cranberry Coconut Smoothie

Yields: 1 serving
Per serving
(8 ounces):

Calories = 130
Cholesterol = 2 mg
Fat = 0 g

    ½ cup skim milk
    ¼ cup low-calorie cranberry juice
    ½ ripe banana
    1 teaspoon sugar
    ½ teaspoon coconut extract
    4 ice cubes

Combine all ingredients in a blender container. Cover and blend on high speed for 1 minute or until smooth. Pour into a glass and serve immediately.

Egg Frothy

Yields: 2 servings
Per serving
(6 ounces):

Calories = 55
Cholesterol = 2 mg
Fat = 0 g

  1 egg
boiling water
¾ cup skim or low-fat milk
  1 teaspoon sugar
½ teaspoon vanilla
  2 crushed ice cubes
⅛ teaspoon ground nutmeg, for garnish

Dip whole egg, in the shell, into boiling water for 30 seconds. Break and separate the egg; put the egg white only in a blender container. Add the milk, sugar, vanilla, and ice cubes. Cover and blend until smooth and frothy. Pour into 2 glasses and sprinkle with nutmeg.

Chill Chaser Punch

Yields: 16 servings
Per serving
(4 ounces):

Calories = 55
Cholesterol = 0 mg
Fat = 0 g

  6 cups unsweetened apple juice
  2 cups low-calorie cranberry juice
½ cup orange juice
½ teaspoon whole allspice
½ teaspoon whole cloves
  3 cinnamon sticks
  1 orange, thinly sliced
  1 teaspoon whole cloves

Combine juices in a large saucepan. Put allspice and ½ teaspoon cloves in a tea ball and add to the juices along with the cinnamon. Heat to boiling. Lower the heat and simmer for 10 minutes. Remove from the heat and let stand for 10 minutes. Remove the tea ball and cinnamon sticks. Pour into punch bowl and top with orange slices that have been studded with 1 teaspoon cloves. Serve hot.

MAKE-A-SHAKE CHART

Combine any of the following protein and carbohydrate ingredients for a high-protein, high-calorie shake.

POSSIBLE INGREDIENTS	AMOUNT	CALORIES	PROTEIN (gm)
PROTEIN SOURCES:			
Whole milk	1 cup	180	8
2% milk	1 cup	120	8
Skim milk	1 cup	100	8
Evaporated milk	½ cup	137	7
Evaporated skim milk	½ cup	99	10
Fruit-flavored yogurt	1 cup	240	9
Powdered milk (nonfat)	¼ cup (dry)	110	11
Egg	1 medium	80	7
Ice cream	1 cup	255	4
Ice milk	1 cup	100	4
Wheat germ	1 tablespoon	36	3
Cottage cheese	½ cup	120	15
Peanut butter (natural)	1 tablespoon	115	5
CARBOHYDRATE SOURCES:			
Orange juice	1 cup	110	0
Banana	1 medium	100	0
Strawberries	1 cup	55	0
Peaches in syrup	1 cup	200	0
Honey	1 tablespoon	65	0

Yields: 1 serving
Per serving
(8 ounces):

Calories = 290
Cholesterol = 20 mg
Fat = 6 g

Orange Citrus Shake

¾ cup orange juice
1 tablespoon nonfat powdered milk
1 cup ice milk

Combine all ingredients in blender container. Cover and blend on high speed for 1 minute or until smooth. Pour into a glass and serve immediately.

Orange Yogurt Shake

8 ounces flavored low-fat yogurt
1 cup orange juice
1 tablespoon nonfat powdered milk
6 ice cubes
½ orange, for garnish

Yields: 2 servings
Per serving
(8 ounces):

Calories = 200
Cholesterol = 17 mg
Fat = 5 g

Combine all ingredients in blender container. Cover and blend on high speed for 1 minute or until smooth. Pour into 2 glasses and serve immediately. Garnish with an orange quarter on side of glass.

Strawberry Smoothie

1 cup low-fat milk
½ cup fresh strawberries
½ cup strawberry ice cream
whole strawberries, for garnish

Yields: one 12-
ounce serving or
three 4-ounce
servings
Per serving
(12 ounces):

Calories = 265
Cholesterol = 48 mg
Fat = 12 g

Combine all ingredients in blender container. Cover and blend on high speed for 1 minute or until smooth. Pour into a glass and serve immediately. Place a whole strawberry on top of each drink.

Variation: To decrease fat and calories, use skim milk and ice milk to replace the low-fat milk and ice cream in this recipe. (Per 12-ounce serving: 190 calories, 13 mg cholesterol, 3 g fat.)

Creamy Chocolate Shake

Yields: 1 serving
Per serving
(8 ounces):

Calories = 190
Cholesterol = 20 mg
Fat = 5 g

¼ cup low-fat cottage cheese
⅓ cup ice milk (vanilla or chocolate)
½ cup low-fat chocolate milk

Combine all ingredients in blender container. Cover and blend on high speed for 1 minute or until smooth. Pour into a glass and serve immediately.

Chocolate Banana Shake

Yields: 1 serving
Per serving
(8 ounces):

Calories = 250
Cholesterol = 18 mg
Fat = 7 g

½ cup ice milk (vanilla or chocolate)
½ cup low-fat chocolate milk
½ ripe banana

Combine all ingredients in blender container. Cover and blend on high speed for 1 minute or until smooth. Pour into a glass and serve immediately.

Banana Blast

Yields: 1 serving
Per serving
(8 ounces):

Calories = 290
Cholesterol = 24 mg
Fat = 6 g

1 ripe banana
6 ounces flavored yogurt
1 tablespoon nonfat powdered milk
½ cup orange juice

Combine all ingredients in blender container. Cover and blend on high speed for 1 minute or until smooth. Pour into a glass and serve immediately.

Rise-and-Shine Special Shake

Yields: 1 serving
Per serving
(8 ounces):

1 cup low-fat milk
1 tablespoon nonfat powdered milk
¼ cup low-fat cottage cheese
1 small ripe banana
2 tablespoons wheat germ

Calories = 320
Cholesterol = 25 mg
Fat = 8 g

Combine all ingredients in blender container. Cover and blend on high speed for 1 minute or until smooth. Pour into a glass and serve immediately.

Purple Cow

Yields: 2 servings
Per serving
(8 ounces):

1 cup low-fat milk
1 cup vanilla ice cream
¼ cup grape juice
1 tablespoon nonfat powdered milk

Calories = 230
Cholesterol = 40 mg
Fat = 10 g

Combine all ingredients in blender container. Cover and blend on high speed for 1 minute or until smooth. Pour into 2 glasses and serve immediately.

Skinny Purple Cow

Yields: 2 servings
Per serving
(8 ounces):

1 cup low-fat milk
1 cup ice milk (vanilla)
¼ cup grape juice
3 tablespoons nonfat powdered milk

Calories = 210
Cholesterol = 20 mg
Fat = 5 g

Combine all ingredients in blender container. Cover and blend on high speed for 1 minute or until smooth. Pour into 2 glasses and serve immediately.

Chocolate Peanut Butter Shake

Yields: 1 serving
Per serving
(8 ounces):

Calories = 300
Cholesterol = 18 mg
Fat = 13 g

1 cup low-fat chocolate milk
1 tablespoon natural peanut butter
1 tablespoon nonfat powdered milk

Combine all ingredients in blender container. Cover and blend on high speed for 1 minute or until smooth. Pour into a glass and serve immediately.

Gelatin Jewels

4 envelopes unflavored gelatin
1 cup cold fruit juice
3 cups hot fruit juice

Yields: 9 servings
Per serving (thirteen
1-inch square
blocks):

Calories = 64
Cholesterol = 0 mg
Fat = 0 g

In a bowl, sprinkle gelatin over cold fruit juice. Let stand for 1 minute Add the hot fruit juice and stir until the gelatin is dissolved. Pour into a 9- × 13-inch pan. Chill until firm. Cut into 1-inch square blocks.

Tasty Tapioca Pudding

2 tablespoons instant tapioca
2 cups skim milk
¼ cup egg substitute
¾ teaspoon vanilla
2 egg whites
2 teaspoons sugar
raisins or cinnamon, for garnish (optional)

Yields: 4 servings
Per serving (½ cup):

Calories = 85
Cholesterol = 2 mg
Fat = 0 g

Cook tapioca and milk in a double boiler over boiling water until tapioca becomes transparent. Slowly add hot tapioca and milk mixture to egg substitute; return mixture to double boiler. Cook, stirring constantly, until the mixture thickens. Cool on counter for 15 minutes and add the vanilla. Beat the egg whites until very stiff; fold into tapioca mixture. Add the sugar by lightly sprinkling over the top of mixture and fold in. Cool in refrigerator for 2 hours. Spoon pudding into individual bowls. Children can decorate their pudding with raisins or sprinkle with cinnamon in a smiling face design.

Festive Fruit-Filled Yogurt Dessert

Yields: 2 servings
Per serving (½ cup):

Calories = 116
Cholesterol = 4 mg
Fat = 2 g

3 almonds
1 small banana
1 apricot (fresh, canned, or dried)
5 cherries (fresh or canned)
1 date (dried)
½ cup low-fat yogurt

Crush almonds with a rolling pin. Chop banana, apricot, cherries, and date separately. Place banana and apricot in the bottom of 2 individual bowls. Cover with yogurt and sprinkle cherries, date, and almonds on top. Chill until served.

Terrific Tapioca Dessert

Yields: 12 servings
Per serving (2¼-inch × 3-inch piece):

Calories = 265
Cholesterol = 3 mg
Fat = 11 g

½ cup canola oil
2 teaspoons vanilla
1 cup brown sugar
4 egg whites*
2 teaspoons ground cinnamon
1 teaspoon salt
2 tablespoons baking soda
1 teaspoon baking powder
2 cups cooked tapioca
2 cups flour
maraschino cherries, strawberries, pecans, or grapes, for garnish

Preheat oven to 350°. Mix the oil, vanilla, sugar, egg whites, cinnamon, and salt. Carefully blend in baking soda, baking powder, tapioca, and flour. Pour mixture into a nonstick 9- × 9-inch baking pan. Bake for 40 minutes. If toothpick inserted near center does not come out clean, bake for a few more minutes until toothpick does come out clean. Top each piece with a maraschino cherry, strawberry half, pecan half, or grape.

*May substitute 2 eggs.

Pumpkin Pie

Yields: 8 servings
Per serving (1 slice):

Calories = 375
Cholesterol = 85 mg
Fat = 16 g

1 prepared graham cracker pie crust*
2 eggs, separated
Pinch of salt
¼ cup firmly packed brown sugar
1 cup canned pumpkin
1 cup part-skim ricotta cheese
2 tablespoons lemon juice
1 teaspoon grated lemon peel
½ teaspoon ground cinnamon
⅛ teaspoon ground ginger
⅛ teaspoon ground nutmeg
½ cup evaporated skim milk
2 tablespoons cornstarch

Preheat oven to 350°. In a large mixing bowl, beat egg yolks with 2 tablespoons plus 2 teaspoons of the brown sugar until well combined. Add the pumpkin, ricotta cheese, lemon juice, lemon peel, and spices; stir until combined. In small bowl or 1-cup measure, combine the evaporated milk and cornstarch, stirring to dissolve cornstarch. Stir into the pumpkin mixture. In a medium mixing bowl using an electric mixer on high speed, beat the egg whites with the salt until soft peaks form. Beat in remaining 1 tablespoon plus 1 teaspoon brown sugar and continue beating until stiff peaks form. Gently fold the whites into the pumpkin mixture. Pour the filling into the prepared pie crust and bake for 35 to 40 minutes. Set on a wire rack and let cool completely.

*Either purchase a prepared pie crust or make your own as follows: Crush 23 graham cracker squares. Stir in ¼ cup sugar. Add 6 tablespoons melted margarine and mix well. Press into a 9-inch pie pan. Bake at 300° for 15 minutes. Let cool completely before filling.

Nutritional Strategies for Special Kids

I n this chapter, I'll deal briefly with four nutrition issues that are raised again and again by parents—obesity, eating disorders, feeding young athletes, and vegetarianism.

If your child is facing one of these issues, you may well find that you need much more comprehensive guidance than I can provide in this book. But perhaps some of the points I'll make will at least give you a start toward finding an answer from specialized pediatricians or other experts, such as registered dietitians.

THE NAGGING QUESTION OF OBESITY

We've already considered a number of aspects of obesity, including how to calculate your child's percent of body fat in chapter 7 and the use of weight-control menus in the previous chapter on smart eating. But the question of obesity continues to nag at parents and children, no matter how many programs they try or recommendations they receive.

A major reason for the ongoing concern is that most attempts to lose weight eventually fail. With many weight-loss programs, 80 to 90 percent of the participants regain much or all of the weight they've lost in a matter of months.

So what should you, as a parent, know about the fitness and medical implications of obesity if your child needs to lose weight? Here are some points that may motivate or, at least, inform you:

• A 1983 study by Dr. Kelly Brown in *Pediatrics* reported that helping a child lose weight through education and behavior modification (such as learning more about nutrition and exercise) works best when parents are involved—but not too involved. The study revealed that when the mother and adolescent attended separate groups to pursue a weight-loss program, the adolescents lost significant amounts of weight. But the kids *gained* weight when their mothers attended the group with them or when the mothers didn't participate at all!

• Decreases in the weight of children 8 to 12 years old have been associated with significant decreases in total blood cholesterol and increases in "good" cholesterol (high-density lipoprotein, or HDL cholesterol), according to a 1989 study by Dr. Leonard H. Epstein, reported in *Nutrition & the M. D.*

• Obese adolescents are more prone than other children to having high blood pressure as a result of sodium intake, according to a 1989 report in the *New England Journal of Medicine.*

• A very strong relationship exists between childhood obesity and adult obesity, especially in children 3 years old or older, says Dr. Myron Winick in a 1988 U.S. Department of Agriculture publication. He notes that an obese 3-year-old has a 60 percent or greater chance of becoming an obese adult.

Finally, I recognize that there is a hereditary component to obesity. That is, children of obese parents are more likely to become obese themselves. But at this time, the jury is still out on this subject. We're just not sure about the extent to which a given child's weight is determined by his personal habits and his environment, including his family influences, and to what extent his genes may play a part.

In any case, I believe that commitment and resolve on the part of parents *can* make a difference in weight reduction with most children. In fact, the primary responsibility begins with the parents. The burden is on them to recognize their child's problem as early as possible, participate in a family-supported weight-control program, of the type outlined in the previous chapter, and, if necessary, secure the services of a qualified nutritionist or physician.

WHEN A CHILD LOSES CONTROL

Volumes have been written on eating disorders, such as anorexia nervosa and bulimia, and an in-depth treatment of these problems is well beyond the scope of this book. But I will deal with certain aspects that are linked to kid fitness.

First of all, some basic definitions: Anorexia nervosa is a syndrome that includes tremendous fear of becoming fat; an overwhelming desire to lose weight, to the point of being willing to starve oneself; and a variety of stress-related emotional symptoms. Also, among anorexic girls, there's a tendency to have amenorrhea, or not to menstruate.

Bulimia involves binge eating and then self-induced vomiting. As with anorexics, bulimics are quite fearful of gaining weight and are usually dissatisfied with their bodies.

These problems are considerably more common among teenage girls than boys, in part because girls tend to associate low weight with physical attractiveness. It's important, however, for parents to watch among *both* sexes for symptoms of excessive undereating and loss of weight. In this vein, a 1989 study in *Pediatrics* revealed that 45 percent of boys and girls in grades three through six wanted to be thinner, 37 percent had already tried to lose weight, and nearly 7 percent were in the anorexia nervosa category.

The warning signals are there for parents who have children of any age. The end of the road for this type of behavior may be self-starvation and, eventually, death.

Eating Disorders Among Athletes. Serious weight loss and even anorexia characterize adolescent girls *and* boys who are driven to achieve a perfect body. And certain activities and sports, such as ballet, gymnastics, and long-distance running, may aggravate this tendency.

Research has revealed that 4 to 19 percent of female college students have eating disorders, such as anorexia nervosa or bulimia. The *Physician and Sportsmedicine* reported more specifically in 1987 on the female sports scene: 20 percent of the women athletes in those sports that emphasize leanness (such as distance running) and 10 percent of all female athletes are preoccupied with weight or have tendencies toward eating disorders.

Young male athletes may also have problems, especially in long-distance running or in sports like wrestling, which demand that a participant lose pounds to "make weight."

In a 1970 study reported in the *Journal of the American Medical Association,* wrestlers trying to lose weight rapidly (i.e., 4.9 percent of their initial body weight in 17 days) showed a marked reduction in their serum testosterone (sex hormone) levels. N O T E : The testosterone did return to normal at the conclusion of the season.

Associated with the rapid weight loss among athletes is a decrease in strength and endurance capacity. In one study, five men lost between 5.4 and 6.2 percent of their body weight in five days. Their endurance or aerobic capacity dropped simultaneously by 31.6 percent. Such fast weight loss is also linked to increased susceptibility to infection, decreased immunity, and, surprisingly, increases in the total serum cholesterol level.

In general, I do not recommend rapid weight loss in any situation. It may either produce potentially harmful and irreversible effects on the body or may result in a change in bodily metabolism that leads to accelerated weight gain once the dieting stops. So when it's desirable to lose weight, don't lose control. Instead, follow the sensible, 1 to 2 pounds per week rule, and never let teenage girls consume fewer than 1200 calories, or teenage boys fewer than 1500 calories per day.

Some further recommendations for young athletes: parents and coaches should not require weight loss without (1) consulting with a physician, (2) measuring the athlete's percent body fat, and (3) evaluating the athlete's vulnerability to eating disorders.

THE FEEDING OF YOUNG ATHLETES

Frequent questions I'm asked by parents are "Should my child, who is a serious competitive athlete, be fed differently from other children?" "What should my daughter eat before a tennis match?" and "What's the best liquid to drink before and during an athletic event?"

Here are some guidelines to help you answer these and related questions. Also, some specific "Pre-Athletic Event Meal Samples" are included.

PRE-ATHLETIC EVENT MEAL SAMPLES
"The Last Supper" (7–20 hours before event) (1,000–1,500 calories)

MEAL 1

2 cups spaghetti, cooked
¾ cup tomato/meat sauce
¾ cup spinach, steamed
¾ cup carrots, steamed
3 dinner rolls
3 teaspoons diet margarine
1 tablespoon diet margarine in cooking
8 ounces skim milk
1 cup fruit salad
32 ounces water throughout evening

Computer Analysis:

1,300 calories
59% complex carbohydrates
24% fat
17% protein

MEAL 2

6 ounces baked, skinless chicken with
   ½ tablespoon oil
   1 tablespoon lemon juice
2 cups rice
Salad
1 tablespoon salad dressing
¾ cup green peas
3 dinner rolls
3 teaspoons diet margarine
8 ounces skim milk
1 cup strawberries
32 ounces water throughout evening

Computer Analysis:

1,400 calories
56% complex carbohydrates
20% fat
24% protein

"The First Meal" (the day of the event—2–4 hours before event) (<500 calories)

MEAL 1

1 scrambled egg
1 English muffin
1 teaspoon margarine
8 ounces orange juice
8 ounces skim milk
16 ounces water

Computer Analysis:

470 calories
58% complex carbohydrates
25% fat
17% protein

MEAL 2

2 slices low-fat cheese
1 English muffin or 2 toast
1 banana
8 ounces skim milk
16 ounces water

Computer Analysis:

475 calories
58% complex carbohydrates
19% fat
23% protein

MEAL 3

½ cup raisin bran cereal
8 ounces skim milk
1 banana
8 ounces orange juice
16 ounces water

Computer Analysis:

550 calories
87% complex carbohydrates
   and sugar
1% fat
12% protein

1. As obvious as it may sound, it's important to remember that an athletic child will need more calories when he's in training than when he's not. Parents may tend to forget this point and serve their son or daughter the same amount of food during the athletic season as during the off-season. Unless calories are increased, undesirable weight loss may occur and energy levels may decline.

To give you an idea of how many calories different sports require, consider these calorie needs for a 100-pound child:

Low-energy sports, such as baseball, walking, or bowling: 240–350, calories/hour
Moderate-energy sports, such as basketball, touch football, hiking with a pack, ice-skating: 330–600 calories/hour
High-energy sports, such as fast cycling or distance running: 420–900 calories/hour

2. High complex carbohydrate foods, such as pasta or fruits, may help overcome complaints of fatigue or low energy. A child's muscles can't store body sugars as efficiently as those of adults. So a higher carbohydrate intake can help keep their energy levels up.
3. A pregame meal should be eaten at least 2.5 hours before competition and as much as 3 to 4 hours if the child tends to have trouble digesting food before the event. The meal should contain mainly carbohydrates and not foods that will be digested more slowly such as fats or desserts. A fast-food hamburger or fries is definitely *not* recommended! Also the child should drink plenty of liquids, including water. Every athlete, especially those in sports that involve heavy sweating, should go into the event with a solid fluid base. This means drinking several glasses of water, beginning the night preceding the event. Some recommended pregame foods are low-fat sandwiches, pasta, fruit, or other grain-based foods.

4. Snacking may be required if the event is delayed for some reason. When the young athlete needs a pick-me-up before competition, he could concentrate on foods such as breads, fruits, low-fat dairy products such as yogurt or cottage cheese, and homemade or other low-fat foods such as those contained in the preceding recipe section.

5. After the game, the main purpose is to bring the body's liquids back to normal and also to replenish the sugars (glycogen) in the muscles. So after the game, it's important to take in water and other fluids immediately, and begin to eat regular foods. Some of the protein and higher-fat foods that were avoided before the contest may now be included.

6. During the athletic event, don't stint on water and other fluids!

Cool water can help lower the body temperature and should be consumed liberally, as needed. When a child is very hot, he should avoid very cold liquids. During exercise in a hot environment, however, the child should take in about 4 to 8 ounces of water every 15 minutes, although the exact amount should be adjusted to body size and degree of sweating. N O T E : There are obvious limits to drinking water. If the youngster begins to feel bloated, or waterlogged, he should stop!

Another rule of thumb is that the athlete should drink 16 ounces of water for each pound of fluid lost through exercise. (The amount of weight lost by a child after an event can be checked simply by weighing immediately before and after the activity. The difference in weight will be due mostly to the loss of fluids.)

As mentioned in the exercise section of this book, electrolyte-based drinks should be diluted by about half by water—that is, one part water to one part sports drink.

7. In general, I think children—especially those who haven't reached puberty—should avoid "carbohydrate loading," or the practice of eating an extremely high percentage of carbohydrates in the few days preceding the event. A diet of the type recommended in this book has plenty of carbohydrates to help the average young athlete achieve his best performance.

The loading practice is of help mainly for long-distance running events exceeding 10 miles, or approximately 20 kilometers. However, this approach may result in health problems such as stiffness, diarrhea, or even more serious ailments unless it's closely monitored.

8. If a young athlete is eating a balanced diet, vitamin and mineral supplements should be unnecessary. Excessive consumption of some vitamins and minerals can have undesirable effects. The use of vitamins and supplements in athletes should be based on a proven need (e.g., anemia) and only under the supervision of a physician.

WHAT ABOUT KIDS WHO ARE VEGETARIANS?

Finally, a topic that has become increasingly important in recent years is the use of a vegetarian or near-vegetarian diet for children.

Only about 4 percent of the adults in the United States are true vegetarians and those regimens differ greatly, depending on the philosophy of the individuals involved. Here are a few of the variations:

• The lacto-ovo vegetarian, who eats vegetables, dairy products such as milk, and eggs
• The vegan, who eats plants and *avoids* all animal products, including milk and eggs
• The fruitarian, who eats only the fruits of plants, but *not* leaves, roots, or anything else that requires the destruction of a living thing
• The macrobiotic diet advocate, who eats mostly soy products, grains, and cooked vegetables, but tends to stay away from raw fruits and vegetables
• The hygienist, who eats raw fruits and vegetables rather than those that are cooked

Personal philosophy or religious orientation often plays a major role in the choice of some of these vegetarian diets. But personal convictions aside, there's a potential health danger in imposing adult standards on growing children.

A major problem is that with too few necessary nutrients in the early years, the growth of some children may be retarded. Several studies have shown height and weight deficiencies among kids on vegetarian diets.

The growth problems may be caused in part by a lack of adequate calories, especially during the weaning period, when children first go on solid foods. It's almost impossible to get adequate calories from a strict vegetarian diet in those early years. Also, a vegetarian diet must be planned very carefully if a child is to receive adequate nutrients for growth, such as calcium and iron.

On a more positive note, a report in September 1989 in *Pediatrics* focused on the impact of vegetarian diets on children at a collective community called

The Farm in rural central Tennessee. The 404 participating children, who ranged in age from 4 months to 10 years, were on a vegan diet until 1983, with soybeans as their primary source of protein. In 1983, some members of the community introduced eggs and dairy products into their diets, in effect becoming lacto-ovo vegetarians.

The researchers concluded that even though the growth of the vegetarian children was "modestly less" than that of nonvegetarians, the vegetarians still tested in normal ranges of height, weight, and general development. But remember, the diets in this study were pursued under close supervision by people experienced in finding an adequate nutritional balance with a vegetarian diet.

Because of the possible dangers, I would advise parents not to place children on a completely vegetarian diet until they are well into adolescence—say at least age 15 or 16. If you must go vegetarian, stick with the first option listed above—the lacto-ovo vegetarian diet, which allows for milk, eggs, cheese, and related dairy products. That way, the child will be more likely to receive adequate calories, protein, calcium, iron, and other nutrients essential for growth. Also, encourage beans regularly as a nutrient-dense meat substitute (e.g., black, kidney, ranch, navy, or white).

NOTE: The same approach to nutrition may be applied for the child who simply refuses to eat meat.

These special nutritional issues may not apply to your child right now. But it's well to understand them, regardless of your child's current status, because they may become pressing issues later. For example, your 8-year-old boy may become a wrestler and confront weight-loss problems similar to those we've discussed. Or your daughter may develop an eating disorder. Or your very conventional 6-year-old, who loves junk food, may suddenly have a "conversion" in early adolescence and become a radical vegan-type of vegetarian.

Any of these decisions or changes may have a significant impact on the potential for physical growth and development, as well as on the child's energy level. Knowing the dangers now can help you head off potential problems in the future.

There's one final nutrition-related issue that often overlaps with other fitness and health concerns. That's the question of how your child's school is doing in providing the kinds of food and other programs that will reinforce your strategy at home. If the school fails, then your entire fitness effort may be in jeopardy—so often, it's necessary to stand up and be counted.

CHAPTER ELEVEN

It's Time to Stand Up and Be Counted!

Too often we parents have heard some version of this familiar chorus: "That school lunch was so bad I could hardly even look at it!" "No, I didn't eat. They didn't have anything I like." "We mainly stand around and talk during gym." "I don't like to play those games at school because I get hot and sweaty, and there's hardly ever a chance to shower."

In general, many of our schools have failed to provide adequate health, nutrition, or fitness instruction because of a lack of funds or information. And busy mothers and fathers have failed to stand up and be counted for programs that will promote the physical well-being of their kids. Consider some of the results:

- Only 21 percent of children in grades 3 through 12 say they think a lot about whether the food they eat is good for them, according to a 1989 Harris poll.
- On the usual school day, 19 percent of students skip breakfast and 13 percent don't exercise even twice a week in school, again, according to the Harris poll.
- Of the children surveyed by Harris in grades 3 to 12, 18 percent smoke cigarettes occasionally or more often.
- Almost half of high-school juniors and seniors admit they drive after drinking alcohol.
- About 8 million public-school students receive little or no health education.
- Approximately 25 million American children eat school meals prepared according to the standards of the U.S. Department of Agriculture's National

School Lunch Program; yet those government standards lack adequate guidelines about how food is to be prepared or the amounts of fat, sugar, sodium, fiber, vitamins, or minerals that are appropriate in the meals.

We've discussed in earlier parts of this book the implications of the lack of national and local programs for physical fitness, obesity prevention, and related concerns. So we're well aware of the problems. But how can we overcome these problems and come up with some solutions?

There are three possibilities I want to submit for your consideration—the sack lunch solution, the school program solution, and the social action solution.

THE SACK LUNCH SOLUTION

The *best* solution to inadequate school lunch programs is, of course, to get the school to change. But as we'll see a little later, that often takes time and effort and may never happen while your child is still a student.

As an alternative, parents can fall back on the old-fashioned sack lunch—but with a few new nutritional twists. Here are some tips from our nutritionists on how to prepare a healthy sack lunch:

• Don't assume you have to include a sandwich; easy-to-fix alternatives include hard-boiled eggs (left in the shell), baked chicken, soup or broth in a thermos, turkey slices without the bread, shelled nuts, pinto beans, or cubes of cheese. BUT NOTE: Whole-grain breads can supply much-needed fiber, carbohydrates, and other nutrients, so don't sell the sandwich short!

• Fresh fruits that taste great for lunch are grapes, peaches, plums, apples, melon wedges, pears, bananas, tangerines, and pineapple wedges; those that are "runny" or have excessive juice can be packed tightly in a plastic container. Raisins and dried fruit are enjoyable "sweets" too.

• Low-fat milk is usually an essential ingredient; pour it in a thermos.

• Include natural, 100 percent fruit juices.

• Many children *love* low-fat, fruit-flavored yogurt after they finally try it.

• Homemade cookies, made with oatmeal, raisin, or wheat germ are good examples of nutritious sack lunch desserts.

• Homemade fruit-filled or bran muffins are another great source of fiber and carbohydrate calories.

• And don't forget the snacks described in the recipe section of this book.

What should you avoid in a sack lunch? Here are a few no-no's:

• Avoid commercial snack items such as cookies, cakes, or candy bars; these are usually full of too much sugar and saturated fats.

• Avoid punch and fruit beverages that are mostly colored water and contain too much sugar.

• Avoid hydrogenated, commercial peanut butter, which contains saturated fats; stick to the natural, nonhydrogenated kind.

• Avoid potato chips and related items, which typically are loaded with saturated fats.

Too often, sack lunches, as well as school lunches, contain high amounts of fat, which tend to weigh heavily in the digestive tract and may cause drowsiness. Also, kids may tend to consume too much salt and sugar from even homemade fare, which may cause problems with high blood pressure and obesity, respectively.

In general, in preparing a sack lunch, if you follow the basic nutritional guidelines outlined in chapter 9, you'll find that your child will have all the fuel he needs for proper growth and efficient school performance.

THE SCHOOL PROGRAM SOLUTION

An even better solution for the school nutrition and fitness problem is to encourage your school to institute a program that will promote basic health principles. This way, other children will be helped along with your own. A few pilot programs in this area have been given high marks by various researchers, including the Heart Smart program, which is based on the extensive Bogalusa Heart Study in Louisiana.

Focusing on elementary schools, Heart Smart was designed to institute school programs that reduce cardiovascular risk factors in children. Specifically, the program includes a longitudinal classroom curriculum, an aerobic fitness program (as part of regular physical education classes), a health-oriented school lunch program, and a teacher-staff development program.

Some of the objectives of the program, according to a 1988 report in the *Health Education Quarterly,* include the following:

• Limiting student dietary fat intake to levels below 30 percent of the total calorie consumption

• Keeping saturated fats below 10 percent of total calories

• Restricting sodium consumption to 5 grams or less during a 24-hour period

- Increasing students' knowledge of cardiovascular health and risk factors
- Helping students to resist peer pressure to smoke or use drugs
- Developing skills and habits consistent with lifetime physical fitness

Those interested in further information on this program can write to Dr. Gerald S. Berenson, Director; National Research and Demonstration Center—Arteriosclerosis; Louisiana State University Medical Center; 1542 Tulane Avenue; New Orleans, LA 70112-2865.

Another program, designed for children from kindergarten through the seventh grade, is Growing Health, which was developed by the National Center for Health Education; 30 East Twenty-ninth Street; New York, NY 10016. This program, which was funded through a grant from the federal Centers for Disease Control in Atlanta, provides practical multimedia health training for children, along with special instruction for teachers. Some of the topics covered include smoking, the workings of the cardiovascular system, and emotional difficulties.

Despite the availability of these and other programs, however, many schools may not respond positively. Officials may say, "We already have adequate programs" or "We don't have money for this sort of thing." What can parents do if they run up against this sort of scholastic brick wall?

THE SOCIAL ACTION SOLUTION

If your school won't respond to your personal efforts to get them to improve their nutrition and fitness programs, the next step is to combine with other parents and start putting pressure on them to change. This is part of the social action tradition in our democratic system; if government agencies and officials won't listen to an individual plea, then hit them with a group. Here's an action plan that has been suggested by experts at our Institute for Aerobics Research and that has worked in a number of practical school situations.

Step 1. Contact as many parents as you can who are concerned about the issue and call a meeting to formulate your action plan.

Step 2. Approach the physical education teacher, the director of the lunch program, or the principal of the school as a group. This can be done by drafting a short petition, or letter, signed by all the concerned parents. Then have one or two spokespersons for the group present it to the school officials. The petition might read as follows:

We, the undersigned, are deeply concerned about the school lunch program at _____ because we have learned that our children either are not eating the food served or are concentrating only on high-fat items. We would like to meet with you as soon as possible to work out a plan to improve this situation. Our representative, _____, will be in touch with you shortly.

[Signatures]

Step 3. If you fail to get satisfaction on the school level, go to the administration above the school officials. Use the same techniques, with a letter signed by all concerned parents.

Step 4. If you *still* fail to get an acceptable answer, public-school parents should go to the school board. The local school board is usually one of the most responsive agencies to public opinion and pressure, and so if you approach them properly, you should get some action.

At this stage, the more parents you have behind you, the better. Also, an endorsement by the school's parent-teacher group will be a big plus. It may even be possible to contact representatives from other schools and get them on your team.

How should you approach the school board? Sending petitions to each board member is a good idea. Also, it will help to start a letter-writing campaign, with scores of individualized letters pouring in from around the school district.

Once this groundwork has been laid, you'll have to present the issue from the floor of the school board meeting. For this role, choose a committed leader of the movement who is a good speaker and highly presentable. If he or she holds some prominent position in the community, that's even better. N O T E : A *reasonable* presentation is always preferable, whether you're writing or speaking to the school or school board officials. Those in public positions hear more than their share of emotional parents, and so you want to set yourself and your movement apart. What you're promoting makes very good sense, and your presentation must reflect that rationality.

Be sure to avoid finger pointing or accusing individuals or officials. Instead, talk in terms of a "serious problem in our system." Also, emphasize that your main concern is the "health and welfare of our children."

Finally, be well prepared to present your case. Use pertinent facts and statistics, such as those sprinkled throughout this book. Undoubtedly, you'll gather plenty more as you prepare for your presentation. The more information you have to back you up, the more reasonable you'll seem in arguing your case.

It's possible, of course, that this effort may fail. But more often, if you're well prepared and have plenty of parents behind you, you can expect results.

And positive results will work to the benefit not only of your child and his schoolmates, but also to the benefit of all future classes.

Exercise and good nutrition are obviously essential elements in any fitness program. But even more fundamental is the fostering of basic good health. The next two chapters will thus focus on some of the key health principles and practices that must undergird fitness.

CHAPTER TWELVE

The Hearts of Kids

To all outward appearances, Andy was a typical, healthy 17-year-old boy. From an early age, he had participated in playground and community sports, although his activity level had tapered off since junior-high school. He just hadn't been a good enough athlete to make any of his junior-high or high-school teams.

Also, Andy had always had plenty to eat—and therein lay a major root of his problem. From the time he was a preschooler, he had developed a taste for high-fat, high-cholesterol foods, including ice cream, shakes, fries, and cheeseburgers. His parents, who couldn't seem to get him interested in dieting, finally gave up and allowed him to eat practically anything he wanted. "After all," they rationalized, "some kids don't eat at all. At least we don't have to worry about malnutrition!"

As a result of these eating habits, Andy became, in a number of ways, a prototype of the many children in our society who are in serious danger of developing heart disease.

To understand what was happening inside Andy's cardiovascular system, it's necessary to begin at the beginning, during his infancy and toddlerhood. His heart, the center of his cardiovascular system, developed quite normally. His heart probably weighed about 24 grams, or 0.73 ounce, at birth and stayed that size for about four weeks. By this time, all the elements found in the adult electrocardiogram could also be found in Andy's.

Then his heart started to grow, doubling in size by the end of his first year of life. By age 5, the weight of Andy's heart had quadrupled and when he reached 9 years of age, his heart was six times the size of its birth weight.

As Andy went through his big growth spurt as a teenager, his heart followed along accordingly, reaching 220 grams at age 14. Now, at age 17, his heart is nearly full adult size, at just under 300 grams, or 10.5 ounces.

What about the rate at which Andy's heart was beating during this period of development? His average heart rate at rest dropped from about 140 beats per minute at birth, to 110 beats at age 1, to 98 beats at age 9, to 84 beats at age 14, to 72 to 80 beats at age 17.

As Andy's heart was growing, so was the rest of his circulatory system. The blood vessels developed and spread as the rest of his body grew, thus feeding and nourishing his new tissues with plenty of blood. Throughout this growth, his blood pressure remained within normal limits: his readings were 100/60 millimeters of mercury (mm Hg) at ages 2 to 6, 105/64 at age 9, 115/70 at age 14, and 120/75 now, at age 17.

What are the normal blood pressure limits for children? In my book *Overcoming Hypertension* (Bantam 1990), I recommend the following *upper* limits for normal blood pressure among youngsters of different ages:

- Age 5 and younger: 110/75
- Ages 6 to 10: 120/80
- Ages 11 to 14: 125/85
- Ages 15 to 18: 135/90

Clearly, Andy's measurement had remained well within these limits throughout his life.

But along with this normal cardiovascular growth, there were signs that things might not be quite perfect inside Andy's heart and blood vessels. For one thing, his total cholesterol had been on the high side from a very young age. When he was only 6 years old, a blood lipid test revealed that his cholesterol was 174 mg/dl—slightly above the average for his age and also above the 170 mg/dl that I consider the upper safe limit for a child.

When he was 10 years old, further testing showed that Andy's total cholesterol had risen to 185, and it had increased even further, to 200, when he was 16. In general, I encourage parents of children with total cholesterol levels between 170 and 185 to consider dietary counseling and to restrict the intake of foods high in cholesterol and saturated fats. Those with cholesterol levels above 185 should definitely seek professional counseling, and children with measurements of 200 or above may be candidates for medications that will lower their cholesterol.

NOTE: You may have heard or read that cholesterol levels below 200 mg/dl are desirable and safe—and that's usually quite true for adults. But the standards for children are different. A boy like Andy with cholesterol ranging from 174 to 200 throughout his youth will typically have much higher cholesterol levels when he reaches adulthood.

Furthermore, blood tests over the years indicated that this boy had relatively low levels of high-density lipoproteins (HDLs), also known as "good cholesterol." HDLs are linked to the ability of the body to clean excess cholesterol out of the vessels and prevent the buildup of plaque associated with atherosclerosis. So the higher your HDL level, the more protection you have against heart and vessel disease.

Specifically, Andy's HDL level was 36 mg/dl (normal for males is 45 mg/dl). At his age, this level is unusually low and indicates an increased risk for developing cardiovascular disease.

An important relationship between the total cholesterol and HDL readings—known as the total cholesterol to HDL cholesterol ratio—was also high. In numerical terms, Andy's ratio was 200/36, or 5.5, a number that placed him in a high-risk category. In children his age, the ratio should be less than 3.6. (At birth, the ratio is usually less than 2.0.)

Finally, the blood test revealed that another component of Andy's cholesterol, his "bad" cholesterol, or low-density lipoprotein (LDL), was relatively high at 142 mg/dl. (Normal is less than 130 mg/dl.)

What were the implications of these findings for Andy's future health? Our *precise* knowledge about what was going on inside Andy was still quite limited at age 16. He hadn't displayed any symptoms that would warrant a coronary arteriogram (an X ray of his blood vessels supplying blood to the heart) or other tests that would provide a definitive picture of his circulatory system.

But in light of various studies of children and young people, including the Bogalusa Heart Study of 1973–1975, it *is* possible to make some reasonable, educated guesses about what was happening inside Andy.

A LOOK INSIDE ANDY'S HEART AND BLOOD VESSELS

If we could actually have peered inside Andy's heart and blood vessels over the short duration of his life, here's what we might have found: During his preschool and early elementary school years, his arteries and veins remained relatively clean. That is, the fatty streaks that begin to line the vessels as a sign of early atherosclerosis (hardening or clogging of the arteries) hadn't yet taken hold. But the eating habits that Andy developed from a very early age stayed with him, and the resulting high cholesterol finally caused the fatty streaking to appear in his large arteries during his teenage years.

Andy's experience was similar to that of children evaluated as part of the Bogalusa Heart Study between 1973 and 1983 in Bogalusa, Louisiana. At one point in that investigation, autopsies were done on 35 young people, from birth to age 26, who had died from accidents, suicides, or homicides. The researchers found fatty streaks both in the coronary arteries leading into the heart and in the aorta, the large artery that originates in the heart and channels blood to other parts of the body.

Unfortunately, the fatty streaking of the vessels is only the beginning. Autopsies done on young men killed in action during the Korean and Vietnam wars have shown it only takes a few years for the clogging of the arteries to grow much worse.

Specifically, researchers William F. Enos, James C. Beyer, and Robert H. Holmes reported in 1955 that of 200 men averaging about 22 years of age who were killed in Korea, 77.3 percent had "some gross evidence of coronary disease." The evidence ranged from some thickening of the coronary arteries leading to the heart, to complete blockage of one or more of the main coronary branches. These investigators concluded that the blood fats that caused the plaque buildup and blockages most likely resulted from high-fat foods in the American diet.

A 1971 study of 105 soldiers of the same age killed in Vietnam presented a somewhat brighter picture. There, coronary atherosclerosis (clogging of the arteries leading to the heart) occurred in only 46 percent of the young men; narrowing of more than one vessel happened in 26 percent, and severe atherosclerosis occurred in 5 percent.

The researchers conducting the Vietnam study suggested that part of the difference in results was a difference in methods used to measure the buildup of fat in the vessels. But even when different methodologies are taken into account, I find it alarming that nearly half of the young men studied from Vietnam still had some evidence of atherosclerosis!

As for Andy, I suspect that he was squarely in the position of the young people whose autopsies showed that they were suffering from significant degrees of atherosclerosis. He not only had a high total cholesterol level, a low "good" (HDL) cholesterol level, and high-fat eating habits, he also exhibited other risk factors associated with heart disease. These included a father and grandfather who had been diagnosed with heart problems when they were in their late forties and early fifties.

Because Andy didn't display any particular symptoms of heart disease, such as chest pain, unusual fatigue, or shortness of breath, there was no need to pursue expensive diagnostic studies. Yet, we can predict with reasonable accuracy his future propensity to having a heart problem. Our method was to develop a cardiovascular risk profile—a procedure that I'll now discuss in some detail so that you can evaluate more intelligently Andy's risk and perhaps that of your own children.

RISK FACTORS THAT THREATEN THE HEARTS OF KIDS

The same risk factors that make adults more prone to cardiovascular disease are a threat to children—but these common risk factors also carry some special kid-related concerns for parents. As we move through these different factors, you'll see better why Andy was at such high risk. In addition, you'll get a clearer idea about how to protect the heart of your own child.

Kid Risk Factor #1. Cholesterol As I've already said, the general rules about cholesterol risk are these:

- *Low Risk*. Cholesterol levels should be 169 mg/dl or below.
- *Moderate Risk*. Any child with total cholesterol of 170 to 185 mg/dl should seek nutritional counseling and prepare to shift to a diet lower in saturated fats and cholesterol. Specifically, as the nutritional section of this book recommends, total daily intake of fats should be less than 30 percent of total calories; no more than 10 percent of fats should consist of saturated fats. Also, total daily intake of dietary cholesterol should be restricted to no more than 100 milligrams of cholesterol for every 1,000 calories consumed. (But in no event should the daily consumption of cholesterol exceed 300 milligrams.)
- *High Risk*. Those with cholesterol levels in the 186 to 200 mg/dl range will most likely have to embark on an even stricter low-fat diet under the supervision of a physician.
- *Very High Risk*. Those with cholesterol readings in excess of 200 mg/dl may have a genetic problem with their cholesterol and in some cases may have to use drugs to lower it.

In a recent attempt to refine according to sex the degree of risk associated with various cholesterol levels (*LabNote*, April 1990, p. 3), the National Cholesterol Education Program (NCEP) suggested these guidelines for boys and girls:

Boys, Ages 5 to 18. Those with cholesterol levels of 183 to 202 (the 75th percentile) are at moderate risk for heart disease; those with levels of 203 or higher (the 90th percentile) are at high risk.
Girls, Ages 5 to 18. Those with cholesterol levels of 192 to 216 (the 75th percentile) are at moderate risk for heart disease; those with levels of 217 or higher (90th percentile) are at high risk.

The NCEP arrived at these guidelines by identifying the percentile of boys and girls at various cholesterol levels and then matching those percentiles with the percentiles associated with known risk groups among adults. Specifically, the 75th percentile of adults was known to carry a moderate risk, while the 90th percentile of adults was linked to high risk.

NOTE: The 75th percentile of adults included cholesterol ranging from 200 to 240 mg/dl, while the 90th percentile was above 240. For children, the cholesterol values in the respective percentiles for both boys and girls were lower, as indicated in the above guidelines.

I have a couple of observations on the NCEP's approach: first of all, it's natural that the levels of cholesterol for the different risk groups would be lower for children than for adults. On this general point, I can understand the variation between children and adults.

On the other hand, I'm concerned that the NCEP has still set the moderate- and high-risk categories for children at such relatively high levels of cholesterol. The Bogalusa Heart Study and other authoritative investigations have determined that for purposes of determining risk of heart disease, children's cholesterol values should be even lower than the levels recommended by the NCEP—and I concur.

In the April 1990 issue of *Pediatrics,* for example, researchers from the Bogalusa Study reported that the 75th percentile of boys of different races, aged 5 to 17, had cholesterol ranging from 162 to 182, and boys in the 95th percentile had ranges of 195 to 218. Black and white girls, aged 5 to 17 years, also had lower cholesterol values: those in the 75th percentile ranged from 172 to 188, while those in the 95th percentile were measured at 196 to 229 mg/dl.

As you can see, the Bogalusa findings were lower than those in the NCEP study. Until other facts emerge, I prefer to be more conservative and stick with lower cholesterol values in determining risk. My conclusion: as I've already said, I regard all children, boys and girls, in the low-risk category if their cholesterol is 169 mg/dl or less. They move up to the moderate-risk category if their readings are in the 170 to 185 range, to the high-risk category if they are at the 186 to 200 level, and to the very high-risk category if cholesterol is above 200.

The Role of "Good" Cholesterol. Another important factor in evaluating children's cholesterol is the role played by the so-called good cholesterol, or high-density lipoproteins (HDL). For adults, it's generally accepted that relatively high levels of HDL are protective against heart disease. A popular evaluation of the impact of HDL is the total cholesterol to HDL ratio: the lower the ratio, the more protection the person gets.

For example, if a 45-year-old adult male has a total cholesterol of 200 mg/dl and HDLs of 50 mg/dl, his ratio is 200/50 or 4.0—a perfectly acceptable measurement. Those with such a ratio enjoy excellent protection from heart disease, according to our studies and those of other groups.

N O T E : While total cholesterol and its largest component, low-density lipoprotein (LDL), can usually be lowered with a low-fat, low-cholesterol diet, the same isn't true of HDL. To *raise* the HDL level, which should be the objective of everyone, the best, most effective approach is to increase the person's level of endurance-type aerobic exercise. The aerobic exercise programs described in chapter 8 are the best way to achieve this goal.

Do these general principles about HDL cholesterol apply to children as well as adults? From all indications, a high HDL level and low total cholesterol to HDL cholesterol ratio are important in the younger years as they are in later life. But there are some special considerations that have to be taken into account with children.

First of all, as we've already seen, total cholesterol levels should be lower in children than they are in adults. A 200 mg/dl measurement would be quite satisfactory for most adults, but would be cause for serious concern in a child.

Second, because total cholesterol levels in children are not as high as in adults, the ratio of total cholesterol to HDL cholesterol should be lower. For example, in my book *Controlling Cholesterol* (Bantam 1988), I recommended a ratio range of less than 3.6 for 20-year-old males, and less than 2.8 for 20-year-old females—far lower ratios than the 4.0 that is acceptable for a 45-year-old male!

What should be the recommended ratios for children?

For children under 5 years of age, the ratio for both boys and girls should be less than 2.5.

For older children, the following ratios and risk categories should apply:

Boys 5 to 14 Years Old
Excellent protection: < 2.9
Moderate risk: 2.9 to 3.3
High risk: 3.4 to 3.5
Very high risk: > 3.5

Girls 5 to 14 Years Old
Excellent protection: < 3.1
Moderate risk: 3.1 to 3.4
High risk: 3.5 to 3.7
Very high risk: > 3.7

Boys 15 to 19 Years Old
Excellent protection: < 3.7
Moderate risk: 3.7 to 5.1
High risk: 5.2 to 6.1
Very high risk: > 6.1

Girls 15 to 19 Years Old
Excellent protection: < 2.9
Moderate risk: 2.9 to 3.6
High risk: 3.7 to 4.2
Very high risk: > 4.2

As you can see from the above categories, Andy in our initial example fell into the high-risk category in total cholesterol *and* in the moderate category of the total cholesterol to HDL cholesterol ratio. Consequently, he was a prime candidate for further medical consultations and dietary adjustments, especially with an eye to lowering his intake of saturated fats and cholesterol.

Formulating risk levels for younger children is more challenging. For one thing, there are some special variations in HDL levels that occur among boys and girls of different ages, probably as a result of hormonal changes that occur with adolescence.

Specifically, from about ages 6 to 10, the average HDL levels are *lower* in girls than in boys, according to the Lipid Research Clinics Program Prevalence Study and other investigations. In a 1985 study from the Centers for Disease Control in Atlanta, for example, the average HDL level for boys aged 5 to 9 was 57, while the measurement for girls in that age range was 54. In the 10 to 14 age group, the boys' average dropped slightly to 56, and the girls' declined to 53.

But after age 14, the HDL picture changed dramatically: the average HDL levels of boys aged 15 to 19 dropped to 47, while the girls' held at 53. Other studies show that as the HDL levels for boys decline, the levels for girls increase above the prepubescent levels. This tendency of females to have higher HDL levels—and greater protection from heart disease—continues throughout the childbearing years.

As a result of the fluctuation of HDL levels among the younger age groups, it's difficult to provide specific numerical recommendations for these children. Consequently, I'd suggest that parents follow these recommendations:

• Before age 15, pay closest attention to the risks I've already described that are associated with *total* cholesterol levels.

• As a general guideline, *both* boys and girls younger than age 15 may be evaluated using the above risk categories for ratios of 15- to 19 year-old *girls*.

• Beginning with ages 15- to 19, distinguish between the risks of boys and girls by using the above ratios.

• At *all* ages, remember that regular aerobic exercise, such as walking, running, cycling, and swimming, will usually increase the levels of the protective HDL cholesterol. There is every reason to assume that HDL levels are important in the youngest years just as they are later, even if we don't yet have all the tools to measure the risks associated with various ratios.

Finally, how young and how often should your child be tested for cholesterol? Here are my recommendations:

• Before age 2, the general consensus is that children do not need to be tested. The only exception would be if one or more family members have a history of a serious hyperlipidemia (very high blood fat levels). In any event, very young children should not be placed on a restrictive diet because of the danger that too few fats and calories may impair general physical development. Medications to lower cholesterol in this group are not appropriate.

• Sometime between ages 2 and 6, I believe that all children should be tested for total cholesterol. The independent American Health Foundation follows this approach, although the American Academy of Pediatrics is less aggressive about this sort of testing.

In the view of the American Academy of Pediatrics, children in this age range only need to be tested if they have (1) a family history of early heart disease (i.e., a father or grandfather who has had a heart attack before age 50, or a mother or grandmother who has had one before age 60), or (2) a family history of cholesterol levels higher than 200 mg/dl. Then, if the child's cholesterol turns out to be 176 or higher, further tests may be conducted by the physician.

Certainly, it's important not to leap to any conclusions or lapse into panic when your child's cholesterol results come back. If the level is elevated, the test should be repeated at least once. Furthermore, some of the researchers in the Bogalusa Heart Study cautioned in the April 1990 issue of *Pediatrics* that screening children aged 5 to 17 for total cholesterol levels may fail to pick up many who have high levels of the "bad" cholesterol (LDL). Specifically, the investigation focused on youngsters with very high levels of cholesterol (i.e., those in the 95th percentile). Of these, the exam detected only 44 to 50 percent of those who had elevated LDL levels.

Despite the limitations on cholesterol screening for kids, I prefer to get the first test out of the way by age 6—and definitely by age 10. This way, any possible problems with the child's blood lipids will be picked up early, and also the family and child will have a baseline set of cholesterol measurements for the later years. (I'll deal further with testing for cholesterol in chapter 13. Dietary programs to lower cholesterol have already been covered in chapter 9.)

Risk Factor #2. Hypertension High blood pressure, or hypertension, has been generally accepted as an important risk factor for stroke, heart disease, and a variety of other ills. So it's important to detect any inclination toward hypertension as early as possible and take steps to lower the pressure and minimize the risks.

For children, the upper limits of normal blood pressure—as listed in my book *Overcoming Hypertension* and recommended by the 1988 Joint National Committee on Detection, Evaluation, and Treatment of High Blood Pressure—are as follows for different age groups (all measurements are stated in mm Hg):

Below Age 6: 110/75
Ages 6 to 10: 120/80
Ages 11 to 14: 125/85
Ages 15 to 18: 135/90

The first, or upper, number in the blood pressure measurement is known as the systolic reading. This reading indicates the pressure of the blood against the vessel walls as the heart is pumping. The second, or lower, number is the diastolic reading. It indicates the pressure of the blood between heartbeats, when the heart is resting. An elevation in *either* the systolic or diastolic measurement is cause for concern as a risk for hypertension.

The child's blood pressure gradually increases as he or she grows older, until adulthood has been reached. The upper limit of normal for an adult is now considered to be less than 140/90. A measurement above 140/90 moves the adult into the mild or borderline level of hypertension.

Of course, it's best that a child's blood pressure be below the upper limits of normal and be in the average range for his age group. What are these averages? A 1989 study by Dr. Myung K. Park of the department of pediatrics, University of Texas Health Science Center in San Antonio, with Shirley M. Menard (R.N.), found these *average* blood pressure readings in 1,554 very young children, aged 2 weeks to 5 years:

Ages 2 to 3 weeks: 78/47
Ages 1 to 5 Months: 95/60
Age 2 Years: 96/56
Age 5 Years: 104/58

As you can see, although systolic pressure went up steadily with age, the diastolic pressure (the lower reading) didn't change significantly after 1 month of age.

For older age groups, the Bogalusa Heart Study found the following average blood pressure values—figures that begin slightly lower than those in the Park-Menard investigation because of the normal variations found in the different study populations:

Ages 5 to 6: 96/60
Ages 7 to 8: 95/59
Ages 9 to 10: 98/61
Ages 11 to 12: 103/65
Ages 13 to 14: 107/67

An additional note: as documented previously in Andy's case, the average heart rate of children decreases as they grow older. In the Park-Menard study, the rate went down from the 2- to 3-week measurement of 153 beats per minute to the 5-year value of 97 beats per minute. Other studies on older children show that the typical average heart rate for 6 to 10 year olds is 95, for 10 to 14 year olds is 85, and for 14 to 18 year olds is 82. (The normal rate for adults varies from 60 to 80 beats per minute, although those for highly conditioned athletes may drop as low as 30 to 40 beats per minute.)

A few words should be said about *how* the blood pressure of children should be taken. In the Park-Menard study, an electronic device, the Dinamap Monitor, with an automatic inflation-deflation feature, was used in the doctors' offices. In accordance with sound medical practice, three readings were taken on all of the children 3 years old and older and on 87 percent of those younger than 3. Then the average of those readings was listed as the patient's blood pressure.

One of the biggest problems in getting a true blood pressure measurement with young children is finding a device with a cuff that fits the child's arm properly. Another is creating a relaxed atmosphere so that the child's pressure doesn't rise in response to stress or anxiety connected primarily with the exam itself. Pediatricians may have to experiment with a variety of cuffs for the upper arm and also try several different approaches to taking the pressure to ensure that the child remains calm—and thus avoids the "white coat" syndrome. This syndrome causes the patient's pressure to rise dramatically with any contact with an examining physician or even at a clinic.

There are also important maturity issues that arise in measuring a child's blood pressure. In a symposium concerning hypertension and pediatrics, Dr. Norman Siegel advised in the October 1985 issue of *Contemporary Pediatrics* that it's important to evaluate pressure of kids in the 11- to 18-year group with an eye "not to age, but to developmental changes."

"We have all seen the 14-year-old who is almost fully developed and the 14-year-old who has not begun to go through pubertal changes," says Dr. Siegel, echoing a theme I've already established earlier in this book. "So in that age group, going to a chart and looking at a normal standard for a given age can cause a real problem."

Instead, Dr. Siegel recommends that the Tanner stages or some other developmental yardstick be used for blood pressure: "I am much more worried about the prepubertal child who does not have much secondary sexual development and begins pushing 85 to 90 mm Hg diastolic than I am with the individual who has been doing a lot of isometrics and weight lifting and flexes his arm against the cuff every time I try to blow it up."

What are the prospects for a child who is diagnosed as hypertensive or borderline hypertensive—and what can be done about the situation? First of all, the fact that a young child, up to about 10 years of age, has elevated blood pressure doesn't mean that he'll necessarily be hypertensive as an adult. Studies that have tracked children over a number of years show only a mild correlation with hypertension later in life. On the other hand, a high reading as an older adolescent tends to correlate more closely with high readings as an adult.

Your pediatrician will prescribe the best course of action for the particular needs of your child. But here are some possibilities: In many cases of mild or borderline hypertension, a nondrug program such as the type I advocated for adults in my previous book *Overcoming Hypertension* will lower the readings. The features of such a program often include reducing the salt intake and otherwise adjusting the diet, taking off excess weight, and increasing the level of aerobic exercise.

In more serious circumstances, the child may have to be placed on medications to lower the blood pressure. But even in these cases, Dr. Siegel and other physicians have reported some success in being able to take these boys and girls off medications as they grow older.

Risk Factor #3. Smoking—Including Exposure to Passive Smoke In a statement released June 1, 1990, U.S. Surgeon General Dr. Antonia Novello, predicted that 5 million of today's children will die of smoking-related diseases in their later years if the current rate of tobacco use by young people continues.

More than 3,000 teenagers become smokers each day due primarily to peer pressure, a smoking family member, or successful advertising. Tobacco companies spend more than $3.3 billion annually to advertise and promote their products, often in ways that appeal to children and adolescents.

Because only a very small percentage of smokers begin smoking as adults, efforts at prevention must focus on children. There must be a ban on cigarette machines, a minimum age of 19 must be required for tobacco purchase (and this last must be enforced), and tobacco advertising must be curtailed if this problem of children smoking is to be controlled.

The danger exists on two major fronts: *passive* smoking (inhaling smoke from others) and *active* smoking (being the "villain" yourself!).

Passive Smoking. The evidence continues to accumulate that passive smoking—that is, the consistent inhaling of smoke by nonsmokers—will cause health problems. Here are some of the highlights:

• Passive smoking causes heart disease, according to findings of medical researcher Stanton Glantz of the University of California at San Francisco. In a paper prepared for the World Conference on Lung Health in Boston, Glantz explained, "Passive smoking reduces the ability of the heart to obtain and profit from oxygen. What you end up with is this: The blood doesn't carry oxygen well. The heart doesn't pump as well, and what oxygen gets to the heart isn't used as well."

• A 1988 study in the *American Journal of Epidemiology* reported a "small but measurable risk for arteriosclerotic heart disease" among nonsmokers who live with smokers.

• Two Swedish doctors reported in February 1990 that more than one-fourth of infant deaths linked to the sudden infant death syndrome (SIDS) could be attributed to smoking by mothers during pregnancy. Furthermore, pregnant women who smoked "moderately"—i.e., 1 to 9 cigarettes a day—were twice as likely as nonsmokers to lose infants to SIDS. Infants of those who smoked heavily (more than 10 cigarettes a day) faced a threefold risk of SIDS.

The main lesson from these and related studies: don't smoke around your children and work hard to maintain a smoke-free home.

Active Smoking. Although laws in 43 states prohibit the sale of tobacco to minors, children and teenagers buy $1.25 billion in tobacco products annually, according to a May 1990 report in the *Journal of the American Medical Association.* The study found that kids between the ages of 8 and 18 use 947 million packs of cigarettes and 26 million packages of smokeless tobacco each year.

To make matters worse, smoking among youngsters appears to be on the rise. The Gallup Youth Survey reported that the percentage of teenage smokers aged 13 to 15 increased from 7 percent in 1988 to 11 percent in 1989.

The danger in these trends has been well established in the medical literature: smoking is responsible for an estimated 390,000 deaths annually, or more than one out of every six deaths in the United States. The major cause of the smoking-related deaths are, first, heart and blood vessel disease and, second, lung cancer.

What is the mechanism by which smoking leads to cardiovascular disease? One concern is that smoking reduces the level of "good" cholesterol (HDL) in the blood and thereby undercuts the protection against heart disease. The famous Framingham Heart Study, conducted over several decades in Framingham, Massachusetts, has revealed significantly lower levels of HDLs among smokers, with an average decrease in HDL levels of 3 to 4 mg/dl in men and 5 to 6 mg/dl in women.

A subsequent study of children—done at the Institute for Health Promotion and Disease Prevention Research at the University of Southern California School of Medicine—confirmed the Framingham studies: the HDL levels decreased in 12- to 14-year-old children who began to smoke, but didn't decrease for those who refrained from smoking.

How Can You Discourage a Child from Becoming a Smoker? A number of studies have dealt with this problem and have come to the general conclusion that health education and other training can be extremely helpful. The Bogalusa Heart Study concluded that although "nearly all children try smoking at one time or another," programs designed to intervene and prevent the habit can succeed, especially with those who are merely experimenters. For example, children on the borderline can be convinced that cigarette smokers are insecure, shy, have "bad breath," or are otherwise socially inept—characteristics that no child wants applied to him.

In another investigation, reported in the June 1985 issue of the *American Journal of Public Health,* 689 adolescents who received health information and skills training had less inclination to smoke and used cigarettes less than those who were either provided with no information or were given the information without any instruction in how to use it. Among other things, the children in the program learned how to resist the urge or temptation to smoke, to deal with pressure from peers, and to solve other problems presented by smoking.

A particularly difficult group to steer away from smoking, however, are 16- to 17-year-old girls, 41 percent of whom are regular smokers, according to the Bogalusa study. These females have been shown to have a higher need for asserting their social power than adolescent men. As a result, they are more responsive to advertising that emphasizes personal freedom and success—such as "You've come a long way, baby." The most effective approach with these older girls, as well as with other adolescents, is to train and educate them at as early an age as possible. They can be influenced and persuaded more easily when they are still in the experimental stage with smoking.

Risk Factor #4. Sedentary Lifestyle As I explained in chapter 1, a long-term study performed at our Institute for Aerobics Research in Dallas has demonstrated that a sedentary lifestyle and a lack of physical fitness are associated with a shorter life span and also with a greater propensity toward cardiovascular disease.

In general, to reduce substantially all risks of mortality, all a person has to do is to walk 2 miles in less than 30 minutes at least 3 days a week. To be in the lowest-risk category, it's necessary to walk 3 miles in less than 45 minutes, five days a week, or to run 2 miles in less than 20 minutes, 4 days a week.

Although this study involved adult men and women, the same principles apply to children. In a related investigation, reported in 1988 in the *American Journal of Epidemiology,* researchers found that the fitness levels of children were directly linked to a healthy cardiovascular risk profile, including normal blood pressure readings, low and properly balanced cholesterol measurements, and a lack of obesity.

"There is consistent evidence in children and adults that physically fit and physically active individuals have more favorable risk profiles," the researchers noted (p. 937). As for guidelines for parents about children, they concluded, "These findings reinforce recommendations that children be provided with opportunities for regular exercise and suggest that increased activity and fitness in childhood may enhance adult cardiovascular risk profiles" (p. 939).

The message from these and other reports seems clear: starting a lifetime aerobic exercise program *now* will greatly reduce your child's risk of dying from sedentary living as an adult. If your child is inactive or out of shape, that problem can be corrected in a matter of weeks by testing him and then beginning one of the fitness programs outlined in chapter 8.

Risk Factor #5. Obesity Excess body fat is associated with cardio-vascular disease in adults and has been linked to adult-onset diabetes, high blood pressure, high cholesterol, and other coronary risk factors. Consequently, establishing good eating habits and weight levels in childhood can be an important step in laying the groundwork for adult health.

For example, a study reported in the September 1989 issue of *Nutrition & the M.D.* showed that the cholesterol levels of 56 obese children, ages 8 to 12, improved dramatically when they took off weight. These kids, who lost an average of 17 percent of their body weight, experienced significant decreases in their total cholesterol and triglyceride levels and significant increases in their HDL levels.

Other aspects of obesity in childhood—including how overweight kids can lose excess pounds—have been covered in chapter 9. Also, techniques for measuring your child's body fat percentage at home, including body fat standards for different age groups, have been described in chapter 7.

Risk Factor #6. Oral Contraceptives Oral contraceptive use by girls up to 17 years of age is associated with higher total cholesterol levels and lower levels of "good" cholesterol, reports the Bogalusa Heart Study in the March 1982 issue of the *American Journal of Public Health.*

These findings are generally consistent with studies of adult women, although in investigations of both adults and children, the levels of "good" (HDL) cholesterol respond inconsistently: sometimes they go up, and sometimes they go down.

As far as blood pressure is concerned, about 5 percent of adult women on the birth control pill experience mild hypertension (above 140/90) within five years. A 1979 study of adolescent females, aged 15 to 19, published in the December 1979 issue of the *Journal of Pediatrics,* found no significant difference in blood pressure among users and nonusers of the pill. But it's reasonable to assume that as some of these girls grow older, they will experience elevations in blood pressure.

Risk Factor #7. Family History of Heart Disease Finally, an ongoing, highly influential coronary risk factor among kids is their family history. Various studies have shown that a child with a parent or sibling who has had a heart attack before the age of 50 is at high risk of developing heart disease. Those with close relatives who have had heart attacks before age 60 are also at risk, although the risk decreases as the age of the relative in question increases.

The same principle applies when family history is applied to specific risk factors. So, a study conducted by the Mayo Clinic and the University of Michigan revealed that the HDL and LDL cholesterol levels in children between the ages of 6 and 16 become predictors of heart disease in their older relatives. The researchers concluded that the correlation between the children's and adult relative's risk profiles makes it possible to identify those kids whose cholesterol levels place them at higher risk for heart disease after they grow up.

In a few cases, there may be a rare genetic defect in the family called "familial hypercholesterolemia" (FH). In some form, this problem may strike 1 percent of the population, according to Dr. Scott Grundy, director of the Center of Human Nutrition at the University of Texas Health Science Center at Dallas. Kids with this genetic deficiency are at extreme risk for a fast buildup of fatty deposits in the blood vessels and for serious heart disease as children or young adults.

Unfortunately, it's not always possible to tell from family medical records exactly which children are at highest risk for this disease. That's one of the reasons I recommend initial cholesterol screening at a relatively young age, preferably by age 6.

Similarly, there's a strong genetic factor at work with hypertension. A number of investigations have demonstrated that certain people are *born* with a tendency toward high blood pressure. So any elevation in blood pressure in youth should be evaluated in light of blood pressure measurements in parents or other close relatives to see if a genetic factor is at work.

What's the best response if you and your physician determine that your child may have inherited a predisposition toward heart disease or toward one or more risk factors that are associated with cardiovascular problems? Certainly, you shouldn't just give up and decide, "There's nothing we can do about it." Instead, it's important to take the genetic determination as a warning signal and then work hard to lower the risk factors that can be influenced by diet, drugs, or other means. A family tendency toward heart disease can often be minimized by serious efforts in other areas.

Understanding the heart of your child can obviously be a challenging and complex topic. Still, it's important for parents to understand their youngster's general level of risk as a means to educate themselves about the health status of their children and to facilitate communication with the medical experts who should be monitoring the overall health of that boy or girl. Of course, in the last analysis it's the family doctor who will have to offer a final judgment on the meaning of the various risk factors in your child's life. But alert and informed parents can be a highly effective front line of defense.

Now, let's delve more deeply into the doctor's role: the various cardio-vascular risk factors we've been discussing can be identified most effectively as part of a regular pediatric medical exam. The frequency of these exams, and the different tests that should be performed by the physician, are the focus of our next chapter.

Monitoring Kid Fitness Through the Medical Exam: Some Tips for Working with Your Family Physician

The pediatrician or family physician is the one who must be in charge of any child's medical examinations. But it behooves all parents to know something about special areas of concern at different ages so that they can ask the right questions and become alert to possible problems before they come to the attention of the doctor.

Medical examinations by a physician should be a regular event during early childhood and then should be scheduled periodically, as needed, as the youngster grows older. Naturally, the precise schedule must be left up to the individual physician. But parents can expect to make several visits immediately following birth and after that, additional, regular checkups that may coincide with the immunization schedules for infants and children.

In fact, the required vaccinations are the first thing you should know about your child's medical checkups. Here are the basic shots that your child should receive and the times they should be given, according to the suggested schedule of the American Academy of Pediatrics:

AGE	VACCINES
2 months	DPT (diphtheria-pertussis-tetanus), OPV (oral poliovirus)
4 months	DPT, OPV
6 months	DPT, OPV in areas where polio risk is great
15 months	MMR (measles-mumps-rubella)
18 months	DPT, OPV, *Haemophilus influenzae* type b (Hib) vaccine (for meningitis and other infections)
4 to 6 years	DPT, OPV
On entry to middle school or junior high	MMR
14 to 16 years	TD (adult tetanus and diphtheria—this shot is to be repeated every 10 years throughout life)

When your child goes in to see the pediatrician for these shots, a general medical exam will often be conducted. The doctor will take the blood pressure, check the pulse, examine the various organs by feeling and pressing them, and in many cases will examine a urine specimen and take a sample of blood to check for cholesterol and other important blood components. More detailed information on the meaning of these tests can be found in chapter 12.

The doctor will be the one to make final determinations on the state of your child's health. But I think it's wise for you to be aware of at least the following three sensitive areas that you should monitor closely. By keeping track of your youngster's health, you may be in a position to schedule a checkup that can ward off problems before they become too serious.

These three major areas of parental monitoring that I think you should focus on are (1) your child's rate of growth in height and weight, (2) several age-related problems that your physician is likely to zero in on during his exam, and (3) the scheduling of gynecologic exams for certain teenage girls.

YOUR CHILD'S RATE OF GROWTH: WHAT'S THE NORMAL RANGE FOR HEIGHT AND WEIGHT?

Because medical exams become less frequent as a child gets older, it's often up to the parents to check whether their child is growing at a normal rate.

Some of the most useful tools for both physicians and parents to monitor the growth rates of boys and girls are the height and weight charts. As you look them over, compare them with the discussion in chapter 2 of normal rates of growth during different developmental stages.

To use the charts, you'll first choose the appropriate one, depending on the sex of your child. Then measure your child barefoot and weigh him unclothed or in underwear.

Next, you match his age with his height and weight in the two separate parts of each chart. The point at which the age-height and age-weight measurements cross the wavy lines will show you the percentile at which your child should be placed according to his height and weight. (You'll note that each of the wavy lines is connected to a percentile number on the edge of the chart.)

How do you interpret your child's standing on these charts? If he is in the 50th percentile range or above, you probably have nothing to be concerned about. Even if he's in a lower percentile, that may be perfectly normal too, especially if short stature runs in your family. On the other hand, if your child seems especially short according to the norms, if your family is of normal height, and also if your child's rate of growth seems to be declining, you should schedule an appointment with your physician.

For some abnormally small children, the administering of a synthetic growth hormone can correct early growth problems before they become irreversible. But to be in a position to obtain a prescription for hormones, you must be in touch with your physician. So if your child is older, say in elementary school, and you rarely see your doctor, it will be up to you to spot the potential problem and make that appointment.

DANGER AREAS FOR DIFFERENT AGES

As your child moves from one age or developmental stage to the next, some problems of childhood fade into the background and others appear. In this section, I want to alert you to a few of those changing conditions that your pediatrician will watch for at these different times of life. With this knowledge, you'll be in a better position to monitor your child between exams and also to ask questions during the medical evaluation.

Birth to 18 Months. Watch for misalignment of the back or eyes, tooth decay, and signs of nutritional inadequacies.

Ages 2 to 6. Watch for vision problems, tooth decay, poor alignment of

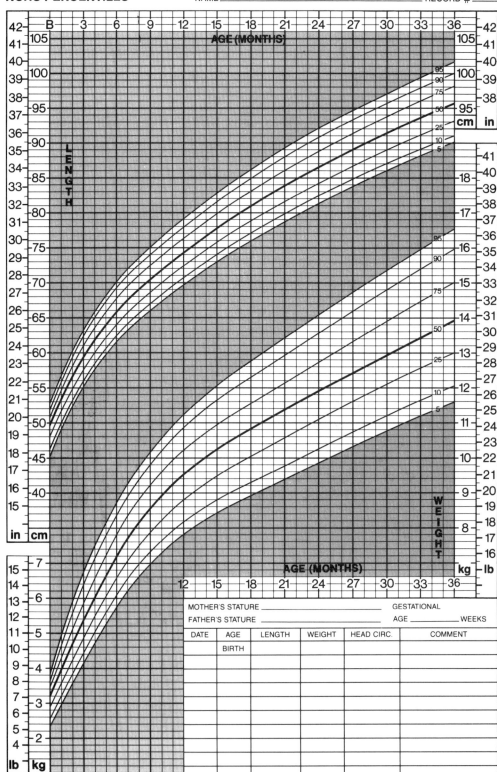

GIRLS: BIRTH TO 36 MONTHS
PHYSICAL GROWTH
NCHS PERCENTILES*

NAME _____ RECORD # _____

Ross
Growth &
Development
Program

HEIGHT AND GROWTH CHARTS FOR GIRLS.

AGE (MONTHS)

LENGTH

WEIGHT

MOTHER'S STATURE _____ GESTATIONAL
FATHER'S STATURE _____ AGE _____ WEEKS

DATE	AGE	LENGTH	WEIGHT	HEAD CIRC.	COMMENT
	BIRTH				

* Adapted from: Hamill PVV, Drizd TA, Johnson CL, Reed RB, Roche AF, Moore WM: Physical growth: National Center for Health Statistics percentiles. AM J CLIN NUTR 32:607–629, 1979. Data from the Fels Longitudinal Study, Wright State University School of Medicine, Yellow Springs, Ohio.

© 1982 Ross Laboratories

GIRLS: 2 TO 18 YEARS
PHYSICAL GROWTH
NCHS PERCENTILES*

NAME _____ RECORD # _____

Ross
Growth &
Development
Program

| MOTHER'S STATURE _____ FATHER'S STATURE _____ | | | | |
DATE	AGE	STATURE	WEIGHT	COMMENT

AGE (YEARS)

STATURE

WEIGHT

AGE (YEARS)

HEIGHT AND GROWTH CHARTS FOR GIRLS.

95
90
75
50
25
10
5

cm in
in cm
lb kg
kg lb

*Adapted from: Hamill PVV, Drizd TA, Johnson CL, Reed RB,
Roche AF, Moore WM: Physical growth: National Center for Health
Statistics percentiles. AM J CLIN NUTR 32:607-629, 1979. Data
from the National Center for Health Statistics (NCHS), Hyattsville,
Maryland.

© 1982 Ross Laboratories

BOYS: BIRTH TO 36 MONTHS
PHYSICAL GROWTH
NCHS PERCENTILES*

NAME _____ RECORD # _____

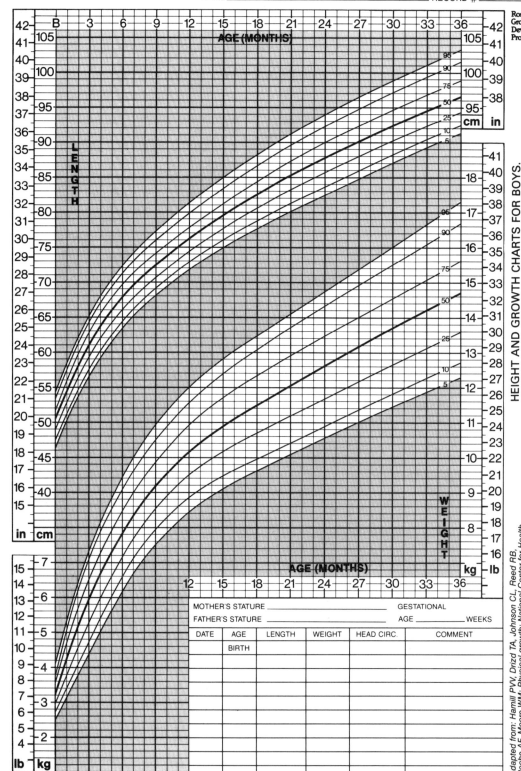

Ross
Growth &
Development
Program

HEIGHT AND GROWTH CHARTS FOR BOYS.

AGE (MONTHS)

LENGTH

WEIGHT

MOTHER'S STATURE _____ GESTATIONAL

FATHER'S STATURE _____ AGE _____ WEEKS

DATE	AGE	LENGTH	WEIGHT	HEAD CIRC.	COMMENT
	BIRTH				

*Adapted from: Hamill PVV, Drizd TA, Johnson CL, Reed RB, Roche AF, Moore WM: Physical growth: National Center for Health Statistics percentiles. AM J CLIN NUTR 32:607-629, 1979. Data from the Fels Longitudinal Study, Wright State University School of Medicine, Yellow Springs, Ohio.

© 1982 Ross Laboratories

BOYS: 2 TO 18 YEARS
PHYSICAL GROWTH
NCHS PERCENTILES*

NAME _____ RECORD # _____

Ross
Growth &
Development
Program

HEIGHT AND GROWTH CHARTS FOR BOYS.

DATE	AGE	STATURE	WEIGHT	COMMENT

MOTHER'S STATURE _____ FATHER'S STATURE _____

AGE (YEARS)

STATURE

WEIGHT

*Adapted from: Hamill PVV, Drizd TA, Johnson CL, Reed RB,
Roche AF, Moore WM: Physical growth: National Center for Health
Statistics percentiles. AM J CLIN NUTR 32:607-629, 1979. Data
from the National Center for Health Statistics (NCHS), Hyattsville,
Maryland.

© 1982 Ross Laboratories

the back or teeth, premature loss of teeth, a tendency to breathe through the mouth (which may indicate upper respiratory problems).

Ages 7 to 12. Note possible vision disorders (such as an inability to read easily or see objects at a distance), hearing problems, tooth decay, tooth malalignment, breathing through the mouth.

Ages 13 to 18. Watch for symptoms of depression (such as listlessness, loss of appetite, excessive sadness), abnormal bereavement, tooth decay, and tooth malalignment. Also, this is the age to begin to watch closely for suicide risk factors, such as recent divorce of parents, separation of parents, unemployment of parent, depression, alcohol or other drug abuse, serious medical illness, and recent bereavement. Signs of child abuse, neglect, or abnormal bereavement are always of great concern to the examining physician, regardless of the patient's age.

You don't have to know what to *do* about these danger signals. That's the doctor's job. Rather, I mention these factors just to give you a handy checklist so that you'll know when a visit to the pediatrician is in order.

GYNECOLOGIC EXAMS FOR CERTAIN GIRLS

Most girls continue to see a pediatrician well into their teenage years, but soon, the time arrives for the first gynecologic exam. Some guidelines that have been widely accepted for the timing of a first exam are these:

- The girl has become sexually active.
- She is complaining about some gynecologic problem.
- She has reached age 16.

It's especially important for sexually active teenage girls to begin to see a physician regularly because intercourse raises the risk of many diseases, including cancer of the cervix. An annual Pap smear can detect this problem at an early stage, at which point the problem is correctable.

As you can see, a number of the problems we've been discussing in this survey of highlights of the kid's medical exam deal with the emotions. Throughout childhood, the pressures and stresses of life can weigh heavily and trigger serious health problems. For this reason, in the next few pages I want to concentrate on the child's way to a low-stress lifestyle.

CHAPTER FOURTEEN

Your Child's Way to a Low-Stress Lifestyle

Alan was a 12-year-old star athlete and musician—who also suffered from bleeding ulcers. The main cause of his problem, according to his pediatrician and a family therapist, was tension between his parents, who were in the process of getting a divorce.

As they fought over custody of the boy, Alan became extremely tense. The many uncertainties in his life were quite literally overwhelming him. Consequently, his performance in the classroom and on the playing field declined.

Alan was particularly worried that he would not be able to compete in a championship soccer game because of an impending visit he had to make to one of his parents. Even without the family problems, he was overloaded with activities and responsibilities and just didn't have the inner resources to deal with the extra stresses being imposed by his parents. His inability to handle the pressure finally emerged physically in the form of a bleeding ulcer.

The solution: the doctor and therapist met with both parents and explained what a devastating effect their squabbling was having on their son. The discussion centered on the stress points and events in Alan's life. Impressed by this explanation, the parents agreed to do everything possible to keep their son's life on a more even keel during their marital discussions. As a result, his medical problems improved.

Alan's case demonstrates several important themes among today's children:

- Outside pressure can have a direct impact on a child's health and fitness.
- A child's academic and athletic performance is almost sure to decline as family stresses rise.
- Parents have the most control over the degree of stress that their child must face.

Again, we return to our well-worn but valid theme that it's the parent's responsibility to identify and deal with their child's stress. More often than not, parents establish the schedules and create the family environments that raise or lower the pressures faced by a child. This is particularly true with younger children like Alan, who are more under parental control than those who are older.

In this chapter, I want to provide you with some guidelines that will enable you to draft a kind of *stress profile* of your child. You should first know the major pressure points in your home and your youngster's schedule and also the way that boy or girl is reacting to those pressures.

Various studies have revealed that the kinds of stresses that children have the most trouble with are different from those that plague adults. In particular, a 1985 study in *Pediatric Annals* reported that children are most concerned about a lack of respect or loss of self-esteem among peers or classmates. For example, it bothers them deeply if they are the last chosen for a team or if they are not invited to a party or to be a member of some "in" group.

Another set of stress factors centers on problems in the family. Like Alan in our example above, many children suffer physical and emotional problems when their parents are going through a divorce. Also, they may experience severe stress when they feel they aren't allowed to spend enough time with their parents or when they sense their parents are being particularly unfair or abusive. The death of a parent or other close family member is another event that may produce heavy stresses on a child.

Finally, children may also suffer the consequences of stress when they experience major uprootings or dislocations, such as moving to another town or changing schools. Those in the early elementary school years may revert to bedwetting or other infantile behavior if they begin having problems with a new teacher or otherwise have difficulty fitting into a new environment.

What signals should you look for as you try to evaluate the pressure that your child is under? Here are some of the main "stress symptoms" that researchers have identified as indicators that children are at risk for serious physical and emotional ills.

Stress Symptom #1. An Increase in Illnesses A 1971 study by Dr. Mary Ann Lewis and Dr. Charles Lewis of the UCLA Center for the Health Sciences reported that children under 7 years of age with significant behavioral and psychosocial problems also accounted for most of the visits to the school nurse. Their main complaint: stomachache.

Those over age 7 with similar emotional problems also had a relatively high number of trips to the nurse. But in their case, the main complaint was headache.

Other studies have shown that children with significant psychosocial problems also develop a relatively large number of medical problems like streptococcal disease and various respiratory ills.

Stress Symptom #2. An Increase in Accidents and School-Related Problems Family pressures on a child may also emerge in accidents and other outside problems, such as difficulties at school. That was the finding of a 1990 study by Deborah Dawson of the National Center for Health Statistics. She discovered that children who live in "nontraditional families"—that is, single-parent households, those run by stepparents, and the like—have a 20 to 30 percent greater risk of an injury than those from two-parent families. Also, children in mother-headed families were 50 percent more likely to have asthma.

On the school front, children living in families headed by mothers, or mothers and stepfathers, were 40 to 75 percent more likely to have to repeat a grade than those living with both biological parents. Finally, children from broken marriages were more than 70 percent more likely to have been expelled or suspended from school.

Stress Symptom #3. Aberrant Behavior by Latchkey Children A 1989 study in *Pediatrics* reported that among the nearly 5,000 eighth-grade students who were studied, the latchkey child—that is, one who spends much of his time alone at home, perhaps because both parents work—was at higher risk for use of alcohol, tobacco, and marijuana. Specifically, the students who took care of themselves for 11 hours or more a week were at twice the risk for substance abuse as those who did not take care of themselves at all.

Stress Symptom #4. An Increase in Physical Complaints Unrelated to Specific Injuries by Young Athletes Sometimes, the pressures of an overwhelming sports training schedule or of too-intense competition may cause Elite Child Athletes to experience unusual aches and pains. The distress may even lead them to say that they want to quit the sport.

It's important for physicians, parents, and coaches to look closely for causes of these complaints. If the problem can be traced to a specific athletic injury that can be treated, well and good. But more often, these generalized complaints may indicate a mental fatigue with the athletic experience.

A remedy that often works in this case: *rest!* Overtraining will make any young child who is most interested just in having fun want to run in the opposite direction. But if some of the pressure can be lifted and the youngster can be given an opportunity to relax and pursue another activity for a week or so, the enthusiasm may return. And frequently, the physical ailment will disappear.

Stress Symptom #5. Deepening Depression or Other Signs That Life Has Little Meaning The ultimate symptom of stress is suicide, a problem that experts in pediatrics have deemed an epidemic in our age. Adolescent and young adult suicides have tripled in the last 25 years. Furthermore, according to the latest statistical compilations available, the suicide rate for white males aged 15 to 19 increased by 60 percent in the decade between 1970 and 1980.

With such ominous trends among our youth, any signals that a child may have "had it" with life should be taken seriously and professional help should be sought immediately. Here are some of the warning signs that have been published by the American Academy of Pediatrics:

- Noticeable changes in the child's eating or sleeping habits
- Unexplained or unusually severe violent or rebellious behavior
- Withdrawal from family or friends
- Running away
- Persistent boredom and/or difficulty concentrating
- Drug and/or alcohol abuse
- Unexplained decline in the quality of schoolwork
- Unusual neglect of appearance
- Radical personality change
- Psychosomatic complaints
- Preoccupation with themes of death
- Giving away prized possessions
- Expressing suicidal thoughts, even jokingly

If you observe any of these behaviors or tendencies in your child, the American Academy of Pediatrics suggests that you take these four simple steps:

Step 1: Listen. Don't dismiss the youngster's problems as trivial because to him they are extremely important and are the source of his unhappiness.

Step 2: Be Honest. If you're worried about your child, tell him. You won't push him over the edge to suicide just by asking questions.

Step 3: Share Your Feelings. Let your youngster know he's not alone—that you and others have felt sad or depressed at times. And furthermore, you've always found a way out of those negative feelings.

Step 4: Get Help. After identifying what you believe may be suicidal tendencies, find a physician, psychologist, or another qualified professional to take over the treatment of your child. Above all, don't wait for the problem to disappear or fade away. It may be that the depression will lift; but there's also a chance that it will get worse, and the young person may decide that suicide is the only answer.

YOUR CHILD'S STRESS PROFILE

You now have enough information to begin to do a preliminary evaluation of the stresses in your child's life and how well he is responding to them. I'm not suggesting that you try to become a therapist or psychologist—just that you gather some basic information and start formulating a picture of your child's mode of handling of stress.

Here's a form you can use to evaluate your child's stress profile:

I. Stress Factors in My Child's Life
    Family-Related
        Divorce
        Presence of stepparent, single-parent household, or other nontraditional
            situation at home
        Parent-child arguments
        Parent-parent fights
        Latchkey child
        Death of loved one
        Other
    School-Related
        Problems with peers
        Drop in grades

        Sports stresses
        Problems with teachers
        Other
      Dislocation-Related
        Move to new home
        Move to new school
        Other
II. Stress Symptoms in My Child's Life
        Physical illnesses
        Emotional complaints
        Accidents
        Acting out at school
        Frequent visits to nurse at school (once a week or more)
        Drug, tobacco, or alcohol use
        Loss of interest in relatively long-standing athletic involvements
        Suicidal expressions
        Other
III. My Evaluation of How the First Two Parts of This Profile May Relate

Now, here's how to personalize this profile for your child. First, you should list those factors that are undoubtedly causing stress, such as the ones I listed earlier. In the second part of the profile, list those symptoms possibly related to stress. Finally, in the third part, try to draw connections between the two lists.

If you determine that your child is having some relatively serious symptoms, like suicidal tendencies, physical illnesses, or destructive behaviors, such as low grades or fights at school, then you should seek professional help. If the symptoms are less severe—such as periodic irritability or occasionally feeling too pressured or overloaded—you should suggest ways to make adjustments before the problems become too serious.

Remember, you have a great deal of control over your child's life, perhaps almost total control if the child is in the Early Team Phase (roughly ages 8 to 10) or younger. So it's up to you to take decisive steps to reduce those stress factors once you've identified them.

CHAPTER FIFTEEN

An Intelligent Approach to the Sports Scene

Sports of all types offer tremendous physical and psychological benefits for kids—and also the promise of deep satisfaction for parents.

Unfortunately, however, the promise often falls short of reality. In too many cases, the underlying reason for participating in the sport becomes distorted or forgotten as a team marches toward the league championship or as an exceptional child begins to demonstrate abilities that might take him or her to the high-school team, a college athletic scholarship, or even beyond.

What are the reasons that kids should participate in sports? Remember what the 6- to 10-year-old children said in a study I cited earlier. The top motivational factors for these kids were

- "Learn to do my best"
- "Learn and improve skills"
- "Have a coach to look up to"
- "Get stronger and healthier"

Responses like "win games" and "become popular" were at the bottom of the list. Young children, in other words, seem to have a more balanced view of sports participation than many adults! In this regard, I'm reminded of several examples that illustrate better than any admonitions or formulas the dangers that parents face on the kid sports scene.

- In one Little League, the parents fell into the habit of arguing incessantly, whether it was the coaches with the umpires, the parents of one team with the parents of another, or coaches and parents with kids who didn't seem to be performing up to par. The bottom line was that no matter what the children wanted, the parents wanted to *win*. Mothers and fathers wanted those championship trophies even more than their sons and daughters.

The final result: as the playoffs approached, a coach and umpire got into a fistfight. The parents of the opposing teams then got into a violent shouting match, which came close to qualifying as a riot. And the head of the Little League in the area canceled the championship playoffs. Not only did no one receive a trophy but the children were left disappointed, discouraged, and unmotivated to try again next season.

- In a local 12-and-under tennis championship, one parent accused another of illegally coaching a child (which is technically an infraction of the rules in U.S. Tennis Association [USTA]–sanctioned tournaments). The parents argued, ended up sitting on opposite sides of the viewing area, and refused to speak to one another when they met in later tournaments. Needless to say, these attitudes increased the stress and pressure on the children and decreased the enjoyment of activity.
- A junior-high-school football coach sent a player back into a game even though the boy was complaining of a problem with his ankle. "Push through that pain, Joe," the coach urged. "Shake it off. We need you in there." The result: Joe sprained his ankle badly and was on crutches for the rest of the season.

If it seems that I'm pointing the finger at parents and coaches of children on competitive athletic teams, you're right—I *am* pointing the finger! For the most part, kids of any age will do what the respected adult in charge tells them to do, even if it hurts. Parents and coaches, who are supposed to be monitoring children to watch for signs of a physical or emotional problem, must step in before any injury results, or before discouragement sets in.

Children who are interested enough and good enough to play on teams and become competitive in a sport have a great opportunity to develop a strong sense of personal identity and to stay in top physical shape. Because of their special gifts, they are a valuable commodity in our society. Consequently, it's up to the adults around them, especially the parents, to protect them.

To understand some of the ways that parental actions and attitudes can and will enhance a child's fun and enjoyment in athletic competition, you may want to consider how the following "principles for responsible sports parents" apply to you.

PRINCIPLES FOR RESPONSIBLE SPORTS PARENTS

The principles listed here can also be used as a kind of checklist to evaluate your attitudes and actions in your child's sports career. These points are certainly not exhaustive; you can probably think of others that apply to your special situation. But at least these guidelines should help you get started in the right direction with your young athlete.

#1. Focus on What Pleases Your Child in Sports, Not on What Pleases You

A corollary to this point: Don't try to relive your youth through your child. This may seem a hackneyed piece of advice, but year after year, generation after generation, I see parents investing a large part of their adult identity, their very being, in how well their youngster does in sports. That attitude is *deadly* to the child's enjoyment and also to the parent's relationship with the young person.

Another corollary: Encourage your child to choose the sport that *he* likes, not simply one that you like. If you pressure your youngster to be a tennis player or golfer because you like those games—and if he really wants to play baseball or basketball—you'll lose in two respects. First, he probably won't be a very good tennis player or golfer, even if he seems to have all the physical equipment. The reason is that the mental requirements, including the commitment to the game, won't be there. Second, you'll be distracting your child from a sport that he might really excel in simply because he likes it.

#2. Keep Your Child's Developmental Age in Mind

Suppose your youngster seems to be having trouble shooting baskets, hitting a baseball, moving with agility around an athletic field, or paying close attention to fixed plays or strategies a coach is trying to teach. In such a case, ask yourself, "How old is my child—really?" What's his *developmental* age, not just his chronological age?

Refer back to chapters 2 and 3 for descriptions of the characteristics of children in the six different developmental phases. It can be quite comforting to know that your 9-year-old, who is having trouble focusing on those complex soccer strategy instructions, is still mostly in the third, or Fitness Phase, of development and not fully into the Early Team Phase. With that insight, the frustration that a parent feels at what looks like a bad attitude or inadequate physical abilities, may be replaced by greater patience and understanding.

#3. Emphasize Good Old-Fashioned Sportsmanship More and more, youth coaches and sports leagues are coming to see the value of good sportsmanship among young athletes. Trophies and other awards for exemplary attitudes and conduct are being offered increasingly to counter the image of pro hockey players who get into fights regularly on the ice or pro tennis players who verbally abuse officials and throw their rackets.

As a parent, you can reinforce this trend by praising your child as much or more if he wins the sportsmanship award, as if he is named the most valuable player. And there's good reason for this approach, beyond the obvious benefits of promoting good behavior.

For one thing, when you, the parent, emphasize sportsmanship, you'll automatically begin to put a higher priority on enjoyable, ethical participation, and less value on the win-at-any-cost attitude. Perhaps just as important, the qualities that make a child a well liked and respected member of the team are the same qualities that will help him get along with colleagues and bosses in his later career. These are among the most important values that any parent can promote.

#4. Monitor Your Child's Physical and Emotional Well-Being during Practices and Competition Often, it's the alert parent who first picks up signs of physical injury or emotional damage. If your child complains of persistent or sharp pain, you should immediately take him to his physician for a checkup. You should also seek professional help if he experiences any marked emotional change, such as excessive secrecy or depression.

A little later in this chapter we'll be dealing in more detail with sports injuries and related conditions. For now, just remember that parents are the child athlete's first line of defense against injury or illness.

THE BENEFITS OF ATHLETIC ACHIEVEMENT

Although there are many dangers to intense athletic activity among children, there are also at least two major benefits—*if* the play remains fun and the outcomes of competition are kept in perspective.

As I see it, the first main advantage of a high level of sports participation through childhood is that the young athlete is in a position to develop high levels of self-confidence. Just making a sports team or being accepted as a peer by other good players is enough to cause the self-esteem of most children to rise significantly. Also, the support of a good coach and the applause and praise of parents and other adults reinforces the sense that "I'm good at what I do, and others know it."

In many cases, achievement in athletics also fosters habits and attitudes that may carry over to other areas of life. Learning to focus on a task, develop skills through hard work and training, and expect success as a result of thorough preparation are all qualities that are potentially transferable to schoolwork, leadership positions, and other extracurricular endeavors.

The second major benefit of sports participation is that the boy or girl automatically has a means to maintain high levels of physical fitness throughout childhood and adolescence. As you already know, many children tend to drop out of sports beginning at about age 10, and the exit intensifies during early adolescence. But those who are committed to one or more sports must stick consistently over the years to a training regimen if they want to continue to compete. This built-in motivation to stay in shape is a major benefit of ongoing sports participation.

Of course, if a child hopes to succeed as an elite athlete, he must put something extra into his training. There should be a continued healthy sense of perspective on winning and losing, and certainly sportsmanlike conduct. But the very best athlete will take things one step further. He will try to gain an edge in his fitness training, as well as in his development of sports skills. This means going beyond the basic fitness programs outlined in chapter 8 and embarking on a special regimen designed to place him a cut above his competitors.

THE ELITE CHILD ATHLETE: SOME TRAINING TIPS

Athletes in practically any sport can benefit from following a basic fitness routine, such as those described in chapter 8. There, you learned how to develop greater aerobic or endurance capacity and also how to build a basic foundation of muscle strength and flexibility. All athletes need this basic level of fitness, both to enhance their performance and also to minimize the risks of injury.

But basic fitness is only the beginning for those who want to excel in sports. First of all, the levels of aerobic fitness given in chapter 8 would not be adequate for many sports that require significantly higher levels of endurance. For those who want to pursue those higher levels of aerobic fitness, my book *The Aerobics Program for Total Well-Being* contains charts to guide you. Second, the kind of strength a child needs as an athlete in a particular sport demands an additional and quite different kind of training.

The Secrets of Specificity and Overloading. One secret to successful strength training in sports can be illustrated by this story shared with me by Dr. Charles Sterling, the executive director of the Institute for Aerobics Research in Dallas. It seems that two boys made a high-school track-and-field squad as shot-putters and, at least to most outward appearances, they followed similar training programs. Both lifted weights regularly and both spent similar amounts of time on the athletic field practicing their technique. But there were a couple of major differences in the two boys. In the first place, one was considerably smaller than the other and, in the second place, the smaller boy could consistently toss the shot farther than the bigger boy!

Puzzled by this situation, the coach took a closer look at their training routines. He noted that the bigger boy, as he expected, could lift more weights during his strength-training workout than the smaller one. But there was a slight difference in the type of exercise routines they followed.

The bigger boy did regular bench presses by lying flat on his back and pushing the weights straight up away from his chest. The smaller boy, in contrast, did his bench presses on an incline bench. That is, he pushed the weights upward, but in a direction that was halfway between a flat-on-the-back bench press and an overhead lift.

The answer to the puzzle now became clear to the coach. The smaller boy was throwing better because he had chosen a form of exercise that closely mimicked the actual throwing of the shot. As a result, he was doing a better job of developing shot-putting muscles than the bigger boy.

This story illustrates the first basic principle of effective fitness conditioning for sports: *specificity training*. This concept refers to the need for top athletes to do exercises that strengthen and improve the specific movements required for their sport.

A second basic principle of sports conditioning—which is related to specificity—is what's often called *overloading*. This idea involves doing enough work, such as repetitions of a certain exercise, to fatigue the muscle. When the muscle becomes tired and then recovers, greater strength results.

There are several ways to create an overload on muscles: (1) increasing resistance, (2) increasing repetitions, (3) decreasing the rest time between sets, and (4) increasing the number of training sessions per week.

Following this principle, many athletes try to increase gradually the number of repetitions they do of a calisthenics exercise, such as push-ups or sit-ups, until their muscles become tired. At first, for instance, it may only take 20 repetitions of a push-up to become tired. But with regular workouts, that fatigue threshold may move up to 30, 50, or even more repetitions.

Now, if you put specificity and overloading together, you can see that doing strength exercises that increase your strength in executing movements required by the sport will most likely produce improved performance. A case in point: if you have the basic hand-to-eye coordination necessary to hit a baseball, doing exercises that mirror the batting motion by using increasing resistance should make you a better hitter.

One technique would be to buy one of the many rubbery stretch exercisers that can be purchased in many sporting goods stores and attach it to a hook or heavy piece of furniture. Then connect the other end of the stretch device to a bat or a short handle that feels like a bat, and begin "batting" with it until you become fatigued. Also, these exercises should be done as quickly as possible to replicate the batting motion.

A similar kind of specificity routine might be devised using light dumbbells or other free weights. The idea would be to determine the important motions in the sport and then use the weights in high repetitions to mirror those movements.

How old should a child be before he or she begins to do specificity exercises by using exercise equipment such as stretch devices or weights? As I've indicated in earlier sections of this book, the current research suggests that prepubescent children—those as young as 8 to 10 years old—can significantly increase their muscle power and strength by systematic strength training, including closely supervised workouts with weights and other equipment.

But, again, before any parents plunge into a massive weight program in an effort to provide their kids with an edge in sports, I want to remind you of some caveats:

• Power lifting with heavy weights, as opposed to strength training with relatively light weights, should be avoided at all costs. Trying to lift too much can seriously damage the growing bones of children and may injure the growth plates.

• Any young child who uses weight-training or other exercise equipment should do so only under the strict supervision of an adult who understands the techniques and knows the dangers to youngsters.

• The use of weights or other equipment should be pursued in conjunction with the principles of specificity and overloading that we've already discussed. It may be a waste of time to concentrate on a set of exercises that has little or nothing to do with the child's favorite sport.

BANISHING THE SPECTER OF SPORTS INJURIES: A BRIEF GUIDE TO UNDERSTANDING AND PREVENTION

A study by the U.S. Consumer Products Safety Commission provided the following overview of injuries among young people:

- Up to age 4, the head and face area are the most commonly injured part of the body.
- From ages 5 to 14, the arms are the most often injured.
- For ages 15 and older, the knees and ankles are hurt most frequently—probably a reflection of the damage resulting from contact sports.

Many of the injuries to the head could be minimized or prevented by wearing protective gear, like bicycle helmets, protective goggles, or batting helmets. The medical literature is full of studies and admonitions about these dangers. But even when the protective equipment is sound, other injuries may occur in sports because of such factors as overuse or poor training techniques.

The Overuse Issue. The term *overuse* refers here to using a part of the body so often that injury results. The two most common types of overuse injuries among children are those involving throwing motions and swimming.

In a 1981 study of young baseball players, researchers found that 20 percent of the pitchers under 12 years old had elbow pain, 48 percent of 13- to 14-year-olds had the same pain, and 58 percent of pitchers 15 or older had pain.

What causes the elbow pain? During the throwing motion, shearing forces are put on the elbow as the arm whips over the shoulder and down in front of the body. Although damage may occur to growth plates in the arm, complete recovery often is possible—*provided the child stops throwing* and rests the arm for an extended period.

A similar overuse problem may develop with young competitive swimmers who begin to experience pain in their shoulders. One study in August 1985 in *The Physician and Sportsmedicine* reported that there was a strong correlation between a lack of flexibility and the incidence of "swimmer's shoulder." Also, male swimmers often had shoulder pain when they increased the intensity and duration of their weight training. In short, the key to prevention is not overdoing it, and the best cure is often rest.

The Specter of Steroids. Finally, a word on steroid use. An estimated half million high-school boys have used steroids, sometimes in an effort to enhance their athletic performance and sometimes just with the objective of looking more muscular and "manly." Unfortunately, those who take these habit-forming drugs often do permanent damage to their bodies, including throwing their blood lipids completely out of balance. The "good" cholesterol (HDLs) in these boys tends to drop precipitously, and they become candidates for heart attacks at a young age.

The increased number of athletic screening programs for steroid and other drug users, along with the health dangers that accompany this practice, make this an eminently stupid choice for anyone. These substances are the shortest way to end an athletic career as well as a life.

The magnitude of this problem was tragically illustrated in an article entitled "Steroids Claims Our Son's Life," published in *The Physician and Sportsmedicine* in August of 1990.

On August 7, 1989, the parents of an 18-year-old boy found the body of their son hanging from a tree by their front door. Five empty bottles of Dionabol (methandrostenolone), a steroid drug, were found in his car.

Investigation of his death revealed that he began using steroids the summer before his senior year in high school to prepare himself for football. Although poor grades made him ineligible to play, he became heavily involved in bodybuilding. Using an intense weight training regimen, he gained about 30 pounds in a short time, and his muscles began to appear very defined.

But the process of physical development seemed to be moving unnaturally quickly. The boy's parents suspected steroid use and advised him to stop, but to no avail.

During the year preceding his death, he had many episodes of abnormal aggressiveness. On several occasions, he had altercations with other auto drivers, and on two occasions he became involved in fights. Other times, he became enraged at his family members over inconsequential events.

In short, there was no way to predict what would set him off. Once he pounded dents into the hood of the family car. Later, he was unable to explain his rage, though he said he felt confused and angry at himself for "acting so stupid."

After he began taking steroids, this boy's body became covered with hives. He also started having nosebleeds and complained of stomach pain. Headaches became frequent, and he began having insomnia. During the day, his mental state fluctuated from sluggishness to hyperactivity.

In his last few months of life, he could not make decisions and acted increasingly confused and frustrated. He alternated between rational and irrational thoughts. A month prior to his death, he quit taking steroids, but by then it was too late to overcome the depression that led to his suicide.

This is not an isolated case. There are too many accounts of other young men who have committed suicide while using or withdrawing from anabolic-androgenic steroids. Although no scientific proof ties these psychiatric symptoms to steroids, the evidence of linkage is compelling.

Parents who suspect their children are using such drugs should take immediate steps to secure medical or psychological help for their kids. As you can see from the above case, it's absolutely *essential* to move quickly.

CHAPTER SIXTEEN

The Meaning of a Competitive Edge

"**M**y goal is to give my child a competitive edge," exclaimed one overenthusiastic parent whose daughter seemed to have the potential to become a gymnastics star.

In pursuit of his goal, he pushed the girl beginning in her early elementary-school years to work out for several hours every day, to the exclusion of many childhood activities, such as attending parties with friends or romping about with neighborhood kids after school.

The final result of this father's efforts presents us with a now-familiar scenario: when she turned 12, the girl became one of those fitness drop-out statistics that worry us so much. He became frustrated and angry and accused her of falling short of her potential and letting him down.

Did this girl ever have a real "competitive edge"? I think not because as far as I'm concerned, the genuine advantages that come with competition should enhance life, not detract from the joys of childhood.

As you now know, this is a book not about developing super child athletes but about encouraging *all* children to develop health and fitness habits that will last over a lifetime. I want *every* child to develop a competitive edge, in the sense of becoming healthier and pursuing athletic activities for fun. Also, kids should train and play sports at a level of intensity at which *they* feel comfortable, not simply in a way that pleases their parents or coaches.

Granted, the more deeply a child becomes involved in athletics, the more demanding the training and the competition will become. But regardless of the plateau of excellence at which the athlete is functioning, there must be some enjoyment. The moment that a sport becomes distasteful or "all work" marks the same moment that the athlete begins to withdraw from the activity and search for other outlets that promise greater satisfaction.

To me, achieving a competitive edge means first gaining a basic level of physical fitness and nutritional balance, so that sound health is ensured. Then the edge is sharpened as fitness increases, and along with this intensification of conditioning, energy levels, and the capacity to enjoy life more fully than ever before. As one's endurance, strength, and flexibility improve, so does the ability to embark on longer physical adventures, perform ever-greater feats of strength, and shine ever brighter in sports.

As adults, we can turn back the clock to some extent by getting into top physical shape. But we can never recapture our youth. In the last analysis, being young is a special gift of childhood. That's something our children have and something we don't have, and we must be careful not to rob them of the special benefits that accompany that time of their life. So if a competitive edge is to exist at all in childhood, it must be combined with the joys of youth and the loving guidance of parents committed to the reasonable, sound pursuit of health and fitness.

Selected References

CHAPTER 1

Appenzeller, Otto, M.D., Ph.D., and Ruth Atkinson, M.D. *Sports Medicine*. Baltimore, Maryland: Urban & Schwarzenberg, second edition, 1983.

Blair, S. N., et al. "Physical Fitness and All-Cause Mortality: A Prospective Study of Healthy Men and Women." *Journal of the American Medical Association*, vol. 262, 1989, pp. 2395–2401.

Christophersen, Edward R., Ph.D., Jack W. Finney, Ph.D., and Patrick C. Friman, Ph. D., guest editors. *The Pediatric Clinics of North America*, vol. 33, no. 4, August 1986.

"Does Physical Fitness of Today's Children Foretell the Shape of Tomorrow's Adult America?" *Journal of the American Medical Association*, vol. 259, no. 16, April 1988.

Forbes, Gilbert B., M.D., editor, and Calvin W. Woodruff, M.D., associate editor. *Pediatric Nutrition Handbook*. Elk Grove Village, Illinois: Committee on Nutrition, American Academy of Pediatrics, second edition, 1985.

Gisolfi, Carl V., Ph.D., and David R. Lamb, Ph.D., editors. *Perspectives in Exercise Science and Sports Medicine, Volume 2: Youth, Exercise, and Sport*. Indianapolis, Indiana: Benchmark Press, Inc., 1989.

Litt, Iris F., guest editor. *The Pediatric Clinics of North America*, vol. 27, no. 1, February 1980.

Lowrey, George H., M.D. *Growth and Development of Children*. Chicago: Year Book Medical Publishers, Inc., eighth edition, 1986.

Martens, Rainer. "The Uniqueness of the Young Athlete: Psychological Considerations." *American Journal of Sports Medicine*, vol. 8, no. 5, 1980, pp. 362–385.

Milverstedt, Fred. "Are Kids Really So Out of Shape?" *Athletic Business*, January 1988, p. 24.

Morgan, Beverly C., M.D., guest editor. *The Pediatric Clinics of North America,* vol. 25, no. 4, November 1978.

Pencharz, Paul B., M.B., Ph.D., F.R.C.P.(C), editor. *The Pediatric Clinics of North America,* vol. 32, no. 2, April 1985.

Raithel, Kathryn Simmons. "Are American Children Really Unfit?" *The Physician and Sportsmedicine,* vol. 16, no. 10, part 1, October 1988.

Rogers, Elaine. "An Unfit Generation." *U.S. Air,* November 1987, p. 92.

Rogers, Peter D., M.D., guest editor. *The Pediatric Clinics of North America,* vol. 34, no. 2, April 1987.

Rosenthal, Amnon, M.D., guest editor. *The Pediatric Clinics of North America,* vol. 31, no. 6, December 1984.

Simons-Morton, Bruce G., et al. "Children and Fitness: A Public Health Perspective." *Research Quarterly for Exercise and Sport,* vol. 58, no. 4, pp. 295–302.

Simons-Morton, Bruce G., et al. "Health-Related Physical Fitness in Childhood: Status and Recommendations." *Annual Review of Public Health,* vol. 9, 1988, pp. 403–425.

Smith, Nathan J., M.D., guest editor. *The Pediatric Clinics of North America,* vol. 29, no. 6, December 1982.

Stern, Patrick H., M.D., et al. "Young Children in Recreational Sports—Participation Motivation," *Clinical Pediatrics,* vol. 29, no. 2, February 1990, pp. 89–94.

Strasburger, Victor C., M.D., guest editor. *The Pediatric Clinics of North America,* vol. 36, no. 3, June 1989.

Strong, William B., M.D. "Physical Fitness of Children: *Mens Sana in Corpore Sano.*" *American Journal of Diseases of Children,* vol. 141, May 1987, p. 488.

Zuckerman, Barry, M.D., Michael Weitzman, M.D., and Joel J. Alpert, M.D., guest editors. *The Pediatric Clinics of North America,* vol. 35, no. 6, December 1988.

NOTE: References in this first chapter have been used in other sections of the book but have not necessarily been included in later reference listings.

CHAPTER 2

Caine, Dennis J., M.Ed., and Jan Broekhoff, Ph.D. "Maturity Assessment: A Viable Preventive Measure against Physical and Psychological Insult to the Young Athlete?" *The Physician and Sportsmedicine,* vol. 15, no. 3, March 1987, pp. 67–79.

Caine, Dennis J., M.Ed., and Koenraad J. Lindner, Ph.D. "Overuse Injuries of

Growing Bones: The Young Female Gymnast at Risk?" *The Physician and Sportsmedicine,* vol. 13, no. 12, December 1985, pp. 51–64.

Dyment, Paul G., M.D. "Controversies in Pediatric Sports Medicine." *The Physician and Sportsmedicine,* vol. 17, no. 7, July 1989, pp. 57–76.

Groves, David. "Is Childhood Obesity Related to TV Addiction?" *The Physician and Sportsmedicine,* vol. 16, no. 11, part 2, November 1988, pp. 117–122.

Lowrey, George H., M.D. *Growth and Development of Children.* Chicago: Year Book Medical Publishers, Inc., eighth edition, 1986.

Morgan, Beverly C., M.D., guest editor. *The Pediatric Clinics of North America,* vol. 25, no. 4, November 1978.

Pappas, Arthur M., M.D. "Osteochondroses: Diseases of Growth Centers." *The Physician and Sportsmedicine,* vol. 17, no. 6, June 1989, pp. 51–62.

Pencharz, Paul B., M.B., Ph.D., F.R.C.P.(C). *The Pediatric Clinics of North America,* vol. 32, no. 2, April 1985.

Rogers, Peter D., M.D., guest editor. *The Pediatric Clinics of North America,* vol. 34, no. 2, April 1987.

Rosenthal, Amnon, M.D., guest editor. *The Pediatric Clinics of North America,* vol. 31, no. 6, December 1984.

Shaffer, Thomas E., M.D. "The Uniqueness of the Young Athlete: Introductory Remarks." *American Journal of Sports Medicine,* vol. 8, no. 5, 1980, pp. 370–371.

Simmons-Raithel, Kathryn. "Are Girls Less Fit Than Boys?" *The Physician and Sportsmedicine,* vol. 15, no. 11, November 1987, pp. 157–163.

———. "Are American Children Really Unfit?" *The Physician and Sportsmedicine,* vol. 16, October 1988, p. 152.

Smith, Nathan J., M.D., guest editor. *The Pediatric Clinics of North America,* vol. 29, no. 6, December 1982.

———. "Is That Child Ready for Competitive Sports?" *Contemporary Pediatrics,* vol. 3, March 1986, pp. 30–54.

Speer, Donald P., M.D., and J. Keit Braun, M.D. "The Biomechanical Basis of Growth Plate Injuries." *The Physician and Sportsmedicine,* vol. 13, no. 7, July 1985, pp. 72–78.

Sports and Your Child. Elk Grove Village, Illinois: American Academy of Pediatrics, 1988.

Strasburger, Victor C., M.D., guest editor. *The Pediatric Clinics of North America,* vol. 36, no. 3, June 1989.

Strong, William B., and Jack H. Wilmore. "Unfit Kids: An Office-Based Approach to Physical Fitness." *Contemporary Pediatrics,* April 1988, p. 34.

Watkins, Bruce, and Amy B. Montgomery. "Conceptions of Athletic Excellence among Children and Adolescents." *Child Development,* vol. 60, 1989.

Zimmerman, David R. "Maturation and Strenuous Training in Young Female

Athletes." *The Physician and Sportsmedicine,* vol. 15, no. 6, June 1987, pp. 219–222.

Zuckerman, Barry, M.D., Michael Weitzman, M.D., and Joel J. Alpert, M.D., guest editors. *The Pediatric Clinics of North America,* vol. 35, no. 6, December 1988.

CHAPTER 3

Committee on the Pediatric Aspects of Physical Fitness, Recreation, and Sports. *Participation in Sports by Girls.* American Academy of Pediatrics.

"For Some of Nation's Young Athletes, Training May Be Too Much of a Good Thing." *Journal of the American Medical Association,* vol. 262, no. 6, August 1989.

Litt, Iris F., guest editor. *The Pediatric Clinics of North America,* vol. 27, no. 1, February 1980.

Lowrey, George H., M.D. *Growth and Development of Children.* Chicago: Year Book Medical Publishers, Inc., eighth edition, 1986.

Malina, Robert M., et al. "Anthropometric, Body Composition, and Maturity Characteristics of Selected School-Age Athletes." *The Pediatric Clinics of North America,* Sports Medicine, December 1982, pp. 1309–1310.

Morgan, Beverly C., M.D., guest editor. *The Pediatric Clinics of North America,* vol. 25, no. 4, November 1978.

Offer, Daniel, M.D., Eric Ostrov, J.D., Ph.D., and Kenneth I. Howard, Ph.D. "Adolescence: What Is Normal?" *American Journal of Diseases of Children,* vol. 35, no. 6, December 1988, pp. 731–736.

Pencharz, Paul B., M.B., Ph.D., F.R.C.P.(C), guest editor. *The Pediatric Clinics of North America,* vol. 32, no. 2, April 1985.

Pratt, Michael, M.D., M.S. "Strength, Flexibility, and Maturity in Adolescent Athletes." *American Journal of Diseases of Children,* vol. 143, May 1989, p. 560.

Rogers, Peter D., M.D., guest editor. *The Pediatric Clinics of North America,* vol. 34, no. 2, April 1987.

Rosenthal, Amnon, M.D., guest editor. *The Pediatric Clinics of North America,* vol. 31, no. 6, December 1984.

Smith, Nathan J., M.D., guest editor. *The Pediatric Clinics of North America,* vol. 29, no. 6, December 1982.

Strasburger, Victor C., M.D., guest editor. *The Pediatric Clinics of North America,* vol. 36, no. 3, June 1989.

Zuckerman, Barry M.D., Michael Weitzman, M.D., and Joel J. Alpert, M.D., guest editors. *The Pediatric Clinics of North America,* vol. 35, no. 6, December 1988.

CHAPTER 4

Blair, Steven N., P.E.D., et al. "Exercise and Fitness in Childhood: Implications for a Lifetime of Health," in Carl V. Gisolfi, Ph.D., and David Lamb, Ph.D., editors, *Perspectives in Exercise Science and Sports Medicine, Volume 2: Youth, Exercise, and Sport.* Indianapolis, Indiana: Benchmark Press, Inc., 1989.

Kraus, Hans, M.D. "Unfit Kids: A Call to Action." *Contemporary Pediatrics,* vol. 5, April 1988, pp. 18–30.

Rogers, Peter D., M.D., guest editor. *The Pediatric Clinics of North America,* vol. 34, no. 2, April 1987.

Rosenthal, Amnon, M.D., guest editor. *The Pediatric Clinics of North America,* vol. 31, no. 6, December 1984.

Smith, Nathan J., M.D., guest editor. *The Pediatric Clinics of North America,* vol. 29, no. 6, December 1982.

Stern, H. Patrick, M.D., et al. "Young Children in Recreational Sports: Participation Motivation." *Clinical Pediatrics,* vol. 29, no. 2, February 1990, pp. 89–94.

Strasburger, Victor C., M.D., guest editor. *The Pediatric Clinics of North America,* vol. 36, no. 3, June 1989.

Zuckerman, Barry, M.D., Michael Weitzman, M.D., and Joel J. Alpert, M.D., guest editors. *The Pediatric Clinics of North America,* vol. 35, no. 6, December 1988.

CHAPTER 5

Brownell, Kelly D., Ph.D., Jane H. Kelman, M.S., and Albert J. Stunkard, M.D. "Treatment of Obese Children with and without Their Mothers: Changes in Weight and Blood Pressure." *Pediatrics,* vol. 71, no. 4, April 1983, pp. 515–552.

Christophersen, Edward R., Ph.D., Jack W. Finney, Ph.D., and Patrick C. Friman, Ph.D., guest editors. *The Pediatric Clinics of North America,* vol. 33, no. 4, August 1986.

Hellstedt, Jon C., Ph.D. "Kids, Parents, and Sports: Some Questions and Answers." *The Physician and Sportsmedicine,* vol. 16, no. 4, April 1988, pp. 59–71.

Litt, Iris F., guest editor. *The Pediatric Clinics of North America,* vol. 27, no. 1, February 1980.

Morgan, Beverly C., M.D., guest editor. *The Pediatric Clinics of North America,* vol. 25, no. 4, November 1978.

Murphy, Joseph K., Ph.D., et al. "Physical Fitness in Children: A Survey Method

Based on Parental Report." *American Journal of Public Health,* vol. 78, no. 6, June 1988, pp. 708–709.

Pencharz, Paul B., M.B., Ph.D., F.R.C.P.(C), guest editor. *The Pediatric Clinics of North America,* vol. 32, no. 2, April 1985.

Rogers, Peter D., M.D., guest editor. *The Pediatric Clinics of North America,* vol. 34, no. 2, April 1987.

Rosenthal, Amnon, M.D., guest editor. *The Pediatric Clinics of North America,* vol. 31, no. 6, December 1984.

Smith, Nathan J., M.D., guest editor. *The Pediatric Clinics of North America,* vol. 29, no. 6, December 1982.

Strasburger, Victor C., M.D., guest editor. *The Pediatric Clinics of North America,* vol. 36, no. 3, June 1989.

Zuckerman, Barry, M.D., Michael Weitzman, M.D., and Joel J. Alpert, M.D., guest editors. *The Pediatric Clinics of North America,* vol. 35, no. 6, December 1988.

CHAPTER 6

Glover, Bob. "Child's Play." *Runner's World,* June 1989, pp. 60–66.

Laser, Michael. "Advice from Kids." *Well Street Journal* (Mercy Medical Center, Cedar Rapids, Iowa), vol. 7, no. 8, November–December 1988, p. 1.

Litt, Iris F., guest editor. *The Pediatric Clinics of North America,* vol. 27, no. 1, February 1980.

Lowrey, George H., M.D. *Growth and Development of Children.* Chicago: Benchmark Press, Inc., eighth edition, 1989.

Morgan, Beverly C., M.D., guest editor. *The Pediatric Clinics of North America,* vol. 25, no. 4, November 1978.

Pencharz, Paul B., M.B., Ph.D., F.R.C.P.(C), guest editor. *The Pediatric Clinics of North America,* vol. 32, no. 2, April 1985.

Rogers, Peter D., M.D., guest editor. *The Pediatric Clinics of North America,* vol. 34, no. 2, April 1987.

Rosenthal, Amnon, M.D., guest editor. *The Pediatric Clinics of North America,* vol. 31, no. 6, December 1984.

Rowland, Thomas W., M.D. "Motivational Factors in Exercise Training Programs for Children." *The Physician and Sportsmedicine,* vol. 14, no. 2, February 1986, pp. 122–128.

Shephard, Roy J., M.D., Ph.D. "Motivation: The Key to Fitness Compliance." *The Physician and Sportsmedicine,* vol. 13, no. 7, July 1985, pp. 88–101.

Smith, Nathan J., M.D., guest editor. *The Pediatric Clinics of North America,* vol. 29, no. 6, December 1982.

Strasburger, Victor C., M.D., guest editor. *The Pediatric Clinics of North America,* vol. 36, no. 3, June 1989.

Zuckerman, Barry, M.D., Michael Weitzman, M.D., and Joel J. Alpert, M.D., guest editors. *The Pediatric Clinics of North America,* vol. 35, no. 6, December 1988.

CHAPTER 7

Christophersen, Edward R., Ph.D., Jack W. Finney, Ph.D., and Patrick C. Friman, Ph.D., guest editors. *The Pediatric Clinics of North America,* vol. 33, no. 4, August 1986.

Clark, Debra G., and Steven N. Blair. "Physical Activity and Prevention of Obesity in Childhood." In *Childhood Obesity: A Biobehavioral Perspective.* N. A. Krasnegor, G. D. Grave, and N. Kretchmer, editors. Canfield, New Jersey: Telford Press, 1988, p. 218.

Dennison, Barbara A., M.D., et al. "Childhood Physical Fitness Tests: Predictor of Adult Physical Activity Levels?" *Pediatrics,* vol. 82, no. 3, September 1988, pp. 324–329.

"Fitness of American Children." *Coaching & Training Times,* vol. 3, no. 2, 1989, p. 1.

Forbes, Gilbert B., M.D., editor, and Calvin W. Woodruff, M.D., associate editor. *Pediatric Nutrition Handbook.* Elk Grove Village, Illinois: Committee on Nutrition, American Academy of Pediatrics, second edition, 1985.

Graham, George, Shirley Ann Holt/Hale, and Melissa Parker. *Children Moving: A Teacher's Guide to Developing a Successful Physical Education Program.* Mountain View, California: Mayfield Publishing Co., second edition, 1987.

Institute for Aerobics Research, developer. *Fitnessgram®: User's Manual* (IBM PC version). Dallas, Texas: Institute for Aerobics Research, 1987.

Johnson, Barry L., and Jack K. Nelson. *Practical Measurements for Evaluation in Physical Education.* Minneapolis, Minnesota: Burgess Publishing Co.

Kraus, Hans, M.D. "Unfit Kids: A Call to Action." *Contemporary Pediatrics,* vol. 5, April 1988, pp. 18–30.

Litt, Iris F., guest editor. *The Pediatric Clinics of North America,* vol. 27, no. 1, February 1980.

Lohman, Timothy G., Ph.D. "Applicability of Body Composition Techniques and Constants for Children and Youths."

Lohman, Timothy G., Richard A. Boileau, and Mary H. Slaughter. "Body Composition in Children and Youth." In Richard Boileau, editor, *Advances in Pediatric Sports Sciences,* vol. 1, Human Kinetics, 1984.

McGinnis, J. M. "Introduction." In *Summary of Findings from National Children and Youth Fitness Study I. Journal of Physical Education, Recreation, and Dance,* January 1985.

————."Introduction." In *Summary of Findings from National Children and Youth Fitness Study II*. Public Health Service, Office of Disease Prevention and Health Promotion, U.S. Department of Health and Human Services, *Journal of Physical Education, Recreation, and Dance*, November–December 1987.

Morgan, Beverly C., M.D., guest editor. *The Pediatric Clinics of North America*, vol. 25, no. 4, November 1978.

Murphy, Patrick. "Youth Fitness Testing: A Matter of Health or Performance?" *The Physician and Sportsmedicine*, vol. 14, no. 5, May 1986, pp. 189–190.

Pencharz, Paul B., M.B., Ph.D., F.R.C.P.(C), guest editor. *The Pediatric Clinics of North America*, vol. 32, no. 2, April 1985.

"Press Toward Achieving the 1990 National Objectives for Physical Fitness and Exercise." *Journal of the American Medical Association*, vol. 262, no. 6, August 1989.

Rogers, Peter D., M.D., guest editor. *The Pediatric Clinics of North America*, vol. 34, no. 2, April 1987.

Rosenthal, Amnon, M.D., guest editor. *The Pediatric Clinics of North America*, vol. 31, no. 6, December 1984.

Ryan, Allan J., M.D. "America's Youth Not in Bad Shape." *The Physician and Sportsmedicine*, vol. 13, no. 1, January 1985, p. 41.

Slaughter, M. H., et al. "Influence of Maturation on Relationship of Skinfolds to Body Density: A Cross-Sectional Study." *Human Biology*, vol. 56, no. 4, December 1984, pp. 681–689.

Smith, Nathan J., M.D., guest editor. *The Pediatric Clinics of North America*, vol. 29, no. 6, December 1982.

Sterner, Major Thomas G., M.S., and Edmund J. Burke, Ph.D. "Body Fat Assessment: A Comparison of Visual Estimation and Skinfold Techniques." *The Physician and Sportsmedicine*, vol. 14, no. 4, April 1986, pp. 101–107.

Strasburger, Victor C., M.D., guest editor. *The Pediatric Clinics of North America*, vol. 36, no. 3, June 1989.

Summary of Findings from National Children and Youth Fitness Study. Public Health Service, Office of Disease Prevention and Health Promotion, U.S. Department of Health and Human Services.

Thelen, Esther. "Treadmill-Elicited Stepping in Seven-Month-Old Infants." *Child Development*, vol. 57, 1986, pp. 1498–1506.

"Today's Children Are Fatter Not Fitter, Say Experts." *Environmental Nutrition*, vol. 12, no. 4, April 1989, p. 1.

Zuckerman, Barry, M.D., Michael Weitzman, M.D., and Joel J. Alpert, M.D., guest editors. *The Pediatric Clinics of North America*, vol. 35, no. 6, December 1988.

CHAPTER 8

American Academy of Pediatrics, "Policy Statement: Infant Exercise Programs." *The Physician and Sportsmedicine,* vol. 18, no. 6, June 1990, p. 142.

Bar-Or, Oded, M.D. "Trainability of the Prepubescent Child." *The Physician and Sportsmedicine,* vol. 17, no. 5, May 1989, pp. 65–81.

Christophersen, Edward R., Ph.D., Jack W. Finney, Ph.D., and Patrick C. Friman, Ph.D., guest editors. *The Pediatric Clinics of North America,* vol. 33, no. 4, August 1986.

Cimons, Marlene. "Stroll Models: How Can You Run and Spend Time with Your Baby? Take Your Running Stroller for a Spin." *Runner's World,* June 1989, pp. 74–76.

Clark, Debra G., and Steven N. Blair. "Physical Activity and Prevention of Obesity in Childhood." In *Childhood Obesity: A Behavioral Perspective,* N. A. Krasnegor et al., editors. Canfield, New Jersey: Telford Press, 1988, pp. 121–141.

Committee on Pediatric Aspects of Physical Fitness, Recreation, and Sports. "Fitness in the Preschool Child." *Pediatrics,* vol. 58, no. 1, July 1976, p. 88.

Committee on Sports Medicine. "Infant Exercise Programs." *Pediatrics,* vol. 82, no. 5, November 1988, p. 800.

Committee on Sports Medicine and Committee on School Health. "Organized Athletics for Preadolescent Children." *Pediatrics,* vol. 84, no. 3, September 1989, pp. 583–584.

Corbin, Charles B., and Robert P. Pangrazi. *Teaching Strategies for Improving Youth Fitness: Fitnessgram®.* Dallas, Texas: Institute for Aerobics Research.

Cureton, Kirk J., and Gordon L. Warren. "Criterion-Referenced Standards for Youth Health-Related Fitness Tests: A Tutorial." *Research Quarterly for Exercise and Sport,* vol. 61, no. 1, 1990, pp. 7–19.

DeBenedette, Valerie. "Exercise Helps Hypertensive Children." *The Physician and Sportsmedicine,* vol. 15, no. 4, April 1987, p. 39.

Duda, Marty. "Prepubescent Strength Training Gains Support." *The Physician and Sportsmedicine,* vol. 14, no. 2, February 1986, pp. 157–161.

Dyment, Paul G., M.D. "Controversies in Pediatric Sports Medicine." *The Physician and Sportsmedicine,* vol. 17, no. 7, July 1989, pp. 57–71.

Landry, Gregory L., M.D. "What Is the Role of a Pediatrician within a Sports Medicine Program?" *The Physician and Sportsmedicine,* vol. 13, no. 1, January 1985, pp. 51–52.

Lee, Amelia M., Jo A. Carter, and Kare M. Greenockle. "Children and Fitness: A Pedagogical Perspective." *Research Quarterly for Exercise and Sport,* vol. 58, no. 4, pp. 321–325.

Litt, Iris F., guest editor. *The Pediatric Clinics of North America,* vol. 27, no. 1, February 1980.

Lubell, Adele. "Potentially Dangerous Exercises: Are They Harmful to All?" *The Physician and Sportsmedicine,* vol. 17, no. 1, January 1989, pp. 187–192.

Morgan, Beverly C., M.D., guest editor. *The Pediatric Clinics of North America,* vol. 25, no. 4, November 1978.

Nash, Heyward L. "Hyperthermia: Risks Greater in Children." *The Physician and Sportsmedicine,* vol. 15, no. 2, February 1987, p. 29.

Nichols, Beverly, Ph.D. *Moving and Learning: The Elementary School Physical Education Experience.* St. Louis: Times Mirror/Mosby, College Publishing, 1988.

Pencharz, Paul B., M.B., Ph.D., F.R.C.P.(C). *The Pediatric Clinics of North America,* vol. 32, no. 2, April 1985.

"Principles of Strength Training." In *The Strength Connection.* Dallas, Texas: INR Press, 1990.

Rogers, Peter D., M.D., guest editor. *The Pediatric Clinics of North America,* vol. 34, no. 2, April 1987.

Rosenthal, Amnon, M.D., guest editor. *The Pediatric Clinics of North America,* vol. 31, no. 6, December 1984.

Rowland, Thomas W. "The Health-Exercise Link." In *Exercise and Children's Health.* Human Kinetics Books, 1990.

Siedentop, Daryl, Jacqueline Herkowitz, and Judith Rink. *Elementary Physical Education Methods.* Englewood Cliffs, New Jersey: Prentice-Hall Press, 1984.

Smith, Nathan J., M.D., guest editor. *The Pediatric Clinics of North America,* vol. 29, no. 6, December 1982.

Strasburger, Victor C., M.D., guest editor. *The Pediatric Clinics of North America,* vol. 36, no. 3, June 1989.

Taswell, Ruth. "Weight-Training Women Won't Look Like Men." *The Physician and Sportsmedicine,* vol. 17, no. 3, March 1989, p. 56.

Teaching Physical Education in Elementary Schools. Philadelphia: Saunders College Publishing, sixth edition, 1982.

Tillman, Kenneth G., and Patricia Rizzo Toner. *You'll Never Guess What We Did in Gym Today!* West Nyack, New York: Parker Publishing Co., Inc., 1985.

Ward, Amy. "Born to Jog: Exercise Programs for Preschoolers." *The Physician and Sportsmedicine,* vol. 14, no. 12, December 1986, pp. 163–167.

Weber, Debra G., Harold W. Kohl, Marilu D. Meredith, and Steven N. Blair. "An Automated System for Assessing Physical Fitness in School Children." In *Proceedings of the 1985 Public Health Conference on Records and Statistics.* Washington, D.C.: National Center for Health Statistics (U.S. Government Printing Office: DHHS Pub. No. [PHS] 86-1214), 1986.

Zuckerman, Barry, M.D., Michael Weitzman, M.D., and Joel J. Alpert, M.D., guest editors. *The Pediatric Clinics of North America,* vol. 35, no. 6, December 1988.

CHAPTER 9

American Heart Association. "Diet in the Healthy Child." *Circulation,* vol. 67, 1983, p. 1411A.

Appenzeller, Otto, M.D., Ph.D., and Ruth Atkinson, M.D. *Sports Medicine.* Baltimore, Maryland: Urban & Schwarzenberg, second edition, 1985.

"Calcium Supplements." *The Medical Letter on Drugs and Therapeutics,* vol. 31 November 17, 1989, p. 101.

Clark, Nancy, M.S., R.D. "Dairy Tales." *Runner's World,* June 1989, p. 44.

Creger, C. P., chairman. Proceedings: Texas Human Nutrition Conference, February 17, 1989, College Statia, Texas, The Texas A&M University System.

Forbes, Gilbert B., M.D., editor, and Calvin W. Woodruff, M.D., associate editor. *Pediatric Nutrition Handbook.* Elk Grove Village, Illinois: Committee on Nutrition, American Academy of Pediatrics, second edition, 1985.

Heird, William C., M.D. "Nutrition During the Second Six Months of Life." Paper presented at the Second Annual Carnation Symposium, July 12–14, 1989, Columbia University.

Massachusetts Medical Society Committee on Nutrition. "Sounding Board: Fast-Food Fare." *The New England Journal of Medicine,* vol. 321, no. 11, September 1989, p. 752.

Walker, W. Allan, M.D., and Kristy M. Hendricks, R.D., M.S. *Manual of Pediatric Nutrition.* Philadelphia: W. B. Saunders Co., 1985.

CHAPTER 10

Allen, Thomas Wesley, M.D. "Wrestling Termed Most Dangerous Youth Contact Sport." *Family Practice News,* February 15–28, 1989, p. 14.

Borgen, Jorunn Sundgot, M.S., and Charles B. Corbin, Ph.D. "Eating Disorders among Female Athletes." *The Physician and Sportsmedicine,* vol. 15, no. 2, February 1987, p. 89.

Clark, Debra G., and Steven N. Blair. "Physical Activity and Prevention of Obesity in Childhood." In N. A. Krasnegor et al., editors. *Childhood Obesity: A Biobehavioral Perspective.* Canfield, New Jersey: Telford Press, 1988, pp. 121–142.

Clark, Nancy. *Nancy Clark's Sports Nutrition Guidebook.* Leisure Press, 1990, pp. 116–123.

Collipp, Platon J., M.D., guest editor. "Childhood Obesity Update: Part I." *Pediatric Annals,* vol. 13, no. 6, June 1984.

———. "Childhood Obesity Update: Part II." *Pediatric Annals,* vol. 13, no. 7, July 1984.

Comerci, George D., M.D. "Eating Disorders in Adolescents." *Pediatrics in Review,* vol. 10, no. 2, August 1988, p. 1.

Forbes, Gilbert B., M.D., editor, and Calvin W. Woodruff, M.D., associate editor. *Pediatric Nutrition Handbook.* Elk Grove Village, Illinois: Committee on Nutrition, American Academy of Pediatrics, second edition, 1985.

Goldberg, Harold L., M.D. "Unlocking the Family Door: A Systemic Approach to the Understanding and Treatment of Anorexia Nervosa" (book review). *The New England Journal of Medicine,* vol. 321, no. 9, August 31, 1989, p. 623.

Loosli, Alvin, M.D. "Athletes, Food, and Nutrition." *Food Nutrition News,* vol. 62, no. 3, May–June 1990, p. 1.

Maloney, Michael J., M.D., et al. "Dieting Behavior and Eating Attitudes in Children." *Pediatrics,* vol. 84, no. 3, September 1989, p. 482.

Mellin, Laurel M., M.A., R.D., Lee Ann Slinkard, M.S., and Charles E. Irwin, Jr., M.D. "Adolescent Obesity Intervention: Validation of the SHAPEDOWN Program." *Journal of the American Dietetic Association,* vol. 87, no. 3, March 1987, p. 1.

O'Connell, Joan M., M.H.S., et al. "Growth of Vegetarian Children: The Farm Study." *Pediatrics,* vol. 84, no. 3, September 1989, p. 475.

Primos, William A., M.D., and Gregory L. Landry, M.D. "Fighting the Fads in Sports Nutrition." *Contemporary Pediatrics,* vol. 6, September 1989, p. 14.

Rocchini, Albert P., M.D., et al. "The Effect of Weight Loss on the Sensitivity of Blood Pressure to Sodium in Obese Adolescents." *The New England Journal of Medicine,* vol. 321, August 1989, p. 580.

Strauss, Richard H., M.D., Richard R. Lanese, Ph.D., and William B. Malarkey, M.D. "Weight Loss in Amateur Wrestlers and Its Effect on Serum Testosterone Levels." *Journal of the American Medical Association,* vol. 254, no. 23, December 1985, p. 3337.

Tipton, Charles M., Ph.D., and Tse-Kia Tcheng, Ph.D. "Iowa Wrestling Study: Weight Loss in High School Students." *Journal of the American Medical Association,* vol. 214, no. 17, November 1970, p. 1269.

"Today's Children Are Fatter Not Fitter, Say Experts." *Environmental Nutrition,* vol. 12, no. 4, April 1989, p. 1.

"The Young Athlete." *Sportswatch,* vol. 4, no. 1, p. 1.

CHAPTER 11

Butcher, Ann H., R.N., M.P.H., et al. "Heart Smart: A School Health Program Meeting the 1990 Objectives for the Nation." *Health Education Quarterly,* vol. 5, no. 1, 1988, pp. 17–34.

Caldwell, Frances. "City Parks: Untapped Resource for Fitness." *The Physician and Sportsmedicine,* vol. 13, no. 7, July 1985, p. 120.

Duda, Marty. "Gauging Steroid Use in High School Kids." *The Physician and Sportsmedicine,* vol. 16, no. 8, August 1988, p. 16.

Gaskins, Samuel E., M.D., and William F. deShazo, III, M.D. "Attitudes Toward Drug Abuse and Screening for an Intercollegiate Athletic Program." *The Physician and Sportsmedicine,* vol. 13, no. 9, September 1985, p. 93.

Mann, George V. "Sports in Education." *Perspectives in Biology and Medicine,* vol. 31, Autumn 1987, pp. 34–41.

Murphy, Patrick. "The Cincinnati Academy of Physical Education: Using Fitness to Aid Learning." *The Physician and Sportsmedicine,* vol. 15, no. 4, April 1987, p. 173.

"Physical Fitness and the Schools." *Pediatrics,* vol. 80, no. 3, September 1987, p. 449.

"Preventing Drug Abuse." *Parent Currents,* vol. 3, no. 3, 1989.

Rice, Stephen G., M.D., Ph.D. "Is Athletic Health Care a Primary Concern in Secondary Schools?" *The Physician and Sportsmedicine,* vol. 13, no. 3, March 1985, p. 169.

Rogers, Peter D., M.D., guest editor. *The Pediatric Clinics of North America,* vol. 34, no. 2, April 1987.

Sintek, Stephanie, M.A.Ed., and Paul Bishop, Ed.D. "Physicians' Perceptions of Using Physical Education for Managing Childhood Obesity." *The Physician and Sportsmedicine,* vol. 13, no. 5, May 1985, p. 119.

CHAPTER 12

Bailie, Michael D., M.D., Ph.D., et al. "Hypertension: More Than Ever, A Pediatric Concern." *Contemporary Pediatrics,* October 1985, p. 30.

"Biochemical, Clinical, Epidemiologic, Genetic, and Pathologic Data in the Pediatric Age Group Relevant to the Cholesterol Hypothesis." *Pediatrics,* vol. 78, no. 2, August 1986, p. 349.

The Centers for Disease Control. "Tobacco Use by Adults: United States, 1987." *Journal of the American Medical Association,* vol. 262, no. 17, November 1989, p. 2364.

Chasnoff, Ira J., et al. "Temporal Patterns of Cocaine Use in Pregnancy: Perinatal

Outcome." *Journal of the American Medical Association,* vol. 261, no. 12, 1989, p. 1741.

"Cholesterol Clues within Genes." *Nutrition & Health News,* vol. 6, no. 3, Summer 1989, p. 1.

"Cholesterol Screening: For All or Only Some?" *Contemporary Pediatrics,* October 1989, p. 125.

"Cholesterol Values in Children." *LabNote,* April 1990, p. 3.

Christensen, Bobbe, et al. "Plasma Cholesterol and Triglyceride Distributions in 13,665 Children and Adolescents: The Prevalence Study of the Lipid Research Clinics Program." *Pediatric Research,* vol. 14, 1980, pp. 194–202.

Christophersen, Edward R., Ph.D., Jack W. Finney, Ph.D., and Patrick C. Friman, Ph.D., guest editors. *The Pediatric Clinics of North America,* vol. 33, no. 4, August 1986.

"Chronic Disease Reports: Coronary Heart Disease Mortality—United States, 1986." *Morbidity and Mortality Weekly Reports,* vol. 38, no. 16, April 28, 1989, pp. 285–287.

"Cigarette Advertising: United States, 1988." *Morbidity and Mortality Weekly Report,* vol. 39, no. 16, April 27, 1990, pp. 261–265.

Committee on Nutrition. "Childhood Diet and Coronary Heart Disease." *Pediatrics,* vol. 49, no. 2, February 1972, p. 305.

Cooper, Gerald R., Ph.D., M.D., and David D. Bayse, Ph.D. "Standardization of Lipid and Lipoprotein Determinations for Pediatric Screening Procedures." *Progress in Clinical and Biological Research,* vol. 188, 1985, pp. 1–17.

Cresanta, James L., et al. "Serum Lipoprotein Levels in Children: Epidemiologic and Clinical Implications." *Journal of Chronic Diseases,* vol. 35, 1982, pp. 41–51.

———. "Serum Lipid and Lipoprotein Cholesterol Grids for Cardiovascular Risk Screening of Children." *American Journal of Diseases of Children,* vol. 138, April 1984, p. 379.

Croft, Janet B., et al. "Transitions of Cardiovascular Risk from Adolescence to Young Adulthood—The Bogalusa Heart Study: I. Effects of Alterations in Lifestyle." *Journal of Chronic Diseases,* vol. 39, no. 2, 1986, pp. 81–90.

Dennison, Barbara A., M.D., et al. *Pediatrics,* vol. 85, no. 4, April 1990, p. 472.

Enos, William F., Jr., M.D., Captain James C. Beyer, M.C., and Robert H. Holmes, M.D. "Pathogenesis of Coronary Disease in American Soldiers Killed in Korea." *Journal of the American Medical Association,* p. 912.

Fixler, David E., M.D., and W. Pennock Laird, M.D. "Validity of Mass Blood Pressure Screening in Children." *Pediatrics,* vol. 72, no. 4, October 1983, p. 459.

Forbes, Gilbert B., M.D., editor, and Calvin W. Woodruff, M.D., associate editor. *Pediatric Nutrition Handbook.* Elk Grove Village, Illinois: Committee on Nutrition, American Academy of Pediatrics, second edition, 1985.

Frank, Deborah A., M.D., et al. "Cocaine Use During Pregnancy: Prevalence and Correlates." *Pediatrics,* vol. 82, no. 6, December 1988, p. 888.

Frankowski, Barbara L., M.D., and Roger H. Secker-Walker, M.B. "Advising Parents to Stop Smoking." *American Journal of Diseases of Children,* vol. 143, September 1989, p. 1091.

Freedman, David S., Ph.D., et al. "Tracking of Serum Lipids and Lipoproteins in Children Over an 8-Year Period: The Bogalusa Heart Study." *Preventive Medicine,* vol. 14, 1985, pp. 203–216.

Freedman, David S., Ph.D., et al. "Serum Lipids and Lipoproteins." *Pediatrics,* vol. 80 (supplement), 1987, pp. 789–796.

Fulroth, Richard, M.D., Barry Phillips, M.D., and David J. Durand, M.D. "Perinatal Outcome of Infants Exposed to Cocaine and/or Heroin in Utero." *American Journal of Diseases of Children,* vol. 143, August 1989, p. 905.

Helsing, K. J., D. P. Sandler, G. W. Comstock, and E. Chee. "Heart Disease Mortality in Nonsmokers Living with Smokers." *American Journal of Epidemiology,* vol. 127, no. 5, 1988, p. 915.

Hunter, Saundra, Larry S. Webber, and Gerald S. Berenson. "Cigarette Smoking and Tobacco Usage Behavior in Children and Adolescents: Bogalusa Heart Study." *Preventive Medicine,* vol. 9, 1980, pp. 701–712.

Jacobsen, Bjarne K., and Dag S. Thelle. "Risk Factors for Coronary Heart Disease and Level of Education." *American Journal of Epidemiology,* vol. 127, no. 5, 1988, p. 923.

Kaplan, Norman M., M.D. "Calcium Entry Blockers in the Treatment of Hypertension." *Journal of the American Medical Association,* vol. 262, no. 6, August 1989, p. 817.

Kavey, Rae-Ellen W., M.D. "An Office-Based Program of Preventive Cardiology." *Contemporary Pediatrics,* July 1989, p. 46.

Killen, Joel D., Ph.D., et al. "Cardiovascular Disease Risk Reduction for Tenth Graders." *Journal of the American Medical Association,* vol. 260, no. 12, September 1988, p. 1728.

Kleinman, Joel C., et al. "The Effects of Maternal Smoking on Fetal and Infant Mortality." *American Journal of Epidemiology,* vol. 127, no. 5, 1988, pp. 274–289.

Litt, Iris F., guest editor. *The Pediatric Clinics of North America,* vol. 27, no. 1, February 1980.

McNamara, Major J. Judson, M.C., U.S.A., et al. "Coronary Artery Disease in Combat Casualties in Vietnam." *Journal of the American Medical Association,* vol. 216, May 1971, pp. 1185–1187.

"Making Sure Your Children's Hearts Stay Healthy." *Tufts Diet & Nutrition Letter,* vol. 7, no. 2, April 1989, p. 3.

Morgan, Beverly C., M.D., guest editor. *The Pediatric Clinics of North America,* vol. 25, no. 4, November 1978.

Palumbo, P. J., M.D. "Cholesterol Lowering for All: A Closer Look" (editorial). *Journal of the American Medical Association,* vol. 262, no. 1, July 7, 1989, p. 91.

Park, Myung K., M.D., and Shirley M. Menard, R.N., M.S.N. "Normative Oscillometric Blood Pressure Values in the First 5 Years in an Office Setting." *American Journal of Diseases of Children,* vol. 143, July 1989, p. 860.

Pencharz, Paul B., M.B., Ph.D., F.R.C.P.(C), guest editor. *The Pediatric Clinics of North America,* vol. 32, no. 2, April 1985.

Persaud, Deanna, R.N., M.S., Julia Shovein, R.N., M.S., and Carol Leedom, R.N., M.S. "Reducing Passive Exposure to Smoke." *Respiratory Management,* vol. 19, no. 4, p. 98.

Rogers, Peter D., M.D., guest editor. *The Pediatric Clinics of North America,* vol. 34, no. 2, April 1987.

Rosenthal, Amnon, M.D., guest editor. *The Pediatric Clinics of North America,* vol. 31, no. 6, December 1984.

Sallis, James F., et al. "Relation of Cardiovascular Fitness and Physical Activity to Cardiovascular Disease Risk Factors in Children and Adults." *American Journal of Epidemiology,* vol. 127, no. 5, 1988, p. 933.

Schinke, Steven Paul, Ph.D., Lewayne D. Gilchrist, Ph.D., and William H. Snow, M.A. "Skills Intervention to Prevent Cigarette Smoking among Adolescents." *American Journal of Public Health,* vol. 75, 1985, pp. 665–667.

"Screen All Kids for Cholesterol?" Bulletin Board, *Contemporary Pediatrics,* September 1989, p. 159.

Sly, R. Michael, M.D. "The Role of Physicians in Smoking Cessation" (editorial). *Annals of Allergy,* vol. 63, September 1989, p. 163.

Smith, Nathan J., M.D., guest editor. *The Pediatric Clinics of North America,* vol. 29, no. 6, December 1982.

Strasburger, Victor C., M.D., guest editor. *The Pediatric Clinics of North America,* vol. 36, no. 3, June 1989.

Waldron, Ingrid, Ph.D., and Diane Lye, M.A. "Family Roles and Smoking." *American Journal of Preventive Medicine,* vol. 5, no. 3, 1989, p. 136.

Webber, L. S., et al. "Tracking of Cardiovascular Disease Risk Factor Variables in School-age Children." *Journal of Chronic Diseases,* vol. 36, no. 9, 1983, pp. 647–660.

Wilson, Peter W. F., M.D., et al. "Impact of National Guidelines for Cholesterol Risk Factor Screening." *Journal of the American Medical Association,* vol. 262, no.1, July 1989, p. 41.

Winick, Myron, M.D. "Childhood Antecedents to Adult Coronary Artery Diseases." In *Special Reference Briefs,* Beltsville, Maryland: National Agricultural Library, 1988.

Zuckerman, Barry, M.D., Michael Weitzman, M.D., and Joel J. Alpert, M.D., guest editors. *The Pediatric Clinics of North America,* vol. 35, no. 6, December 1988.

CHAPTER 13

American Academy of Pediatrics. *Protecting Your Child Against Diphtheria, Tetanus, Pertussis* (brochure). Elk Grove Village, Illinois: 1988.

Braunwald, Eugene, M.D. "Hypertrophic Cardiomyopathy: Continued Progress." *The New England Journal of Medicine,* March 1989, p. 800.

"Cefuroxime Axetil." *The Medical Letter on Drugs and Therapeutics,* vol. 30, June 3, 1988, p. 57.

Centers for Disease Control. "Influenza Activity: United States, 1989." *Journal of the American Medical Association,* vol. 263, no. 4, January 1990, p. 497.

Centers for Disease Control. "Progress Toward Achieving the 1990 Objectives for the Nation for Sexually Transmitted Diseases." *Journal of the American Medical Association,* vol. 263, no. 8, February 1990, p. 1057.

Centers for Disease Control. "Update: Acquired Immunodeficiency Syndrome—United States, 1989." *Journal of the American Medical Association,* vol. 263, no. 9, March 2, 1990, p. 1191.

Christophersen, Edward R., Ph.D., guest editor. *The Pediatric Clinics of North America,* vol. 29, no. 2, April 1982.

Christophersen, Edward R., Ph.D., Jack W. Finney, Ph.D., and Patrick C. Friman, Ph.D., guest editors. *The Pediatric Clinics of North America,* vol. 33, no. 4, August 1986.

Cocaine: Your Child and Drugs. Elk Grove Village, Illinois: American Academy of Pediatrics, 1986.

Cohen, Michael I., M.D. "Adolescent Gynecology: Sweeping Issues, Pressing Needs" (editorial). *Contemporary Pediatrics,* October 1989, p. 7.

Committee on Nutrition. "Iron-Fortified Infant Formulas." *Pediatrics,* vol. 84, no. 6, December 1989, p. 1114.

Cowell, Carol A., M.D., guest editor. *The Pediatric Clinics of North America,* vol. 28, no. 2, May 1981.

Farrell, Katherine P., M.D. "Lead Poisoning and Public Policy." Letter, *American Journal of Diseases of Children,* vol. 142, March 1988, p. 251.

Gilliam, Thomas B., Ph.D., et al. "Exercise Programs for Children: A Way to Prevent Heart Disease." *The Physician and Sportsmedicine,* vol. 10, no. 9, September 1982, p. 96.

Grumbach, Melvin, M.D. "Growth Hormone Therapy and the Short End of the Stick." *The New England Journal of Medicine,* July 1988, p. 238.

Hoekelman, Robert A., M.D., and I. Barry Pless, M.D. "Decline in Mortality among Young Americans during the 20th Century: Prospects for Reaching National Mortality Reduction Goals for 1990." *Pediatrics,* vol. 82, no. 4, October 1988, p. 582.

Immunization and Your Child's Health. Wayne, New Jersey: Lederle Laboratories, March 1987.

"Immunization Schedule for Normal Infants and Children." *Contemporary Pediatrics,* September 1989, p. 121.

Immunizing Your Child Against Haemophilus b. Disease at an Earlier Age. Connaught Laboratories, Inc., 1988.

"Iron Deficiency Anemia: Adverse Effects on Infant Psychomotor Development." Domestic Abstracts. *Journal of the American Medical Association,* vol. 263, no. 1, January 1990, p. 100.

Johnson, Jennifer, M.D., et al. "A Sexually Transmitted Diseases Curriculum in Adolescent Medicine." *American Journal of Diseases of Children,* vol. 143, September 1989, p. 1073.

Kaplan, Edward L., M.D. "The Startling Comeback of Rheumatic Fever." *Contemporary Pediatrics,* vol. 4, November 1987, p. 20.

Lantos, John, M.D., Mark Siegler, M.D., and Leona Cuttler, M.D. "Ethical Issues in Growth Hormone Therapy." *Journal of the American Medical Association,* vol. 261, no. 7, February 1989, p. 1020.

Lanzkowsky, Philip, M.D., F.R.C.P., D.C.H. "Problems in Diagnosis of Iron Deficiency Anemia." *Pediatric Annals,* vol. 14, September 1985, p. 618.

Linder, Barbara, M.D., Ph.D., and Fernando Cassoria, M.D. "Short Stature Etiology, Diagnosis, and Treatment." *Journal of the American Medical Association,* vol. 260, no. 21, December 1988, p. 3171.

Litt, Iris F., guest editor. *The Pediatric Clinics of North America,* vol. 27, no. 1, February 1980.

McFaul, Richard C., M.D. "Mitral Valve Prolapse in Young Patients." *The Physician and Sportsmedicine,* vol. 15, no. 6, June 1987, p. 194.

McGill, A. Thomas, M.D., and Frederick L. Ruben, M.D. "Preventing Influenza This Winter: Update on Vaccine and Antivirals." *Journal of Respiratory Diseases,* vol. 10, no. 11, November 1989, p. 85.

Meller, Janet L., M.D., and Dennis W. Shermeta, M.D. "Falls in Urban Children." *American Journal of Diseases of Children,* vol. 141, December 1987, p. 1271.

Morgan, Beverly C., M.D., guest editor. *The Pediatric Clinics of North America,* vol. 25, no. 4, November 1978.

Needleman, Herbert L., M.D., et al. "The Long-Term Effects of Exposure to Low Doses of Lead in Childhood." *The New England Journal of Medicine,* vol. 322, no. 2, 1990, p. 83.

Pencharz, Paul B., M.B., Ph.D., F.R.C.P.(C), guest editor. *The Pediatric Clinics of North America,* vol. 32, no. 2, April 1985.

Phillips, Carol F., M.D. "Immunizations: Let's Keep Kids on Schedule." *Contemporary Pediatrics,* October 1988, p. 106.

Primosch, Robert E., D.D.S, M.S., M.Ed., guest editor. "Dental Issues for the Pediatrician." *Pediatric Annals,* vol. 14, no. 2, February 1985.

"Recommendations of the Immunization Practices Advisory Committee (ACIP) Mumps Prevention." *American Journal of Diseases of Children,* vol. 143, October 1989, p. 1141.

Resnicow, Ken, Ph.D., Jane Morley-Kotchen, M.D., and Ernst Wynder, M.D. "Plasma Cholesterol Levels of 6,585 Children in the United States: Results of the Know Your Body Screening in Five States." *Pediatrics,* vol. 84, no. 6, December 1989, p. 969.

Rivara, Frederick P., M.D., M.P.H., et al. "Risk of Injury to Children Less Than 5 Years of Age in Day Care Versus Home Care Settings." *Pediatrics,* vol. 84, no. 6, December 1989, p. 1011.

Rogers, Peter D., M.D., guest editor. *The Pediatric Clinics of North America,* vol. 34, no. 2, April 1987.

Root, Allen W., M.D., Frank B. Diamond, Jr., M.D., and Barry B. Bercu, M.D. "Short Stature: When Is Growth Hormone Indicated?" *Contemporary Pediatrics,* vol. 4, February 1987, p. 26.

Rosenthal, Amnon, M.D., guest editor. *The Pediatric Clinics of North America,* vol. 31, no. 6, December 1984.

Rowland, Thomas W., M.D., et al. "The Effect of Iron Therapy on the Exercise Capacity of Nonanemic Iron-Deficient Adolescent Runners." *Sports Medicine,* vol. 142, February 1988, p. 165.

Schwartz, Joel, Ph.D., Carol Angle, M.D., and Hugh Pitcher, M.S. "Relationship between Childhood Blood Lead Levels and Stature." *Pediatrics,* vol. 77, no. 3, March 1986, p. 281.

Smith, Nathan J., M.D., guest editor. *The Pediatric Clinics of North America,* vol. 29, no. 6, December 1982.

Spirito, Paolo, M.D., et al. "Clinical Course and Prognosis of Hypertrophic Cardiomyopathy in an Outpatient Population." *The New England Journal of Medicine,* vol. 320, no. 12, March 1989, pp. 749–753.

Spitzer, Mark, M.D., and Burton A. Krumholz, M.D. "Pap Screening for Teenagers: A Lifesaving Precaution." *Contemporary Pediatrics,* May 1987, p. 41.

"State-Specific Changes in Cholesterol Screening and Awareness: United States, 1987–1988." *Morbidity and Mortality Weekly Report,* vol. 39, no. 18, May 11, 1990, pp. 304–305.

Strasburger, Victor C., M.D., guest editor. *The Pediatric Clinics of North America,* vol. 36, no. 3, June 1989.

Strong, William B., M.D., and Jack H. Wilmore, Ph.D. "Unfit Kids: An Office-

Based Approach to Physical Fitness." *Contemporary Pediatrics,* April 1988, p. 33.

Strunk, Robert C., M.D., et al. "Cardiovascular Fitness in Children with Asthma Correlates with Psychologic Functioning of the Child." *Pediatrics,* vol. 84, no. 3, September 1989, p. 460.

Talbot, Christopher W., M.D. "The Gynecologic Examination of the Pediatric Patient." *Pediatric Annals,* vol. 15, no. 7, July 1986, p. 501.

"Tetanus: United States, 1987 and 1988." *Morbidity and Mortality Weekly Report,* vol. 39, no. 3, January 26, 1990, pp. 37–41.

"Update: Measles Outbreak—Chicago, 1989." *Morbidity and Mortality Weekly Report,* vol. 39, no. 19, May 18, 1990, pp. 317–319.

Wegman, Myron E., M.D. "Annual Summary of Vital Statistics—1987." *Pediatrics,* vol. 82, no. 6, December 1988, p. 817.

Zuckerman, Barry, M.D., Michael Weitzman, M.D., and Joel J. Alpert, M.D., guest editors. *The Pediatric Clinics of North America,* vol. 35, no. 6, December 1988.

CHAPTER 14

American Academy of Pediatrics. "Surviving Coping with Adolescent Depression and Suicide." Elk Grove Village, Illinois: 1985.

Blackman, James A., M.D., and Melvin D. Levine, M.D. "A Follow-up Study of Preschool Children Evaluated for Developmental and Behavioral Problems." *Clinical Pediatrics,* vol. 26, no. 5, May 1984, p. 248.

Christophersen, Edward R., Ph.D., Jack W. Finney, Ph.D., and Patrick C. Friman, Ph.D., guest editors. *The Pediatric Clinics of North America,* vol. 33, no. 4, August 1986.

Committee on Adolescence. "Suicide and Suicide Attempts in Adolescents and Young Adults." *Pediatrics,* vol. 81, no. 2, February 1988, p. 322.

Davidson, Lucy E., M.D., et al. "An Epidemiologic Study of Risk Factors in Two Teenage Suicide Clusters." *Journal of the American Medical Association,* vol. 262, no. 19, November 1989, p. 2687.

Flint, Patricia A. "Aerobic Exercise Raised Delinquents' Outlook." *The Physician and Sportsmedicine,* vol. 17, July 1989, p. 46.

Goldenring, John M., M.D., M.P.H., and Eric Cohen, M.D. "Getting into Adolescent Heads." *Contemporary Pediatrics,* July 1988, p. 75.

Gould, Madelyn and Shaffer, "The Impact of Suicide in Television Movies." *The New England Journal of Medicine,* vol. 315, 1986, p. 690.

Green, Morris, M.D. "Helping Children and Parents Deal with Grief." *Contemporary Pediatrics,* October 1986, p. 84.

Green, Morris, M.D., et al. "When Somatic Complaints Mask Psychosocial Disorders." *Contemporary Pediatrics,* January 1985, p. 20.

Kirn, Timothy F. "Studies of Adolescents Indicate Just How Complex the Situation Is for This Age Group." *Journal of the American Medical Association,* vol. 261, no. 23, June 1989, p. 3362.

Levine, Milton I., M.D. "Stress: Also a Pediatric Problem" (editorial). *Pediatric Annals,* vol. 14, August 1985, pp. 535–537.

Litt, Iris F., guest editor. *The Pediatric Clinics of North America,* vol. 27, no. 1, February 1980.

MacLean, George, M.D. "The Suicide of Children and Adolescents." Editorial, *Canadian Journal of Psychiatry,* vol. 32, no. 8, November 1987, p. 647.

Morgan, Beverly C., M.D., guest editor. *The Pediatric Clinics of North America,* vol. 25, no. 4, November 1978.

Murphy, George E., M.D. "Suicide and Substance Abuse." *Archives of General Psychiatry,* vol. 45, June 1988, p. 593.

Murphy, Patrick. "Stress and the Athlete: Coping with Exercise." *The Physician and Sportsmedicine,* vol. 14, no. 4, April 1986, p. 141.

Pencharz, Paul B., M.B., Ph.D., F.R.C.P.(C), guest editor. *The Pediatric Clinics of North America,* vol. 32, no. 2, April 1985.

Phillips, David P., Ph.D., and Lundie L. Carstensen, M.S. "Clustering of Teenage Suicides After Television News Stories About Suicide." *The New England Journal of Medicine,* vol. 315, no. 11, 1986, p. 685.

Phillips, David P., Ph.D., and Daniel J. Paight, B.A. "The Impact of Televised Movies about Suicide." *The New England Journal of Medicine,* vol. 317, no. 13, 1987 p. 809.

Reich, Peter, M.D. "Panic Attacks and the Risk of Suicide." *The New England Journal of Medicine,* vol. 321, November 1989, p. 1260.

Rich, Charles L., M.D., et al. "San Diego Suicide Study. III: Relationships Between Diagnoses and Stressors." *Archives of General Psychiatry,* vol. 45, June 1988, p. 589.

Richardson, Jean L., M.D., P.H., et al. "Substance Use Among Eighth-Grade Students Who Take Care of Themselves After School." *Pediatrics,* vol. 84, no. 3, September 1989, p. 556.

Rogers, Peter D., M.D., guest editor. *The Pediatric Clinics of North America,* vol. 34, no. 2, April 1987.

Rosenthal, Amnon, M.D., guest editor. *The Pediatric Clinics of North America,* vol. 31, no. 6, December 1984.

Shanahan, Karen M., B.S., et al. "The Children's Depression Rating Scale for Normal and Depressed Outpatients." *Clinical Pediatrics,* vol. 26, May 1987, p. 245.

Smith, Nathan J., M.D., guest editor. *The Pediatric Clinics of North America,* vol. 29, no. 6, December 1982.

Strasburger, Victor C., M.D., guest editor. *The Pediatric Clinics of North America,* vol. 36, no. 3, June 1989.

Zuckerman, Barry, M.D., Michael Weitzman, M.D., and Joel J. Alpert, M.D., guest editors. *The Pediatric Clinics of North America,* vol. 35, no. 6, December 1988.

CHAPTER 15

"Allergy Proceedings." *The Official Journal of Regional and State Allergy Societies,* vol. 10, no. 3, May–June 1989.

American Academy of Pediatrics. *Sports and Your Child.* Elk Grove Village, Illinois: 1987.

American Academy of Pediatrics Committee on Sports Medicine. "Climatic Heat Stress and the Exercising Child." *Pediatrics,* vol. 69, no. 6, June 1982, p. 808.

"Anabolic-Androgenic Steroid Use by Athletes." Sounding Board, John B. Hallagan, et al. *The New England Journal of Medicine,* October 1989, p. 1042.

Appenzeller, Otto, M.D., Ph.D., and Ruth Atkinson, M.D. *Sports Medicine.* Baltimore, Maryland: Urban & Schwarzenberg, second edition, 1985.

Berg, Kris E., Joseph C. LaVoie, and Richard W. Latin. "Physiological Training Effects of Playing Youth Soccer." *Medicine and Science in Sports and Exercise,* vol. 17, 1985, p. 656.

Bonen, Arend, Ph.D., and Hans A. Keizer, M.D., Ph.D. "Athletic Menstrual Cycle Irregularity: Endocrine Response to Exercise and Training." *The Physician and Sportsmedicine,* vol. 12, no. 8, August 1984, p. 78.

Buckley, William E., Ph.D., et al. "Estimated Prevalence of Anabolic Steroid Use among Male High School Seniors." *Journal of the American Medical Association,* vol. 260, no. 23, December 1988, p. 3441.

Chandy, Thomas A., M.D., and William A. Grana, M.D. "Secondary School Athletic Injury in Boys and Girls: A Three-Year Study . . ." *The Physician and Sportsmedicine,* vol. 13, no. 3, March 1985, p. 106.

"Chest Pads Advised in Youth Baseball." *The Physician and Sportsmedicine,* vol. 15, no. 2, February 1987, p. 31.

Christophersen, Edward R., Ph.D., Jack W. Finney, Ph.D., and Patrick C. Friman, Ph.D., guest editors. *The Pediatric Clinics of North America,* vol. 33, no. 4, August 1986.

Committee on Children with Disabilities and Committee on Sports Medicine. "The Asthmatic Child's Participation in Sports and Physical Education." *Pediatrics,* vol. 69, no. 1, July 1984, p. 155.

Cowart, Virginia S. "Support Lags for Research on Steroid Effects." Medical News, *Journal of the American Medical Association,* vol. 262, no. 18, November 1989, p. 2500.

DiGuiseppi, Carolyn G., M.D., M.P.H., et al. "Bicycle Helmet Use by Children." *Journal of the American Medical Association,* vol. 262, no. 16, October 1989, p. 2256.

Duda, Marty. "Which Athletes Should Wear Mouth Guards?" *The Physician and Sportsmedicine,* vol. 15, no. 9, September 1987, pp. 179–183.

Forbes, Gilbert B., M.D., editor, and Calvin W. Woodruff, M.D., associate editor. *Pediatric Nutrition Handbook.* Elk Grove Village, Illinois: Committee on Nutrition, American Academy of Pediatrics, second edition, 1985.

Francaux, M., R. Ramyead, and X. Sturbois. "Physical Fitness of Young Belgian Swimmers." *Sports Medicine,* vol. 27, 1987, p. 197.

Garbarino, James, Ph.D. "Preventing Childhood Injury: Developmental and Mental Health Issues." *American Journal of Orthopsychiatry,* vol. 58, no. 1, January 1988, p. 25.

Georgiades, George, and Vassilis Klissouras. "Assessment of Youth Fitness: The European Perspective." *American Journal of Clinical Nutrition,* vol. 49, 1989, pp. 1048–1053.

Greipp, Joseph F., M.Ed. "Swimmer's Shoulder: The Influence of Flexibility and Weight Training." *The Physician and Sportsmedicine,* vol. 13, no. 8, August 1985, p. 92.

Hansen, Byron L., M.S., A.T.C., Jack C. Ward, R.P.T., A.T.C., and Richard C. Diehl, Jr., M.D. "The Preventive Use of the Anderson Knee Stabler in Football." *The Physician and Sportsmedicine,* vol. 13, no. 9, September 1985, p. 75.

Haywood, K. M., B. A. Clark, and J. L. Mayhew. "Differential Effects of Age-group Gymnastics and Swimming on Body Composition, Strength, and Flexibility." *Journal of Sports Medicine,* vol. 26, 1986, p. 416.

Huang, Shih-Wen, M.D., et al. "The Effect of Swimming in Asthmatic Children: Participants in a Swimming Program in the City of Baltimore." *Journal of Asthma,* vol. 26, no. 2, 1989, pp. 117–121.

Karofsky, Peter S., M.D. "Hyperventilation Syndrome in Adolescent Athletes." *The Physician and Sportsmedicine,* vol. 15, no. 2, February 1987, p. 133.

Keates, Richard H., M.D. "Preventing Eye Injuries in Sports: Some Questions and Answers." *The Physician and Sportsmedicine,* vol. 16, no. 8, August 1988, p. 122.

Kizilos, Peter J. "Skateboarding Injuries Worry Pediatrics Group." *The Physician and Sportsmedicine,* vol. 17, no. 8, August 1989, p. 15.

Litt, Iris F., guest editor. *The Pediatric Clinics of North America,* vol. 27, no. 1, February 1980.

Lombardo, John A., M.D., and Douglas B. McKeag, M.D. "Football Player with a Persistent Headache." *The Physician and Sportsmedicine,* vol. 15, no. 10, October 1987, p. 75.

McLain, Larry G., M.D., and Scott Reynolds, A.T.C. "Sports Injuries in a High School." *Pediatrics,* vol. 84, no. 3, September 1989, p. 446.

McMaster, William C., M.D. "Painful Shoulder in Swimmers: A Diagnostic Challenge." *The Physician and Sportsmedicine,* vol. 14, no. 12, December 1986, p. 108.

Maehlum, Sverre, M.D., Erik Dahl, M.D., and Odd A. Daljord, M.D. "Frequency of Injuries in a Youth Soccer Tournament." *The Physician and Sportsmedicine,* vol. 14, no. 7, July 1986, p. 73.

Magazanik, Abraham, et al. "Iron Deficiency Caused by 7 Weeks of Intensive Physical Exercise." *European Journal of Applied Physiology,* vol. 57, 1988, pp. 198–202.

Moore, Wayne V., M.D. "Anabolic Steroid Use in Adolescence." Editorial, *Journal of the American Medical Association,* vol. 260, no. 23, December 1988, p. 3484.

Morgan, Beverly C., M.D., guest editor. *The Pediatric Clinics of North America,* vol. 25, no. 4, November 1978.

Moskwa, C. Alexander, Jr., M.D., and James A. Nicholas, M.D. "Musculoskeletal Risk Factors in the Young Athlete." *The Physician and Sportsmedicine,* vol. 17, no. 11, November 1989, p. 49.

Murphy, Patrick. "Youth Sports Coaches: Using Hunches to Fill a Blank Page." *The Physician and Sportsmedicine,* vol. 13, no. 4, April 1985, p. 136.

Orlando, Richard G., M.D. "Soccer-Related Eye Injuries in Children and Adolescents." *The Physician and Sportsmedicine,* vol. 16, no. 11, November 1988, p. 103.

Pacelli, Lauren C. "Conditioning Can Help Girls Avoid Injuries." *The Physician and Sportsmedicine,* vol. 17, no. 6, June 1989, p. 27.

Pencharz, Paul B., M.B., Ph.D., F.R.C.P.(C), guest editor. *The Pediatric Clinics of North America,* vol. 32, no. 2, April 1985.

Pitman, Mark I., M.D. "Sports Injuries in Children." *Resident & Staff Physician,* vol. 32, September 1986, p. 47.

"Recommendations for Participation in Competitive Sports" (American Academy of Pediatrics Policy Statement). *The Physician and Sportsmedicine,* vol. 16, no. 5, May 1988, p. 165.

"Risks in Long Distance Running for Children" (American Academy of Pediatrics Policy Statement). June 1982, p. 11.

Rogers, Peter D., M.D., guest editor. *The Pediatric Clinics of North America,* vol. 34, no. 2, April 1987.

Rosenthal, Amnon, M.D., guest editor. *The Pediatric Clinics of North America,* vol. 31, no. 6, December 1984.

Rowland, Thomas W., M.D., and Peter P. Hoontis, B.S. "Organizing Road Races for Children: Special Concerns." *The Physician and Sportsmedicine,* vol. 13, no. 3, March 1985, p. 126.

Rowland, Thomas W., M.D., and Coleen A. Walsh, B.S. "Characteristics of

Child Distance Runners." *The Physician and Sportsmedicine,* vol. 13, no. 9, September 1985, p. 45.

Smith, Nathan J., M.D., guest editor. *The Pediatric Clinics of North America,* vol. 29, no. 6, December 1982.

———. "Is That Child Ready for Competitive Sports?" *Contemporary Pediatrics,* vol. 3, March 1986, p. 30.

Strasburger, Victor C., M.D., guest editor. *The Pediatric Clinics of North America,* vol. 36, no. 3, June 1989.

Thompson, Robert S., M.D., Frederick P. Rivara, M.D., M.P.H., and Diane C. Thompson, M.S. "A Case-Control Study of the Effectiveness of Bicycle Safety Helmets." *The New England Journal of Medicine,* vol. 320, no. 21, May 1989, pp. 1361–1367.

Ward, Amy. "Are Playground Injuries Inevitable?" *The Physician and Sportsmedicine,* vol. 15, no. 4, April 1987, p. 162.

———. "Improving Bicycle Safety for Children." *The Physician and Sportsmedicine,* vol. 15, no. 6, June 1987, p. 203.

"Weight Training and Weight Lifting: Information for the Pediatrician" (American Academy of Pediatrics Policy Statement). July 1982, p. 7.

Zuckerman, Barry, M.D., Michael Weitzman, M.D., and Joel J. Alpert, M.D., guest editors. *The Pediatric Clinics of North America,* vol. 35, no. 6, December 1988.

General Index

Page numbers of illustrations appear in italics

Recipe Index